Immediate High Alert . . .
for Flying Saucers!

On December 5, 1950, FBI director J. Edgar Hoover sent a teletype message in which he asked Special Agent in Charge (SAC) Knoxville to investigate "radar jamming" at the Oak Ridge National Laboratory. The laboratory was the home of Project NEPA, the project to develop atomic-powered aircraft, and considered a "vital installation."

The FBI had received word of strange happenings in the Oak Ridge area in October and November of 1950. In October, radar detected unidentified objects in the vicinity of Oak Ridge Laboratory. Over the next month and a half, there were several independent reports made by credible witnesses (many of whom worked as security guards for the laboratory) of strange aircraft, noises, and lights.

On December 8, FBI headquarters received the following message from SAC Richmond, Virginia:

URGENT. December 8. RE: FLYING SAUCERS. This office very confidentially advised by Army Intelligence, Richmond, that they have been put on immediate high alert for any data whatsoever concerning flying saucers. CIC here states background of instructions not available from Air Force Intelligence, who are not aware of reason for alert locally, but any information whatsoever must be telephoned by them immediately to Air Force Intelligence . . .

How very strange for the Counter Intelligence Corps to be put on immediate high alert for any data regarding objects/phenomena/craft that Air Technical Intelligence Center claimed can *all* be explained, *and are no threat to the security of the United States!*

About the Author

Dr. Bruce Maccabee is a physical scientist with a doctorate in physics who became interested in the UFO phenomenon in the 1960s. Dr. Maccabee was the first to obtain the previously secret file of the FBI. He has also collected documents from the CIA, the Air Force, the Army, and other agencies. He has appeared on dozens of radio and TV shows over the past twenty years, and is the coauthor of *UFOs Are Real: Here's the Proof.*

To Write to the Author

If you wish to contact the author or would like more information about this book, please write to the author in care of Llewellyn Worldwide and we will forward your request. Both the author and publisher appreciate hearing from you and learning of your enjoyment of this book and how it has helped you. Llewellyn Worldwide cannot guarantee that every letter written to the author can be answered, but all will be forwarded. Please write to:

Bruce Maccabee, Ph.D.
℅ Llewellyn Worldwide
P.O. Box 64383, Dept. K493-6
St. Paul, MN 55164-0383, U.S.A.

Please enclose a self-addressed stamped envelope for reply,
or $1.00 to cover costs. If outside U.S.A., enclose
international postal reply coupon.

Bruce Maccabee, Ph.D.

UFO FBI
CONNECTION

The Secret History
of the Government's Cover-Up

2000
Llewellyn Publications
St. Paul, Minnesota 55164-0383, U.S.A.

FIRST EDITION
First Printing, 2000

Book design and editing by Michael Maupin
Cover design by Lisa Novak
Cover photo by Leo Tushaus
Interior photos courtesy of the J. Allen Hynek Center for UFO Studies, Wendy Connors of Project Sign Research Center, and FATE magazine.
McMinnville–Trent photos courtesy of Bruce Maccabee

The X-Files is produced by Ten Thirteen Productions in association with 20th Century Fox Television. Fox ® is a registered trademark of 20th Century Fox Film Corporation, used under license from News Digital Media, Inc.

Library of Congress Cataloging-in-Publication Data
[ISBN: 1-56718-493-6   Pending]

Llewellyn Worldwide does not participate in, endorse, or have any authority or responsibility concerning private business transactions between our authors and the public.
   All mail addressed to the author is forwarded but the publisher cannot, unless specifically instructed by the author, give out an address or phone number.

Llewellyn Publications
A Division of Llewellyn Worldwide, Ltd.
P.O. Box 64383, Dept. K493-6
St. Paul, MN 55164-0383, U.S.A.
www.llewellyn.com

Printed in the United States of America.

Also by Bruce Maccabee

UFOs Are Real: Here's the Proof (with Ed Walters)
(Avon Books, 1997)

Contents

Acknowledgments

In order to compile this history of the UFO phenomenon, I have made use of the work of many investigators. In particular I thank the following people for their efforts in obtaining formerly classified government documents other than the FBI documents (in alphabetical order): Jan Aldrich, Don Berliner, Joel Carpenter, Stanton Friedman, Barry Greenwood, Bill LaParl, Bill Moore, Jaime Shandara, and Robert Todd. I also thank the following people for their publications on the subject; publications which provided me with information and helped to clarify details of the history (in alphabetical order): Jan Aldrich, Don Berliner, Jerry Clark, Wendy Connors, Stanton Friedman, Barry Greenwood, Loren Gross, Mike Hall, Bill Moore, Kevin Randle, Edward Ruppelt (long deceased), Jaime Shandara, Don Schmitt, Brad Sparks, and Michael Swords.

I also thank the early readers of this manuscript for their helpful comments, especially Elaine Douglass, Karl Pflock, Michael Swords, and a certain astute person, formerly in military intelligence, who wishes to remain unnamed.

Finally I thank the many investigators, FBI, Air Force, and CIA personnel, who generated these documents and thereby provided a paper trail that shows how the Air Force treated the UFO subject through the early years.

Throughout this manuscript emphasized statements are italicized. Statements which are contained within quotation marks or are contained in indented paragraphs are direct copies from original documents.

Foreword

It is not surprising that Bruce Maccabee, an optical physicist, is frequently called upon to investigate motion picture, video, and still pictures of Unidentified Flying Objects. With thirty years of professional experience working on a wide variety of classified advanced optical research and development programs such as the Strategic Defense Initiative (SDI or "Star Wars"), he certainly knows his optics. He has even had the courage to publish articles in scientific peer reviewed journals about such well-known UFO photographs as those taken in McMinnville, Oregon, in 1950, and the motion picture footage of a UFO filmed from an airplane in New Zealand in 1978. His work on the famous Gulf Breeze, Florida, sightings was reported in the book, *The Gulf Breeze Sightings* by Edward and Frances Walters (Morrow, NY, 1990). More research on those and other pictures and sightings was discussed in detail in *UFOs Are Real: Here's The Proof* by Edward Walters and Bruce Maccabee (Avon, 1997).

In this new work Dr. Maccabee demonstrates his understanding of both government documents and the government lies about the UFO subject. Living in the Washington, D.C., area, he has ready access to a number of archives from which he has obtained information presented here. Because of his persistence back in the 1970s he was able to obtain about 1,600 pages of FBI documents under the then-new Freedom of Information Act (FOIA). In this book he clearly shows that the FBI, and Director John Edgar Hoover in particular, did indeed take UFO sightings, and their observers, seriously. This, despite frequently telling people seeking UFO information that the subject of UFOs "is not and never has been" a responsibility of the FBI.

As a nuclear physicist who has lectured all over the world on the subject "Flying Saucers ARE Real," I have responded to tens of thousands of questions after lectures and from journalists and talk show hosts during interviews. Many have dealt with documents, especially the very controversial Operation Majestic Twelve documents discussed in my book, *TOP SECRET/MAJIC* (Marlowe & Company, 1996). A major problem with those documents is that we don't know their origin or, as document examiners say, their provenance. To avoid that problem, Dr. Maccabee has used only documents with known provenance, namely the government itself. Hence he is able to focus on content instead of debating the origin. It seems clear that the FBI has been much more open about its UFO documents than have been the Central Intelligence Agency, the National Security Agency, the National Reconnaissance Office, the U.S. Air Force Office of Special Investigations, the Office of Naval Intelligence, or the Air Defense Command.

An important aspect of Dr. Maccabee's research involves the cross-connection between the FBI and other agencies such as the Air Force in regard to UFOs. There were meetings among representatives of the FBI, the Atomic Energy Commission, the Army, and the Air Force focusing on UFO observations, especially near highly classified facilities such as the Oak Ridge National Laboratory in Tennessee and the Los Alamos National Laboratory and other government facilities in New Mexico. The people responsible for the security of these national assets took the UFO matter very seriously despite public comments to the contrary by various officials.

An important point to be understood is that very few formerly Top Secret or Top Secret/Code Word (Special Access) documents about UFOs have been released. It is perfectly legal for the government to refuse to release such documents since national security is one of the many exemptions from the FOIA. Unfortunately one can't discuss Top Secret information in Secret or Confidential documents so we have no clue as to how much more material there is in unreleased, highly classified documents. Presidential Executive Order 12958, which becomes law in April 2000, will make it much more difficult for government agencies to keep documents classified. So, one can hope that in the near future Dr. Maccabee will have many more documents to examine.

This book is not sensational tabloid nonsense. It is a sober view of important information giving a new perspective concerning the surprising fact about the FBI and UFOs. Dr. Maccabee may not be Fox Mulder, but he certainly provides many insights into the real "X-Files."

Stanton Friedman

June 1999

Introduction
The "X-Files" Are Real!

The Federal Bureau of Investigation really did investigate sightings of Unidentified Flying Objects, which were called "Flying Saucers," or "Flying Discs," more than fifty-three years ago, when the modern era of UFO sightings began.

The term "X-Files" has been popularized by the Fox network television program, which describes the adventures of two FBI agents who investigate the FBI cases that are too weird for ordinary agents, such as psychic phenomena, reincarnation, vampires, and, especially, UFOs. The UFO plots and subplots revolve around agent Fox Mulder, who not only believes in the existence of UFOs, but he suspects that his "baby" sister was abducted by aliens and never returned to Earth. He continually searches for proof. His partner, Dana Scully, on the other hand, is skeptical of paranormal events. She tries to explain them in conventional ways, even after it becomes apparent that she, too, is directly involved in the UFO phenomenon.

Running through *The X-Files* shows is a subplot of conspiracy: some secret group inside, or outside, the government knows that UFOs are real and uses all means possible to prevent the public from discovering the truth. Certain "Deep Throat" type individuals provide Mulder with some important clues, but they are "terminated" by the insiders who control the truth. Furthermore, it seems that the closer

Mulder and Scully get to finding "the final proof," the closer they get to their own . . . termination.

Chris Carter, creator of *The X-Files,* has struck a responsive chord with the American people. Building on the success of paranormal investigative shows such as NBC's *Unsolved Mysteries,* Paramount's *Sightings,* and Fox network's own *Encounters, The X-Files* brings all of these mysteries together and neatly weaves them into a series of exciting fiction stories. Perhaps the success of *The X-Files* lies partially in the fact that, according to Gallup and other polls over the last forty years, roughly half of the American population believe "UFOs are real." Not only that, but according to a recent Roper poll, as much as seven percent of the population believe they have actually seen a UFO.

The X-Files is very entertaining because it is well written by people who are quite famliar with the phenomena they write about. But it does not accurately portray the FBI interest in UFOs. However, it does get two things right, although probably by accident: one, FBI agents did investigate saucer sightings in the early years; and two, UFO sightings were often filed under the title "FLYING DISCS: SECURITY MATTER – X." These are the *real* "X-files."

The FBI also collected and stored information provided by Air Force investigators who had their own file of secret UFO information, which is revealed here *for the first time.* As you will see, some of the FBI and Air Force information proves top Air Force officials knew there were unexplainable sightings and seriously considered the possibility that some UFOs were *extraterrestrial vehicles!*

But how can that be? It's all fiction, isn't it? After all, everybody knows that only "kooks and nuts," and people looking for publicity, see UFOs, right? Not necessarily. One wonders what skeptical Agent Scully would think if she were allowed to see the *real* "X-Files." Would she reject sightings by responsible citizens of the United States, by Air Force officers, by pilots, and by policemen? Would she reject a two-witness sighting, one witness an employee of the Top Secret National Security Agency and the other an FBI employee? Would she reject information the FBI kept secret from the American people until it was finally released under the Freedom of Information Act?

The government records of these UFO events were not lost, they were merely made unavailable to the American people until recently.

And now, thanks to the Freedom of Information and Privacy Act, and the efforts of many UFO investigators over the last twenty years, you are able to read what the Air Force and FBI knew nearly fifty years ago. Skeptics and perpetrators of the UFO cover-up hope that you won't read this book and find out for yourself that UFOs are real, and may well be interplanetary craft.

The truth is not "out there," it's *in here!*

Read on!

CHAPTER 1

The UFO-FBI Connection

I would do it, but we first must have access to all discs recovered ...

—J. Edgar Hoover, July 11, 1947

A teletype machine at the headquarters of the Federal Bureau of Investigation in Washington, D.C. suddenly sprang to life and began noisily typing out an urgent message from a Special Agent in Charge (SAC):

```
FBI ALBUQUERQUE
5:37 PM MST (Mountain Standard Time) URGENT
TO: DIRECTOR, FBI
FROM SAC, ALBUQUERQUE 62 NEW MEXICO
UNIDENTIFIED FLYING OBJECT SOCORRO, NM
INFORMATION CONCERNING
```

The message described the object sighted by Lonnie Zamora, a respected police officer in Socorro, New Mexico, on April 24, 1964. Zamora had seen a strange, unidentified object, and two humanlike creatures on the ground near Socorro. The object then took off with a roaring noise and left indentations in the ground. He radioed for help, and other officers arrived only minutes after it had disappeared in the distance, but in time to see Zamora looking pale and shaken. Minutes later the FBI arrived. SAC Arthur Byrnes, acting in an unofficial capacity, interviewed Zamora and sent a teletype message to FBI headquarters the next day. Over the next few weeks he sent several more messages to headquarters concerning the results of the Air Force investigation of this incident (described further in chapter 23) which, to this day, remains unexplained.

This is just one of the UFO sightings contained within FBI file #62-83894, the file on flying discs—*the real X-Files!*

But, how can this be? Surely the FBI wouldn't get involved with anything as crazy as UFOs and flying saucers. The FBI does not currently investigate UFO sightings (or so they say). But that wasn't always the case.

Fact: In July 1966 a TV-show writer asked the FBI for help in verifying the identity of a source of UFO information.

Fact: Director John Edgar Hoover responded that "the investigation of unidentified flying objects is not, *and never has been,* a matter within the investigative jurisdiction of the FBI [emphasis added]."

Question: Had Hoover *lied?*

Since 1980, a controversy has raged over exactly what crashed in the desert near Roswell, New Mexico, in early July 1947. On July 8, the Army Air Corps (the Air Corps or Air Force was a branch of the Army until September 18, 1947) at Roswell Army Air Field, by direction of the base commander, Col. William Blanchard, issued a press release that stated a flying saucer had crashed on nearby ranch land and had been retrieved by Army personnel operating under the direction of Maj. Jesse Marcel, the base intelligence officer. The press release said the wreckage was being flown to "higher headquarters." Several hours later Maj. Gen. Clements McMullen, Deputy Commander of the Strategic Air Command at the Pentagon, called Brig. Gen. Roger Ramey, Commander of the 8th Air Force at Fort Worth Army Air Field in Texas. Col. Thomas DuBose, Ramey's Adjutant at the time, took the phone call from McMullen. In interviews forty years later, DuBose reported that McMullen ordered Ramey to squash the story, in order to "get the press

Col. William Blanchard, Roswell base commander (left) and Brig. Gen. Roger Ramey, 8th Army Air Force, Fort Worth (right).

off our back." Gen. Ramey invented an explanation. He told the press reporters that the material retrieved in the desert near Roswell had been identified as a weather balloon, and stated that a special flight to transport the material to Wright Field for analysis (now Wright-Patterson Air Force Base) in Dayton, Ohio, *had been cancelled.*

About thirty years later, Jesse Marcel, retired from active duty in the Air Force, and told UFO investigators that, while the general was telling the press it was a weather balloon device, *the real material was flown by a special flight to Wright Field.* The investigators knew that material from a weather balloon could have been identified by almost anyone. It surely would not have to be flown to Wright Field for analysis and identification.

Could it be, UFO investigators wondered, that Marcel's recollection was incorrect? Was there really no special flight, in which case the material probably was from a weather balloon? It turns out that the answer *was buried in the FBI file!*

Fact: At 6:17 P.M., July 8, 1947, the local FBI agent in Texas filed an urgent report via teletype, which said an object had been found that "resembles a high altitude balloon with a radar reflector." However, "telephonic conversation . . . (with) Wright field had not borne out this belief." The teletype message also said that the material is "being transported to Wright Field by special plane for examination." Thus it appears that Jesse Marcel was correct: the special flight had *not* been cancelled.*

Fact: Immediately after the first publicized reports of flying saucers, starting with Kenneth Arnold's sighting on June 24, 1947, the press asked the Air Force if there was some new, secret aircraft project that could account for the saucer reports. The Air Force said, "No."

Fact: On July 8, 1947, flying saucers were sighted at Muroc Army Air Field (now Edwards Air Force Base) in California by Air Force personnel. (This was the same day that the Roswell press release claimed that a crashed disc had been found.) *The Air Force immediately took a serious interest in flying saucers.*

---

*Thirty years later, Oliver Wendell "Pappy" Henderson confirmed that there was a flight to Wright Field. He was a well-known WWII pilot (thirty missions over Germany) who flew scientists and military observers to and from atomic bomb tests in the late 1940s while he was stationed at Roswell. He had a Top Secret security clearance. In 1977, he told John Kromschroeder of his involvement in the Roswell crash incident. He told Kromschroeder that *he had been the pilot who flew the Roswell material to Wright Field.* Furthermore, he told him that he had seen the wreckage and alien bodies! Four years later Henderson told his wife, Sappho, and his daughter, Mary, the same story. (Henderson died in 1986.)

Gen. Ramey would turn up again five years later in a role of explainer or debunker at another press conference during the peak of the UFO sighting activity in the summer of 1952. (This is discussed in chapter 19.)

In the summer of 1994 the Air Force essentially admitted that Ramey lied when he said the Roswell material was from a weather balloon with a radar target. Instead, said the Air Force, the material was from a formerly Top Secret balloon project intended to detect Soviet nuclear explosions, Project Mogul. This explanation failed to convince many UFO investigators since the Mogul balloon devices were essentially large arrays of balloons like the weather balloons. The balloon materials and associated parts would have been quickly recognized as such by the highly trained Air Force personnel at Roswell Army Air Field. On June 24, 1997, the 50th anniversary of the first widely reported sighting of flying discs or saucers (see below), the Air Force published yet another explanation of the Roswell event. Several of the Roswell witnesses had reported small human-shaped but nonhuman bodies associated with the crash. The Air Force proposed that these were actually parachute test dummies used to test high altitude escape mechanisms. These anthropomorphic dummies were dropped numerous times in the Southwest during experiments in the 1950s. However, the Air Force explanation was rejected by ufologists because the first such dummies were not dropped until six years after the Roswell incident, and none of the dummies landed near the locations of the Roswell debris.

Brig. Gen. George Schulgen, Chief of the Air Intelligence Requirements Division, Army Air Corps Intelligence.

Fact: On July 9, 1947, Brig. Gen. George Schulgen, Chief of the Air Intelligence Requirements Division of the Army Air Corps Intelligence, asked the FBI to help investigate the saucer reports. He wanted to know if the reports were the result of attempts by communist sympathizers or Soviet agents in the United States "to cause hysteria and fear of a secret Russian weapon." Were the witnesses providing honest reports or were they publicity seekers? Did they have a political agenda? The general wanted the FBI to try to answer these questions.

Schulgen told the FBI that his intelligence organization was using "all of its scientists" to determine whether or not "such a phenomenon could, in fact, occur." He, several scientists, and a psychologist, had interrogated an Air Force pilot who saw one. Under the intense questioning the pilot "was adamant in his claim that he saw a flying disc." Schulgen said that the research "is being conducted with the thought that the flying objects might be a celestial phenomenon, and with the view that they might be a foreign body mechanically devised and controlled." In other words, the the craft might have a foreign origin (that is, from Russia) or *a celestial origin.* (This would not be the last time the FBI would learn of the possibility of a "celestial" origin.) Gen. Schulgen assured the FBI that there was no defense project that could account for flying disc reports and offered to work closely with the FBI. He said he would make available to the FBI "reports of his scientists and findings of the various Air Corps installations," and "if the Bureau would cooperate with him in this matter, he would offer all facilities of his office as to results obtained in the effort to identify and run down this matter."

Two years later, a well-publicized magazine story would state that Air Force Intelligence was very reluctant to investigate flying saucer sightings because the intelligence officers thought there was nothing to them.

By this time the nationally distributed newspapers had publicized dozens of sightings of circular, shiny metallic objects, dubbed "flying saucers" by the press. These included the June 24 sighting by Kenneth Arnold (the first widely reported sighting, which *has never been explained!*) and the sighting of nine saucers by Capt. E. J. Smith and crew of a United Air Lines flight on July 4 (which has also *not* been explained). Many years later, UFO investigators, searching through thousands of local newspapers, discovered that there had been not just a few dozen, and not even just a few hundred, but several thousand sightings throughout the United States during this period, and many in other countries, too. Most of the local sightings were not reported in the national newspapers. Therefore, when Gen. Schulgen approached the FBI for help, no one in the government or military knew the true scope of the "flying saucer situation."

Fact: Hoover said, *"I would do it!"*

Assistant FBI Director David M. Ladd thought that interviewing saucer witnesses was a bad idea, "it being noted that a great bulk of those alleged discs reported found have been pranks." However, Clyde Tolson, Hoover's "right hand man" disagreed. "I think we should do this," he wrote to Hoover. Hoover agreed with Tolson, but under a certain condition: "I would do it, but first we must have access to all discs recovered. For example, in the La. case the Army grabbed it and would not let us have it for cursory examination." Hoover required access to any disc recovered because it was the job of the FBI, through its laboratory facilities, to determine the origin of the parts that made up the disc. If

Capt. Edward J. Ruppelt,
first director of the Air
Force's Project Blue Book.

some of the parts did not originate in the United States then there was the possibility that the disc was a form of sabotage or psychological warfare being waged against the U.S. by a foreign country.

The phrase "La. case" refers to a hoax device found in Shreveport, Louisiana on July 7. Someone had put together a model "flying saucer" and tossed it into someone else's backyard as a joke. Army intelligence agents had learned of it, and retrieved it for analysis before the local FBI agent had a chance to look at it. Nothing unusual was found; some electronic and mechanical parts with the words "Made in USA" written on it. The Shreveport case was not the only such hoax case in the FBI files from this time. Apparently some people thought the saucer sightings were a complete joke, and decided to have fun at other people's expense. The files indicate a dozen or so hoaxes among the hundreds of honest reports.

Hoover officially approved of Tolson's recommendation and thus began a two-month period of official investigation followed by many years in which the FBI collected UFO-related information from the Air Force, and other sources. The FBI, with its penchant for collecting all sorts of information that might be of value to Hoover, did all this secretly.

In 1976, when I requested the FBI to release any UFO information under the newly passed Freedom of Information and Privacy Act (FOIPA),

I didn't expect to get anything. There had never been explicit evidence that the FBI was ever involved in UFO investigations. One person who should have known was Capt. Edward J. Ruppelt, the first director of Project Blue Book, which was the publicly known UFO investigation project of the Air Force from 1952 to 1969. He wrote a history of the first eight years of Air Force flying saucer investigations, *The Report on Unidentified Flying Objects* (Doubleday, New York, 1956). According to Ruppelt, the FBI "was never officially interested" in UFO sightings. Therefore I was surprised to learn that there were well over a thousand pages of UFO-related material in the FBI's "X-files." I found that the FBI file contains some early records not in the files of Project Blue Book, which the Air Force claimed was the complete, official Air Force collection of UFO sightings and documents. Of greater interest is the fact that it contains comments and opinions state by Air Force officers who were involved in the early years; comments such as "some military officials are seriously considering the possibility of interplanetary ships"!

CHAPTER 2

Security Matter - X:
The Real "X-Files"

Agents had been sending unoffi-
cial reports on saucers to headquarters for several weeks when, on July
30, 1947, a message went out to all the local offices: "You should investigate each instance which is brought to your attention of a sighting of a
flying disc in order to ascertain whether or not it is a bona fide sighting,
an imaginary one, or a prank . . . The bureau should be notified immediately by teletype of all reported sightings, and the results of your
inquiries . . ." The directive also specified that FBI agents should provide
copies of their reports to the Air Force investigators. According to the
directive, the Air Force Intelligence had "some concern that the reported
sightings might have been made by subversive individuals for the purpose of creating mass hysteria." However, the Air Force had also told the
FBI that it was possible to drag several disc-shaped gliders behind a
plane using a wire towline. Upon release these discs "would obtain
tremendous speed in their descent and would decend [sic] to the earth
in an arc." The fact that the Air Force proposed this rather bizarre
hypothesis indicates that Air Force scientists believed the saucers were

real flying objects and were attempting to determine how they could be explained as devices created by foreign countries.

Over the next two months, the FBI interviewed more than a dozen witnesses and found no evidence of subversion but they did find *evidence of flying saucers.* Here are a few of the reports.

```
REPORTS OF FLYING DISCS September 17, 1947
SECURITY MATTER - X...
```

The above heading introduces the FBI interview of Fred Johnson, a prospector. Johnson had written a letter to the Air Force in which he said he had seen the same objects Kenneth Arnold had seen, at about the same time during the afternoon of June 24.* The Air Force asked the FBI to interview Johnson.

According to the FBI report, Johnson was prospecting near Mt. Adams during the afternoon of June 24. He saw the objects fly overhead. He closely observed them through a telescope. (He is the first person known to have used a telescope to observe flying saucers.) He confirmed Arnold's description of the overall round shape and high speed, and said that they appeared about thirty feet in diameter. He reported they tilted back and forth as they flew, and he last saw them "standing on edge" as they flew into a cloud. As the objects passed overhead, the needle of his compass wobbled back and forth. (This is the first known report of electromagnetic effects of flying saucers.) Johnson told the FBI he had not learned of Arnold's sighting until several days later, and he had written to the Air Force to "lend credence" to Arnold's report. The FBI agent noted that Johnson "appeared to be a very reliable individual" who been prospecting in the northwestern United States for forty years.

In the Project Blue Book records Fred Johnson's sighting occupies an unique position. It is the *first* of about 700 UFO reports the Air Force

---

* Arnold reported seeing nine semicircular, flat, shiny objects fly southward at high speed—1,700 mph!—past Mt. Rainier in Washington state. These objects tilted left and right as they flew. They disappeared from his view near Mt. Adams, about fifty miles south of Mt. Rainier. Although a dozen explanations have been proposed for Arnold's sighting, none has been convincing. His sighting remains unexplained.

admitted it could not explain at the time Project Blue Book closed in 1969.† Inasmuch as Arnold's sighting preceded Johnson's by a minute or so, the astute reader may ask why Arnold's sighting is not the first unexplained sighting, and Johnson's the second. The answer is that the Air Force analysts claim to have explained Arnold's sighting as a mirage! Of course, it is illogical to imply that the objects seen by Arnold and Johnson could be both explained and unexplained. This is just one example of the illogical treatment of UFO sightings by the Air Force.

```
TO: Director, FBI September 4, 1947
FROM: SAC Phoenix
SUBJECT: Reports of Flying Discs...
```

Thus begins a letter to FBI headquarters concerning the interview of William Rhoads of Phoenix, Arizona, who had taken two pictures of a flying saucer near his home. The object in the pictures was somewhat similar to the objects reported by Kenneth Arnold. Rhodes gave the negatives to the FBI with the understanding that they would be turned over to the Air Force Intelligence, and that he probably wouldn't get them back. He never did.

A year and a half later the pictures were published in an intelligence report, originally classified Top Secret, entitled "Analysis of Flying Object Incidents in the U.S." published jointly by the Directorate of Intelligence of the Air Force, and the Office of Naval Intelligence. According to this document, "These photographs have been examined by experts who state they are true photographic images . . ." (This document, which is discussed in chapter 5, was not declassified and released until 1985.)

```
URGENT AUGUST 11, 1947
FLYING DISCS
SECURITY MATTER DASH X...
```

---

† Project Blue Book, 1952–1969, and its predecessors, Project Sign, 1948–1949, and Project Grudge, 1949–1952, are the only publicly known efforts of the Air Force to collect and categorize UFO sightings. The files of these projects were microfilmed and released to the National Archives in 1975.

Thus begins a teletype message from Portland, Oregon, which reports that a former Navy pilot saw a mysterious flying object on two occasions the evening of August 6, 1947. The pilot was near the Tri-City Airport at Myrtle Creek, Oregon, at an altitude of about 400 feet, when he first saw a glistening spherical object at an estimated altitude of 5,000 to 8,000 feet. It appeared to be metallic and traveling eastward while climbing at a speed of about 1,000 mph. He saw no vapor trails.

After it disappeared, he landed the plane and then took off again as part of the instruction for his passenger, a flight student. Once again he saw the spherical object, which again took off at high speed. He estimated the size at about thirty feet. To the flight student, the object appeared to be a fifty-foot sphere. He said that the second object they saw departed straight upward at high speed and disappeared in about forty-five seconds. The sky was clear and the sun low in the west at the time of the sighting.

```
URGENT SEPTEMBER 13, 1947
FLYING DISCS...
```

This teletype message reads, in part:

> [The] chief of Police, Portland [Oregon], states he observed, at about 5:15 P.M. an object similar in size to a weather balloon, which appeared to be made of aluminum or some other bright metal, traveling rapidly northwest to southeast over Portland at an estimated 10,000 ft. Object veered to south and disappeared in the distance in approximately one minute. Also observed by Portland Police officers . . . investigation being conducted.

The follow-up report to the teletype message begins with the heading FLYING DISCS, SECURITY MATTER – X. The report presents the testimony of several other policemen in the northeastern part of Portland who first saw the object coming from the east. By radio, they asked officers further south to look for it. Chief Leon Jenkins then searched the sky and observed what "appeared to be a round, silver object, about 10,000 ft. high, traveling northeast to southwest." Initially he thought it was a weather balloon, but then "further observation convinced him it could not be a weather balloon because of its speed, which was extremely great." He watched the object gradually turn until it was traveling due south. "As it [turned southward] its shape seemed to change until it appeared to be egg-shaped. It disappeared in about thirty seconds."

```
FBI BUTTE 8-15-47 5:45 P.M.
DIRECTOR, FBI
URGENT...
```

The flying disc "X-file" contains many sightings collected by the Air Force and provided to the FBI. These include numerous sightings by pilots, policemen, and others. In most cases, the objects were always quite distant, except for one case.

This case was the sighting by A. C. Urie and his sons, who lived in the Snake River Canyon at Twin Falls, Idaho. At about 1:00 P.M., August 13, 1947, Urie "sent his boys to the river to get some rope from his boat. When he thought they were overdue, he went outside his tool shed to look for them. He noticed them about 300 feet away, looking in the sky and he glanced up to see what he called the flying disc." This strange object was flying at high speed along the canyon which is about 400 feet deep and 1,200 feet across at that point. It was about seventy-five feet above the floor of the canyon and moving up and down as it flew. It seemed to be following the contours of the hilly ground beneath it.

Urie estimated the object was about twenty feet long and ten feet wide and ten feet high, with what appeared to be exhaust ports on the sides. It was almost hat-shaped, with a flat bottom and a dome on top. Its pale blue color made Urie think that it would be very difficult to see against the sky, although he had no trouble seeing it against the walls of the canyon. On each side there was a tubular-shaped fiery glow, like some sort of exhaust. He said that when it went over trees, they didn't sway back and forth but rather the treetops twisted around, which suggests that the air under the object was being swirled into a vortex. He and his sons had an excellent view of the object for a few seconds before it disappeared over the trees about a mile away. He estimated it was going 1,000 miles an hour.

The FBI learned that Urie and his sons were not the only witnesses to a flying saucer on August 13, 1947. County Commissioner and former Sheriff L. W. Hawkins and a companion were near the Salmon River Dam about forty miles southwest of Twin Falls when they saw, high in the sky, two circular, reflective objects. Hawkins said a sound resembling an echo of a motor caused him to look upward and he saw these objects traveling at a great speed.

The sightings presented here are just a small sample of the sightings contained in the FBI "flying disc" files. Several more will be presented here. But first it is necessary to present the history of Air Force activities over the true nature of UFO sightings, because it was this controversy that spilled over into the "real X-files."

CHAPTER 3

Secret Air Force Activities

. . . real and not imaginary or fictitious . . .

—Lt. Gen. Nathan Twining, September 1947

During July, August, and September 1947, FBI headquarters received about two dozen sighting reports and some other documents from the Air Force. All of these reports and documents were supposed to have been contained within the records of Project Blue Book. However, some of these documents were found *only* in the FBI file. One of these provides an early Air Force assessment of the "flying saucer situation." The document, reproduced below, is neither signed nor dated, but its location in the temporal sequence of the FBI file indicates that it was written in late July, after the Air Force had collected and analyzed about two dozen sightings.

From [a] detailed study of reports selected for their impression of veracity and reliability, several conclusions have been formed:

(a) This 'flying saucer' situation is not all imaginary or seeing too much in some natural phenomenon. Something is really flying around.

(b) Lack of topside inquiries, when compared to the prompt and demanding inquiries that have originated topside upon former events, give more than ordinary weight to the possibility that this is a domestic project, about which the President, etc. know.

(c) Whatever the objects are, this much can be said of their physical appearance:

1. The surface of these objects is metallic, indicating a metallic skin, at least.

2. When a trail is observed it is lightly colored, a Blue-Brown haze, that is similar to a rocket engine's exhaust. Contrary to a rocket of the solid type, one observation indicates that the fuel may be throttled which would indicate a liquid rocket engine.

3. As to shape, all observations state that the object is circular or at least elliptical, flat on the bottom and slightly domed on the top. The size estimates place it somewhere near the size of a C-54 or a Constellation.*

4. Some reports describe two tabs, located at the rear and symmetrical about the axis of flight motion.

5. Flights have been reported from three to nine of them, flying good formation on each other, with speeds always above 300 knots.

6. The discs oscillate laterally while flying along, which could be snaking.†

The above statement may well have been written by Lt. Col. George D. Garrett of Air Force Intelligence at the Pentagon who, on August 19, 1947, told FBI liaison Special Agent Reynolds that, whereas the "high brass" of the War Department had exerted "tremendous pressure" on Air Force intelligence to determine the cause of sightings of unidentified objects flying over Sweden in the summer of 1946, in the American

---

* Each of these aircraft had a wingspan of approximately 120 ft. and a length of approximately 95 ft.

† "Snaking" is defined as flying to the left and then to the right, making a track like the shape of a moving snake.

sightings, the "high brass appeared to be totally unconcerned." Garrett said that many of the witnesses were "trained observers . . . reliable members of the community" which, to him, meant that "these individuals saw something." Thus he had concluded that "there were objects seen which somebody in the Government knows all about."

Lt. Col. Garrett's speculation caused the FBI to make further checks with the "high brass" of the Air Force to be certain the FBI was not wasting its time investigating a secret project of the Armed Forces. Brig. Gen. Schulgen, who had initially contacted the FBI, assured the FBI that he would check into it. On September 5, 1947, Gen. Schulgen responded, "A complete survey of research activities discloses that the Army Air Forces has no project with the characteristic similar to those which have been associated with the Flying Discs."

Although Garrett and the writer of the above document (possibly also Garrett) were wrong in guessing that saucers were a secret project of the Armed Forces, his speculation that they were something that the high brass knew about could have been valid. Specifically, if the material retrieved in early July at Roswell, New Mexico (see chapter 1), actually was wreckage of an alien spacecraft, then a few top government civilians and a few members of the "Top Brass" (four-star generals and their associates) who were in charge of the material would not have needed the visual sightings to prove that the saucers were real. They would have *had the hard evidence* as proof.

Then, after the "initial shock of discovery," the Top Brass would realize they needed the sighting reports in order to determine where the saucers were flying, and what they were doing, i.e., the "tactics" of flying saucers. If they wanted the sighting reports but also wanted to keep the knowledge of the Roswell material restricted to very few people, they would have to do two things simultaneously: one, tell their employees (the "lower brass") to collect sighting information, and two, deny that there was proof the saucers were real. The denial could come in two ways: first, *say* that there was no convincing evidence or, second, act as if there were no hard evidence. In order to act as if there were no hard evidence, they would emphasize the importance of collecting *sighting* information in order to determine whether or not the saucers were real. Alternatively, if the lower brass (brigadier generals, colonels, captains, etc.) realized on their own (no prompting from above) that there was a potential threat posed by flying saucers and began collecting and analyzing sighting information as part of their normal intelligence function, the Top Brass wouldn't even have to mention the subject.

Thus, if the Roswell material really was from an extraterrestrial spacecraft, then the above document shows that by late July the cover-up had begun, "the fix" was in and an "iron curtain" had descended over the hard evidence.‡

While the FBI agents were interviewing witnesses and collecting information, Army Air Force intelligence was hard at work trying to make some sense out of the saucer sightings. At some time during the summer of 1947 (date unknown; probably late July or early August), Gen. Schulgen asked the Air Materiel Command (AMC) at Wright Field (now called Wright-Patterson Air Force Base) in Dayton, Ohio, to analyze sightings collected by Air Force Intelligence, and to provide an opinion on them. Within the Air Materiel Command was a technical

---

‡ This book will show that in the late 1940s the Air Force covered up the fact that it had enough evidence based on sightings alone to prove the existence of flying saucers. The Air Force also covered up the fact that some top military officials secretly believed the objects were extraterrestrial. These facts are valid whether or not the so-called Roswell crash incident was actually the retrieval by the military of a crashed alien spacecraft which, of course, would be the hard evidence.

Suppose an alien spacecraft actually was retrieved in July 1947, and suppose that the very top military and civilian officials (President, top generals, top scientists) decided for some reason that the fact of its existence had to be kept absolutely secret. Then, one might logically ask, why is there no specific mention of hard evidence in the formerly secret Air Force documents released over the last twenty years? A person unfamiliar with the way extremely classified military secrets are treated would expect such references. However, the unquestionably authentic government documents released thus far do not indicate that there was a crashed alien craft. In fact, several of the documents indicate that there is no hard evidence in the form of crash debris. Does this prove that the Roswell material was *not* from an alien spacecraft? No, and for the following reason. If the existence of hard evidence had been covered up at the *highest levels* of the military and civilian government, then the references to a lack of hard evidence by several writers could indicate either their lack of knowledge (not being in the "inner circle") or that they knew about the hard evidence but were *ordered to cover up its existence by stating that there was no such evidence*. The fact is that a person in military intelligence could, under orders, lie to cover up evidence. In the following chapters where I refer to the Roswell crash I will describe why the idea that hard evidence was covered up could be consistent with the available information.

Although this book is equivocal on the alien interpretation of the Roswell case, it is not equivocal on the sighting evidence. The bottom line is that some people in the government *knew* a long time ago the true significance of saucer sightings but they didn't tell the American people—they buried this knowledge in their own "X-Files."

Lt. Gen. Nathan Twining, Commanding General of the Air Materiel Command.

intelligence division designated T-2, and an engineering division called T-3. The members of these divisions were scientifically and technically trained Air Force employees whose job it was to analyze foreign aircraft to determine the level of technology and their war-fighting capabilities. Several of the T-2 and T-3 personnel had already taken an interest in saucer reports because they were actively involved in studying designs for saucer-like "low-aspect ratio" aircraft that had been on the drawing boards of the German Air Force in the Second World War. These designs, and even some of the scientists who had worked on them, had been brought to the United States for study after the war. They knew that other German scientists, along with their design plans, had been taken to the Soviet Union at the end of the war. Hence they may well have thought that these designs had actually been built by a military organization in the United States or the Soviet Union. At the very least, they were probably more willing to accept these reports as being reasonably accurate than most people, who thought that an airplane needed wings and an overall "T" shape in order to fly.

As requested, these employees analyzed the sightings and wrote a classified secret report that, over the signature of Lt. Gen. Nathan Twining, the Commanding General of the AMC, was sent to Gen. Schulgen.

The letter, dated September 23, 1947, echoed the positive attitude, and even some of the wording, of the above report found in the FBI file. According to the letter, the opinion of the AMC scientists and engineers was based on "interrogation report data" supplied by Gen. Schulgen. (The letter does not mention any source of information other than sighting reports.) In their opinion, "the phenomenon is something real and not visionary or fictitious," and, "there are objects probably approximating the shape of a disc, of such appreciable size as to appear to be as big as man-made aircraft." The objects were described as metallic in appearance, circular or elliptical in shape and with flat bottoms and domes on top.

The objects were also characterized by their "extreme rates of climb," maneuverability, and general lack of noise. The letter says that, "It is possible within present U.S. knowledge—provided extensive development is undertaken—to construct a piloted aircraft" which would look roughly saucer shaped and "which would be capable of an approximate range of 7,000 miles at subsonic speed." In other words, in the opinion of the AMC scientists and engineers, "saucers" were probably based on reasonably well-understood aerodynamic principles combined with advanced technological means for flight, such as advanced materials for construction and advanced engines for propulsion. In other words, saucers were not only possible, *but probable!*

The letter suggested that the objects might be "of domestic origin-the product of some high security project not known to AC/AS-2 or this Command," or, a more disturbing possibility, that "some foreign nation has a form of propulsion, possibly nuclear, which is outside of our domestic knowledge." However, according to the letter, "a lack of physical evidence in the form of crash recovered exhibits" prevented AMC from conclusively identifying the craft. The letter recommended that a special classified project be set up that would coordinate with the Army, Navy, Atomic Energy Commission, the Joint Research and Development Board, the Air Force Scientific Advisory Group, the RAND project, and other advanced research agencies in order to study the saucer reports. Finally the letter stated that AMC would "continue the investigation within its current resources in order to more closely define the nature of the phenomenon." The letter ended with a promise that Essential Elements of Information (EEI) would be "formulated immediately for transmission through channels." (These EEI were needed in order to help military intelligence operatives throughout the world collect information about any flying saucers that were being made by foreign countries, particularly the Soviet Union and the Soviet Bloc countries.)

The reference to a "lack of physical evidence" suggests that either the Roswell debris did not come from a flying saucer, or, if it did, Twining didn't know about it. A third possibility is that Twining and the AMC analysts knew the Roswell material was hard evidence but couldn't allow it to be mentioned in a letter classified only at the Secret level.

Could it be that Twining had not been informed about the Roswell material? Yes, that is possible. Twining knew that he didn't know everything going on in U.S. military research. The letter suggests that the objects might be "of domestic origin . . . the product of some high security project not known to this command or to [Gen. Schulgen]." Twining's suggestion that *there might be something he didn't know about* is a direct illustration of the way Top Secret information is protected.

Top Secret information is often segmented or divided into "chunks" or "compartments" and a person is allowed access to only the "chunks" of information that he needs to know to do his job. Only a few persons at the very top of the government and defense establishment know everything—or *almost* everything—about individual military research activities. They determine what their employees "need-to-know" in order to carry out their missions and they authorize their employees "special access" to only the needed information. This system of "compartmentalization" of information was developed during the Second World War in order to protect the knowledge about the atomic bomb and other secret technological advances (e.g., radar, bomb site, proximity fuse).

Lt. Gen. Twining, although head of the Air Materiel Command, was nevertheless an "employee" of the Top Brass (a four-star general such as Chief of Staff of the Army Air Force, Gen. Carl Spaatz, in 1947 and, in 1948, Gen. Hoyt Vandenberg). Hence he knew that there *could be* projects, even projects carried out at AMC, *which the Top Brass knew about but for which he had no "need to know" and therefore he hadn't been told.* Furthermore, it appears from the letter that he made the logical assumption that Brig. Gen. Schlugen, also, did not know about any project that was creating the "flying saucer situation."

There is a fourth possibility. Twining knew the Roswell debris was extraterrestrial, but the persons who actually formulated and typed the letter for Twining's signature *did not know.* The T-2 and T-3 personnel who wrote the letter based their conclusions on sighting information from Gen. Schulgen. They mentioned the lack of hard evidence and the possibility that the saucers were some secret project of which "this command" was unaware. When handed this letter, it is possible that *Twining simply signed it as written,* without correcting the statements about a "lack of hard evidence" and a "high security project," in order to maintain the tight security around the debris.

The most important aspect of Twining's letter is that by late September 1947, the AMC technical intelligence analysts had concluded that flying saucers were *real, unexplainable objects.* It is important to know of this early conclusion by Air Force intelligence because a few years later, as the controversy over saucer sightings became popularized and politicized, the Air Force stated publicly that all sightings, including these early ones, could be explained. The claim was wrong, as we will discover.

Air Force intelligence was seriously worried that the Soviet Union had gotten the jump on the United States, by improving on innovative research of the German aeronautical engineers, Walter and Reimar Horton. The Hortons had designed an aircraft in which the main body was not a fuselage but rather a broad wing with the curved front, a "flying wing." The Air Force investigators wondered if the Soviets could have actually constructed such a craft, and flown it over the United States. The Air Force initiated a search by the Army Counter Intelligence Corp (CIC) for the Horton brothers and for any information from foreign countries that might offer an explanation for the saucer sightings. To aid in this search, the Essential Elements of Information (EEI), mentioned at the end of Gen. Twining's letter, were sent to the CIC. These Essential Elements of Information, not released by the Army Security Agency until 1994, show that the Air Force had determined that the saucers had some amazing capabilities. A formerly Secret cover letter for the EEI, found in the files of the Operations Branch of the 970th CIC and dated October 20, 1947 reads as follows:

1. Attached hereto is an EEI written at Wright Field, Ohio, concerning the flying saucers recently sighted over the United States.

2. For your information, the Air Materiel Command at Wright Field is making a study of this subject and is constructing models to be tested in a wind tunnel. As a guide in constructing the models, descriptions from various persons who claimed to have sighted these objects were used. The Air Materiel Command is of the opinion that some sort of object, such as the flying saucer, did exist.

This document makes it clear that AMC considered the saucers to be *real flying craft.* Furthermore, this confirms rumors going back nearly fifty years that the Air Force constructed flying saucer models to test in wind tunnels.

In the EEI document, the AMC investigators discussed the work of the Horton brothers and suggested that, perhaps, the Soviets had pushed the development of flying wing aircraft and had thereby "leapfrogged" our own technological developments. This suggestion, although ultimately proven wrong, caused a considerable amount of confusion in later years as the AMC and lower brass of the Air Force attempted to determine whether flying saucers were craft of another country, meaning Soviet, or spacecraft from another world!

On October 28, 1947, the same day that the 970th CIC sent the EEI to its agents, Gen. Schulgen's Intelligence Requirements Division of the AFI prepared an Intelligence Collection Memorandum and a list of Intelligence Requirements, both of which were based on the EEI document provided by AMC. The Collection Memorandum was written to justify the information collected "in the field of Flying Saucer type aircraft." Most of the Collection Memorandum, most likely written by Lt. Col. George Garrett, is simply a word-for-word copy of a similar portion of the AMC EEI document. Garrett's version of the (formerly Secret) Collection Memorandum begins as follows, with an italic emphasis to indicate words that Garrett added to the original AMC EEI document:

An alleged "Flying Saucer" type aircraft or object in flight, approximating the shape of a disc, has been reported by many observers from widely scattered places, such as the United States, Alaska, Canada, Hungary, the Island of Guam, and Japan. The object has been reported by many competent observers, *including USAF rated officers.* Sightings have been made from the ground as well as the air.

In the summer of 1947, there were few newspaper reports of saucers seen in other countries. Since there were no widely publicized reports of foreign sightings, the skeptics, who did not have access to Air Force information, argued quite correctly that flying saucers couldn't be vehicles from outer space, because, if they were, they would have appeared in other countries as well. From the above memorandum we now know what AFI and the Central Intelligence Agency (CIA), which obtained the reports, knew in 1947: *saucers were sighted in other countries.* The above paragraph also shows that the observers were not all untrained, "average" people who couldn't recognize normal things in the sky. Many of the observers were "rated USAF officers."

Col. Garrett's draft memorandum follows the EEI word-for-word through the list of "commonly reported features":

- a. Relatively flat bottom with extreme light-reflecting ability
- b. Absence of sound except for an occasional roar when operating under super performance conditions
- c. Extreme maneuverability, and apparent ability to almost hover
- d. A plan form approximating that of an oval or disc with a dome shape on the top surface
- e. The absence of an exhaust trail except in a few instances.
- f. The ability to quickly disappear by high speed or by complete disintegration
- g. The ability to suddenly appear without warning as if from an extremely high altitude
- h. The size most reported approximated that of a C-54 or Constellation type aircraft

i. The ability to group together very quickly in a tight for-
    mation when more than one aircraft are together

j. Evasive action ability indicates possibility of being manually
    operated, or possibly by electronic or remote control devices

k. Under certain conditions the craft seems to have the abil-
    ity to cut a clear path through clouds-width of path esti-
    mated to be approximately one half mile, only one inci-
    dent indicated this phenomenon [sic]

This list makes one thing abundantly clear: namely, that there had
been enough credible saucer observations so that the Air Force could
compile a list of specific, and rather startling, characteristics. These
characteristics, which were not publicized, and appeared only in secret
documents, have been reported independently by numerous witnesses
throughout the years since the document was written. Of particular
interest are items b, c, f, g, and j. We had no silent aircraft at the time and
only helicopters could hover. Of course, they are not extremely maneuverable. Hence characteristics b and c could not be correlated with aircraft known at the time. Items f and g indicate that these objects are
capable of extreme acceleration and can travel at *such high speeds that
they are effectively invisible to the observer.*

Over the years many witnesses have reported sudden appearances, dis-
appearances, or sudden changes in location of UFOs, but until recently
the civilian community of ufologists (people who investigate sightings
and study the phenomenon) had no optically recorded evidence, only
personal testimony. However, there are now several video recordings of
UFOs accelerating and moving at extreme speeds. Objects that can
achieve a very large amount of acceleration and move through the sky at
extremely high speeds would, for practical purposes, be "invisible" to
anyone who wasn't looking in exactly the right place at exactly the right
time to see a blur pass by.§ Item j above indicates that saucers were intel-
ligently controlled and not some unusual, previously unknown natural
phenomenon.

§ See "Acceleration" in the Proceedings of the 1996 International Symposium of the Mutual
UFO Network (MUFON), or the World Wide Web at www.webcom.com/kellaher/arti-
cles/maccabee/acceleration.html. Two of these videos are discussed in *UFOs Are Real: Here's
the Proof* by Edward Walters and Bruce Maccabee (Avon Books, 1997).

Garrett's draft of the EEI continued by pointing out that the first sightings occurred around the middle of May 1947 (predating Kenneth Arnold's sighting), the peak activity was in early July, and the "last reported sightings took place in Toronto, Canada, 14 September." It continues to state that "for purposes of analysis and evaluation," the objects were considered to be a "manned craft of Russian origin." (Note: The AMC analysts and Garrett had to *assume* the objects were under intelligent control because they seemed able to take evasive action.)

The AMC at Wright Field was not the only Air Force intelligence agency that took saucer sightings seriously. Documents which have only become available in the last ten years or so prove that the Air Force Office of Intelligence (AFOIN) at the Pentagon (hereafter abbreviated AFI), was carrying out its own study of saucer sightings. The formerly Secret AFI study, "Analysis of Flying Disc Reports," written in the late fall of 1947, was based on single and multiple witness visual sightings, and several radar sightings. "Observers have indicated to be reliable and in some instances several observers have corroborated separate observations of the same phenomenon at the same time," the report stated. The characteristics of flying saucers listed by AFI are essentially the same as in the Intelligence Collection Memorandum discussed above, including the "ability to hover; to appear suddenly as if from a dive; to disintegrate or to disappear, perhaps by increasing speed; to group quickly in a tight formation, and to take evasive action."

According to the report, the AFI thoroughly investigated the flying saucer situation by (a) analyzing sightings (most remained unexplained), (b) checking with all known U.S. agencies that might have developed novel and highly secret circular aircraft (none did), (c) asking AMC to analyze sightings and form its own opinion (AMC responded in Gen. Twining's September 23 letter), (d) asking the FBI to investigate the possibility of communist subversion (none was found), (e) asking the Air Weather Service to analyze the sightings to determine if any could be weather balloons (none were) and (g) analyzing the possibility that a foreign country (for example, the Soviet Union) could have leapfrogged the aeronautical technology of the USA. The AFI could find no reason to believe any country had developed such a unique craft. Furthermore, the AFI analysts argued that even if another country had developed such a craft, that development would not explain the sightings over North America because the country wouldn't fly the craft in an area where the United States could learn its technological secrets if it crashed or was shot down. In spite of their inability to identify the nature or source of the flying discs, the AFI analysts concluded that "flying discs, as reported by widely scattered observers, probably represent something real and tangible, even though physical evidence, such as crash-recovered exhibits, is not available." Whereas some reports might result from natural or man-made phenomena, "the likelihood that some observers actually saw disc-shaped objects sufficiently large to be compared in size with known aircraft cannot be dismissed."

In other words, AFI concluded that flying saucers are real, and probably not flying craft from a foreign country. The AFI study ends with the statement, "The Directorate of Intelligence, USAF, will continue to collect and analyze all reports of sightings of flying objects, lights, trails, etc. in an effort to develop an answer to the puzzling problem which they present."**

On December 18, 1947, Gen. George C. McDonald, the Director of AFI, wrote a letter to Maj. Gen. Craigie, the Director of Air Force Research and Development. The letter presented the overall AFI opinion on flying saucers (they are real and need investigation), and said stated that Gen. McDonald agreed with Gen. Twining's recommendation to set up a special project for investigating and analyzing sightings. On December 30, 1947, Gen. Craigie responded by issuing a directive to Commanding Gen. Twining of AMC to set up a special project with the code name "Sign," at Wright Field. Gen. Craigie directed Project Sign to "collect, collate, evaluate, and distribute to interested government agencies and contractors all information concerning sightings and phenomena in the atmosphere which can be construed to be of concern to national security."††

** The inclusion of the statement that "crash-recovered exhibits are not available" indicates that either no flying disc had crashed (the Roswell material was *not* from a saucer), or that the existence of a crash was being withheld from AFI intelligence analysts, or that the writer of the AFI study was intentionally lying about the absence of crash debris.

†† Note the nonspecific wording of the last part of the sentence. Virtually any atmospheric phenomenon could be investigated if it could be *construed* to be *of concern to national security.* Where is the specific mention of "flying saucers"?

Maj. Gen. George C. McDonald, Director of Air Force Intelligence.

Although initial preparations for a special project had begun weeks before in AMC, the final organization of Project Sign took place in early January and the project officially began on January 22, 1948. It immediately ran into problems. There was little financial support, and the personnel of the project had to be "borrowed" from other projects. Nevertheless, within a few weeks the Air Force and the Army issued their first official requests for information on "Flying Discs." The Army's intelligence collection document was a shortened version of the AMC-EEI document discussed above. The Air Force's intelligence collection request, issued in February 1948, was not based on the EEI. Instead, it asked for basic sighting information such as location and date, time, weather, names of witnesses, number of objects, size, speed, etc.

Thus began the Air Force's twenty-one-year foray into the realm of the impossible—flying saucers. The Project Sign personnel were so impressed by the sightings that, about seven months later, they tried to convince the Chief of Staff of the Air Force, Gen. Vandenberg, that flying saucers *were interplanetary vehicles.* However, Vandenberg rejected this idea and thereby removed interplanetary vehicles as an acceptable explanation for any of the sightings. His rejection had a negative impact on the ATIC investigators. It forced them to use explanations (misidentification or misperception, delusion, hoax) which they really didn't think were correct for many sightings. Possible reasons for the rejection and its impact on the history of UFO research are discussed further in chapter 5.

As we'll see, by this time the FBI was no longer in the saucer business. At least, not *officially.*

CHAPTER 4

Ash Can Covers
and Toilet Seats

FBI agents officially investigated saucer sightings for about a month, and then abruptly ended the investigation as a result of a somewhat "scandalous" situation. In August 1947, FBI agents learned that the Air Force had not been totally honest when it asked for help. In a letter from Lt. Gen. Stratemeyer, Assistant Chief of Staff for Intelligence, to the commanding generals of the 1st, 2nd, 4th, 10th, 11th, and 14th Air Forces, he stated that the FBI had been brought into the investigation "to relieve the numbered Air Forces of the task of tracking down all the many instances which turned out to be ash can covers, toilet seats and whatnot." In other words, "whereas the Air Defense Command Air Forces would interview responsible observers," the FBI "would investigate incidents of discs being found by civilians on the ground," that is, all the hoax cases.

The letter, classified "Restricted" and dated September 3, 1947, was given to the FBI in San Francisco by Lt. Col. Donald Springer. The agent sent a copy of the document to FBI headquarters along with the comment that "the Bureau might desire to discuss this matter further with the Army Air Forces both as to the types of investigations which we will conduct and also to object to the scurrilous wordage which, to say the least, is insulting to the Bureau." On September 27, Director J. Edgar Hoover wrote a letter to Maj. Gen. McDonald. In the letter he mentioned the comment about "ash can covers, toilet seats and whatnot," thereby demonstrating that the FBI had "penetrated" the Air Force secrecy about saucer investigation. He then pointed out that he couldn't "permit the personnel and time of this organization to be dissipated in this manner," and informed the General that the FBI would no longer investigate flying disc sightings. Instead, it would send all sighting investigation reports to the Air Force. On October 1, FBI headquarters sent Bulletin #57 to all FBI offices: "All future reports connected with flying discs should be referred to the Air Force, and no investigative action should be taken by Bureau agents." Thus ended the period of "official" FBI investigation of flying saucer sightings. During this time FBI agents had interviewed witnesses to about two dozen sightings. Roughly one quarter of the sightings they investigated involved hoax devices and models of saucers.

Bulletin #57 did not end the saucer data collection activities of the FBI, nor did it close the "X-File." In a letter to the Special Agent in Charge (SAC) at San Francisco, dated February 20, 1948, and entitled FLYING DISC, SECURITY MATTER – X, the FBI director stated that, in the future, the FBI would collect information from witnesses who volunteered it and turn it over the Air Force and the FBI would "receive any information which the Air Forces volunteer." It is this last phrase which makes the FBI file important for UFO research, because in the following years Air Force representatives provided the FBI with information which was not provided to the American people and, most importantly, *FBI headquarters stored this information.*

Although the period of official investigation had ended, FBI agents interviewed a few more witnesses in the fall of 1947. In March 1948, the FBI received a letter from Senator Kenneth Wherry of Nebraska asking the FBI to comment on a disc observation described in a letter from one of Wherry's constituents, a resident of Benkelman, Nebraska. According to the letter (published here for the first time), on March 13, 1948, at 2:30 P.M. Mountain Standard Time, the man (his name has been blacked out on the document) heard a noise like a motor or a train at a very long distance on a quiet day. He looked into the sky.

At first glance [the object] looked like it might be a vapor trail left by a high flying plane. But the white streak that was in the sky never changed its shape or did it change in the direction of travel. It traveled much faster than any plane I have seen traveling in the sky high enough to leave a vapor trail. As near as I can describe this sight was that it might appear to be a streamlined train traveling at a very high altitude at a very high rate of speed. This rocket or whatever it might have been was high enough to disappear from sight while it was yet far above the horizon. The silver streak in the sky traveled as if it were a long connected streak. This did not resemble a line of smoke left by a train traveling along; it moved altogether as a unit.

The witness saw this object traveling east to west and thought it might have passed over Denver, Colorado. He ended his letter with the following statement:

I am not writing this so that it might seem to be another disc fan or whatever you might call them. I just saw this and it has been on my mind and I thought if there was anything that I could be of help to solve this thing [sic] I would write this to you and you can forward this to the proper Dept. if it is necessary. If it is not against any regulation and if [it is] possible [I] would like to have [an] answer to this object [sic].

Hoover wrote to the witness that he had forwarded the letter to the "Secretary of the Army, National Defense Building, Washington, D.C." Presumably the letter would eventually have gotten to the Air Force and eventually to Project Sign at Wright-Patterson Air Force Base. However, a check of the master case file of Project Blue Book at the National Archives, which is supposed to list all the sightings received by the Air Force since early 1947, does not contain a listing for this sighting.

From April through July 1948, the FBI had only a few communications with the Air Force regarding flying saucers. Then the FBI was called back into action by a postmaster. At noon on August 11, 1948, in Hamel,

Minnesota, two boys, ages eight and ten, saw a silver, two-foot diameter object like two plates lip-to-lip descend to the ground near them. It made a whistling noise and rotated as it contacted the ground with a crunching noise, and then seemed to rebound upward. It hovered momentarily and sped off. The boys ran to their parents and appeared visibly frightened as they told what they had seen. Their parents covered the landing spot with a washtub and then reported the incident to the local postmaster. The postmaster knew of no reason to doubt the boys, so he contacted the local FBI agent who interviewed the boys at their house. He saw a depression in the soil where the saucer had landed. The agent sent his report to the local Air Force intelligence representative. Since there was a depression in the soil, the Air Force decided it would be advisable to have the FBI laboratory analyze the soil. The FBI analyzed a sample for unusual metal particles, evidence of heat, and evidence of radioactivity. Nothing unusual was found.

No one disputed the boys' testimony at the time of the sighting, but a year later the Air Force sighting analysts, who were under pressure to explain every sighting in some way or other, concluded: "This apparent bit of fantasy is hardly worth further consideration."

By the middle of 1948 the FBI had left the ash can covers and toilet seats far behind, with no intent to continue an interest in flying saucers. However, the FBI could not get away that easily. Only a year later the FBI would be leaking to the American people the Air Force "conclusion" that saucers were Soviet aircraft. How that came about is the subject of the next several chapters, which describe the secret internal Air Force controversy over whether or not saucers were *extraterrestrial vehicles!*

CHAPTER 5

Project Sign and the Extraterrestrial Estimate

During much of 1948, the FBI's "X-Files" were mostly dormant, not to awake again until January 1949. The Air Force "X-Files," on the other hand, was active. It contained secret documents that showed it was very active, even approaching red-hot. Although the FBI wasn't involved, it is important to learn what happened within the 1948 Air Force investigation, since that determined to a considerable extent what the Air Force told the FBI in later years.

As pointed out previously, there were two Air Force intelligence groups involved in saucer sighting analysis. One group, herein called AFI, was headquartered in the Pentagon. AFI would collect information related to foreign developments in aircraft for analysis by AFI experts. It would also send copies to the Army Materiel Command (AMC) for an independent analysis by the experts at T-2 and T-3. The available records suggest that the AFI intelligence experts could be divided into two "factions," those who believed that people were seeing real, significant objects, and those who thought the sightings were mistakes, signifying nothing (after all, there was no "hard evidence"). Since it was the AFI which established the liaison with the FBI, the effects of the temporary ascendancy of one or the other of these factions over the ensuing years appears in the FBI records. (The AFI documents were not turned over to the National Archives in 1975. They have been released in more recent years, and many are published here for the first time.)

The other intelligence group, called T-2, or the "Analysis Division," was a part of AMC at Wright Field. In 1948, T-2 became the Technical Intelligence Division and then the Air Technical Intelligence Center (ATIC) while Wright Field, in Dayton, Ohio, was renamed Wright-Patterson Air Force Base (WPAFB; the base was referred to as Wright Field for many years after the name change). Project Sign and its successors, Projects Grudge and Blue Book, were special projects within ATIC. Projects Sign and Grudge were poorly funded and the personnel involved were "borrowed" from other intelligence activities. This low level of support limited their data—gathering ability and their analysis time, but did not limit their enthusiasm for the project.

As mentioned before, several Project Sign investigators had already been studying saucer-like (low-aspect ratio) flying craft for several years because of their interest in advanced airform design. They were also involved with the analysis and exploitation of the German war research into wingless craft. (It is probable that these investigators took the sightings more seriously than most people because they already believed that craft shaped generally like saucers *could* fly.) The AMC/ATIC personnel would analyze sightings and send copies of their work to AFI at the Pentagon. The records from AMC/ATIC and many of the files from the Air Force Office of Special Investigations, which handled most of the witness interrogations (the "legwork" of investigation), were turned over to the National Archives in 1975.

Fact: In a formerly Top Secret study written about nine months after the start of Project Sign, but not released to the general public until 1985, AFI analysts reaffirmed the conclusion, made in the fall of 1947, that flying saucers were *real objects.* Of more importance is the fact that, according to Capt. Edward Ruppelt in *The Report on Unidentified Flying Objects,* in the summer of 1948, the ATIC/Sign investigators tried to convince Gen. Hoyt Vandenberg, Chief of Staff of the Air Force, that flying saucers were *interplanetary vehicles!*

Gen. Hoyt Vandenberg, Air Force Chief of Staff (left) and Maj. Gen. Charles P. Cabell (right).

But how could this be? Aren't all saucer sightings figments of the imagination, or mistakes, or hoaxes? That's what the Air Force told the public, and that's what the skeptics, the press, and most people believed. However that's not what AFI and ATIC believed in 1948, and here's the reason: *there were dozens of sightings by credible witnesses, including Air Force and other military personnel, that could not be explained.* Many of these sightings were obtained through official channels because of the information requests, such as the EEI, discussed previously, which were sent to Air Force, Navy, and Army units stationed throughout the world in early 1948.

In early 1948, Maj. Gen. Charles P. Cabell replaced Maj. Gen. McDonald as the Chief of the Air Intelligence Requirements Division of the Directorate of Intelligence in the Office of the Deputy Chief of Staff for Operations. On February 27, 1948, a month after Project Sign officially began, Lt. Col. Garrett, acting for Gen. Cabell, wrote a letter containing specific instructions that would apply to reporting flying saucer sightings. The letter began:

1. It is Air Force policy not to ignore reports of sightings and phenomena in the atmosphere, but to recognize that part of

its mission is to collect, collate, evaluate and act on information of this nature.

2. In implementing this policy, the Air Materiel Command has been designated as the Air Force agency to collect, collate, evaluate, and distribute to interested government agencies and contractors, all information concerning sightings and phenomena in the atmosphere which can be construed to be of concern to the national security.

Unlike the previously discussed EEI, with its list of intelligence requirements, the instructions included with this letter were to report the location, time, weather, names and occupations of observers, any photographs, the number of objects sighted, color, shape, speed, sound, altitude, maneuvers, etc. In other words, this letter requested specific information that would pertain only to visual sightings of objects in the atmosphere. This sort of information was used by AFI and ATIC analysts to determine saucer activities around the world. The letter specified that, rather than sending sighting reports to AFI headquarters at the Pentagon, the reports were to be sent directly to a special office, MCI-AXO-3*, within ATIC at Wright-Patterson Air Force Base, bypassing AFI and therefore saving time. Army Materiel Command would then send report copies and analyses to AFI. Gen. Cabell's decision to speed up the AMC analysis process by having sightings sent directly to AMC meant that AFI had to rely on AMC for reports and analyses. This procedure allowed AMC to effectively control what AFI received. (Two-and-a-half years later, Gen. Cabell would discover that this procedure had a negative impact on the Air Force saucer investigation. He would discover that *skeptical ATIC analysts invented explanations for all the sightings, whether or not the explanations were reasonable,* and sent these explanations to AFI. He further discovered that they had lied to him when they claimed they were carrying out unbiased investigations!)

By March, Project Sign was well underway at ATIC. Reports from 1947 were analyzed, and new reports were received. According to the Project Blue Book microfilm record in the National Archives, ATIC had

---

* MCIAXO-Office code for Materiel Command, Intelligence, Analysis Division, Special Projects Branch.

Col. Howard McCoy,
Director of Intelligence at
Air Materiel Command.

by this time collected approximately 130 reports by Project Sign. Then, in early 1996, a document was released by the government that suggests the Air Force may have withheld (or lost) some sighting reports.

This document turned up in the transcript of the March 18, 1948 meeting of the Air Force Science Advisory Board (AFSAB). Although most of this Secret level meeting was devoted to presentations about various conventional Air Force advanced technology and technical intelligence projects, for a few minutes Col. Howard McCoy, Director of Intelligence at AMC, discussed an unconventional intelligence project at ATIC:

> We have a new project—Project SIGN—which may surprise you as a development from the so-called mass hysteria of the past summer when we had all the unidentified flying objects or discs. This can't be laughed off. We have over 300 reports which haven't been publicized in the papers from very competent personnel, in many instances—men as capable as Dr. K.D. Wood, and practically all Air Force, airline people with broad experience. We are running down every report. I can't even tell you how much we would give to have one of those crash in an area so that we could recover whatever they are.

Since Col. McCoy was the head of intelligence at AMC, and therefore responsible for Project Sign, it is important to understand what he has said . . . and what he has not said.

He approaches this subject lightly, almost apologetically. I presume he takes this approach because his audience consists of scientists, most or all of whom were not involved in saucer investigations, and knew only what had been reported in the press. The scientific community was generally skeptical about the sightings, since the press had treated the subject lightly and the Air Force had not publicly reported any convincing evidence of their existence. Most, or perhaps all, of the members of Col. McCoy's audience would not have known any more than what was reported in the press, and therefore would not have been inclined to treat the subject seriously. Col. McCoy, presumably to counter the anti-saucer bias of these scientists, begins by telling them that the sightings were important and couldn't be simply "laughed off." He then states that there were "over 300" *unpublicized* reports by "very competent personnel." This number is surprisingly large, because the Project Blue Book microfilm lists only about 130 sightings collected by March 1948, and many of these *had* been publicized. Perhaps he simply made an error in his recollection of how many sightings had been collected. But taken literally, his statement suggests that there might be more than 160 sightings missing from the first nine months (June 1947 – March 1948) of the Blue Book file.

To lend a weight of authority to his statement about the importance of the sightings, McCoy mentions Dr. Karl D. Wood, an eminent scientist and head of the Aeronautical Engineering Department at the University of Colorado. (Dr. Wood had reported a December 1947, sighting of some sort of "strange aircraft" leaving a trail "not like a usual jet airplane trail." Unfortunately the object was too high for Dr. Wood to see its shape.) McCoy indicated just how seriously ATIC was treating these sightings by saying that every one was being investigated.

His closing remark, about wishing one would crash, indicates his belief that they were solid objects, otherwise they couldn't crash, and also that the Air Force had to wait for one to crash because they couldn't shoot one down (had they been conventional enemy aircraft the Air Force could have shot one down). Of course, the straightforward interpretation of his closing remark is that none *had* crashed. There are (at least) two other possible interpretations of his "wish:" one, McCoy, being only a colonel, did not know about the Roswell debris (in other words, Twining or someone higher up had not told him), or two, a more sinister aspect—he knew, but had been ordered to intentionally mislead his audience in order to avoid any interest that would suddenly arise in the members of the scientifically trained audience if they thought that there were hard evidence of a flying saucer reality.†

During the next seven months of 1948, the AMC collected about 100 sightings, according to the tabulation presented in Project Blue Book Special Report #14 (published in 1955). They could not explain most of these sightings. Furthermore, some sightings seemed to indicate intelligent control of highly maneuverable craft. According to Ruppelt in *The Report on Unidentified Flying Objects,* some of the reports were of average quality, puzzling but not totally convincing. A large proportion, however, came from people whose reliability couldn't be questioned. Ruppelt cited the report by three scientists who, for thirty seconds, watched a "round object streak across the sky in a highly erratic flight path near the Army's secret White Sands Proving Ground," the report by an Air Force C-47 crew of "three UFOs (that came rapidly) in from 'twelve o'clock high' to buzz their transport," and a "curious report from the Netherlands from several persons who had seen a rocket-shaped object with two rows of windows along the side." Ruppelt wrote that this latter report probably would have been ignored "except that four nights later a similar UFO almost collided with an Eastern Airlines DC-3." This is a reference to the famous "Chiles-Whitted" sighting of July 24, 1948. At 2:45 a.m., while flying at 5,000 ft. near Montgomery, Alabama, Capt. Clarence Chiles and copilot John Whitted saw a roughly rocket-shaped, wingless object with what appeared to be windows and a blue glow of light. An FBI document dated January 31, 1949 (to be discussed later) provides a brief summary:

---

† Note: He was speaking at a Secret level meeting to a sizable audience of people, most or all of whom, could do their Air Force work without knowing about crashed saucers, i.e., they had no "need-to-know" about such information. It is important to realize that because of military regulations to protect highly secret information one cannot discuss Top Secret information at the Secret level. In some cases one cannot even mention of the existence of Top Secret information in a discussion at the Secret level (and sometimes not even during a discussion at the Top Secret level) without explicit authorization from the person(s) or agency in charge of the information.

In July 1948, an unidentified aircraft was "seen" by an Eastern Airlines pilot and co-pilot and one or more passengers of the Eastern airline plane over Montgomery, Alabama. This aircraft was reported to be of an unconventional type without wings and resembled generally a "rocket ship" of the type depicted in comic strips. It was reported to have had windows; to have been larger than the Eastern Airlines plane, and to have been traveling at an estimated speed of 2,700 miles an hour. It appeared out of a thunderhead ahead of the Eastern Airlines plane and immediately disappeared in another cloud narrowly missing a collision with the Eastern Airlines plane. No sound or air disturbance was noted in connection with this appearance.

The pilots told the Air Force investigators that the object had square windows, a cherry-red flame or wake from the back end, and that it seemed to be only a few hundred feet higher than the plane. After it passed the plane, it seemed to gain altitude and then disappeared above the broken clouds. Note that the estimated speed was roughly 2,000 mph faster than our aircraft could travel, but was much slower than the speed of a meteor. And, of course, glowing meteors do not fly roughly horizontally through clouds at a 5,000 ft. altitude.

There also seemed to be corroborating sightings. According to Ruppelt, "A crew chief at Robbins Air Force Base at Macon, Georgia, reported seeing an extremely bright light pass overhead, traveling at a high speed . . . A quick check on a map showed that the UFO that nearly collided with the airliner would have passed almost over Macon," about 200 miles away. "The UFO had been turning toward Macon when last seen." There was also a report from a pilot flying over northern North Carolina who said he had seen a bright "shooting star" in the direction of Montgomery at about the exact time of the Chiles-Whitted sighting. Of course, a shooting star would not pass a few hundred feet from a plane flying at 5,000 ft., and then climb into the clouds again. A meteor that low would crash. Hence whatever they saw was not a meteor.

This sighting was the straw that broke the camel's back as far as AFI was concerned. Something had to be done to find out what these saucers were! According to the official Blue Book records, the AFI and ATIC investigators had collected by this time over 200 sightings, most of which they couldn't explain. Maj. Gen. Cabell wanted a definitive analysis of these sightings. On July 27, 1948 he directed the Air Estimates Branch of AFI at the Pentagon to prepare a study to determine the "tactics of flying objects" and the "probability of their existence." In response to this directive the Air Estimates Branch wrote a document, to be discussed, that proposed a most likely explanation and contained recommendations on what to do next. The ATIC/Sign investigators also reacted to the Chiles-Whitted sighting and began writing their own Estimate of the Situation. Whether this was in direct response to Gen. Cabell's July 27 letter to AFI or whether they did it on their own is not clear from the available record. Their written response to the Chiles-Whitted sighting was decidedly more daring than the AFI response, as will be seen.

Air Force Reserve Capt. Kevin Randle, in *The UFO Casebook,* has reported an intriguing story related to the Estimate which he heard during a dinner conversation in 1986.‡ The man telling the story was an Air Force Reserve officer. He told Randle and several others that he had been at Wright Field in 1948 and knew that after the Chiles-Whitted sighting, an Estimate of the Situation was quickly drafted and hand-carried to Gen. Vandenberg in the Pentagon. The Estimate suggested *extraterrestrial.* According to this officer, the initial draft of the Estimate contained not only a listing of unexplained sightings, but also a reference to *physical evidence found in New Mexico.* When the personnel at AMC received the initial draft back from Vandenberg they discovered that the paragraphs which mentioned physical evidence had been marked for deletion. According to this officer, the ATIC personnel rewrote the document leaving out the reference to physical evidence. Yet, they were still sufficiently confident to retain their ET conclusion based on the sighting reports alone. According to Randle's informant, on August 5, the second version of the Estimate was again on Vandenberg's desk and once again Vandenberg rejected the document, *this time for lack of hard evidence!* Unfortunately there is no independent corroboration of this man's story

‡ Randle, *The UFO Casebook,* Warner Books, 1989, pp. 29–31.

(he is now deceased) nor is there any documentary evidence available at the present time which demonstrates that ATIC personnel knew about any physical evidence.

Although there is no confirmation of a version that mentions physical evidence, there is confirmation of a version of the Estimate which used sighting information alone to arrive at the ET conclusion. Ruppelt wrote about it in *The Report on Unidentified Flying Objects.* He calls it "the Estimate," with no reference to a predecessor. Ruppelt's story agrees with what Randle's informant said about the second version, except for a discrepancy in the date.

In the published version of his book, Ruppelt wrote that he personally read the Estimate and that it presented the extraterrestrial conclusion based on sightings by scientists, pilots, and other credible observers. Ruppelt did not state in his book exactly when the Estimate was sent to Gen. Vandenberg for approval, but indicated that it was near the end of September 1948. A better estimate of the date is available in the *draft* of the manuscript of his book, which has become available to researchers only in recent years. The draft lists ten of the sightings discussed in the Estimate, only three of which were published in his book. One of the unpublished sightings occurred at the atomic energy research facility known as Los Alamos in New Mexico (which would play an important role in sighting history in the months and years following the demise of the Estimate). According to Ruppelt's draft manuscript, "A group of people were waiting for an airplane at the landing strip in Los Alamos when one of them noticed something glint in the sun. It was a flat, circular object, high in the northern sky. The appearance and relative size was the same as a dime held edgewise and slightly tipped, about fifty feet away." This sighting occurred on September 23, 1948 (exactly a year after Twining's letter to Schulgen which said flying saucers are real!). Since the Estimate seen by Ruppelt included this sighting, it must have been written and sent to Vandenberg after September 23 rather than in August, as indicated by Randle's source.

According to Ruppelt, the Top Secret Estimate was passed, without comment, upward through the chain of command to Gen. Vandenberg. Vandenberg then rejected it for the same reason as indicated by Randle's source: *"lack of proof."* Several of the Project Sign scientists and officers then went to the Pentagon to discuss the Estimate with Vandenberg. They tried to convince him that all their analyses logically pointed toward interplanetary vehicles but, according to Ruppelt, Vandenberg repeated his rejection. Furthermore, if, as Randle's source suggested, they knew about hard evidence, then I speculate that Vandenberg ordered them to never again mention its existence in any document.

Let's suppose the aircraft and intelligence experts at Project Sign really didn't know about any hard evidence (and that Randle's informant was wrong to suggest that hardware had been mentioned in an early version of the estimate). At the same time, let us suppose that the experts logically and honestly arrived at the interplanetary conclusion, even without hard evidence. Why wouldn't Vandenberg accept it? After all, they were the acknowledged experts in understanding foreign aircraft technology. They had found good reasons to say the saucers were interplanetary, but then Vandenberg, in a discussion which couldn't have lasted more than several hours, and may have lasted less than an hour, had essentially told them, "Sorry, *wrong answer.*" Why tell the *experts* that, in spite of a year of investigation and analysis, they were wrong? Was he truly unconvinced by their logic or did he have a hidden agenda? Was he trying to cover something up?

Since there are (at least as of the time of this book) no documented answers to these questions I can only speculate that he didn't want the ET conclusion to be accepted because, if it were accepted, flying saucer reality, with all the attendant consequences, would become official Air Force policy. The conclusion might then leak out and the Air Force would have a big problem. It would have to admit to the American people that alien craft were flying around, and the *Air Force could do nothing about it.*

Vandenberg's rejection of the Estimate was a very important turning point—a "watershed event"—in the history of the Air Force investigation. When Vandenberg rejected the Estimate, he effectively set forth a policy that UFOs or flying saucers *could not be officially identified as extraterrestrial vehicles.* One may imagine that the civilian scientists and military officials who worked on Project Sign were disappointed, perhaps even stunned, at the rejection. They knew that Vandenberg, because of his rank at the top of the military establishment, knew things they didn't. Perhaps they assumed that he rejected the extraterrestrial conclusion because he knew the objects were something else, although they couldn't imagine what since they had already considered and rejected the "secret U.S. project" and the "advanced foreign aircraft" theories. Perhaps they assumed Vandenberg rejected it simply because he couldn't deal with the consequences of accepting it. Whatever the reasons, they were sent home, tails between their legs, perhaps with orders to find other explanations. Sometime later the order came to destroy all copies of the Estimate. (Evidently at least one survived for Ruppelt to read three years later, but then it, too, was destroyed.)

When a four-star general speaks, lower ranks listen and act accordingly. The saucers appeared to be solid, mechanically engineered objects rather than natural phenomena or figments of the imagination. Therefore, if they couldn't be extraterrestrial vehicles they had to be . . . *man-made aircraft or missiles.*

By early October, the ATIC/Sign investigators were again seriously considering the possibility that the saucers were super-secret developments of the United States military or some civilian agency, developments which Vandenberg may have known about, but wasn't willing to tell them. The problem then was to justify this explanation. During the previous nine months, Project Sign had sent requests to numerous military and civilian intelligence agencies (Air Force, Navy, Army, Counter Intelligence Corps, FBI, etc.) for information on flying discs and aerial phenomena. Now they were going to try again. On October 7, 1948, probably only a few days after the Estimate had been rejected, Col. McCoy wrote the following letter to the Navy, the Army, and the CIA:

> This Headquarters is currently engaged in an intelligence investigation of all reported unidentified aerial phenomena. To date, no concrete evidence as to the exact identity of any of the reported objects has been received. Similarly, the origin of the so called "flying discs" remains obscure. The possibility exists that some of the sighted objects are of domestic origin, i.e., unrecognized configurations of some of our latest aeronautical attainments, or that they are objects not readily recognized by the public—test vehicles in various stages of development, etc.

Where security regulations will permit, it is requested that your office submit to (a long mailing address). . . any available evidence which might serve to indicate that these objects have a domestic origin.

Your cooperation in so doing might greatly assist in identifying our own domestic developments from possible inimical foreign achievements.

Of course, they didn't receive any positive response. The fact that the Col. McCoy would, once again, search for a domestic project to explain saucer sightings is certainly not consistent with the idea that he and those working for him knew of any hard evidence which would prove that saucers were real. If it is assumed that someone at Project Sign did know of hard evidence, then the appeal for help in the above letter must be considered an clever ploy to divert attention away from the hard evidence.

Since the saucers were not our missiles but appeared to be real objects, i.e., *someone's* missiles, they had to be of *foreign* origin. The only way the investigators could imagine the missiles to be of foreign origin was if the Soviets had pushed German WWII technology far beyond anything that we had yet imagined. And yet, they could not really accept that either. They were confident that the United States had the most advanced aircraft technology. Furthermore, they didn't believe that, even if the Soviets had such advanced aircraft, they would fly them over the United States where one might crash, or be shot down.

The analysts were caught on the horns of a dilemma. The objects were not allowed to be identified as what they appeared to be: flying craft not made by any nation on earth. At the same time, the objects were not ours and they couldn't be Soviet craft. The objects appeared to be real but the analysts were being forced to reject that reality. Thus began the decline in quality of the Air Force flying saucer investigation, a decline that would not be reversed, and then only temporarily, until late 1951.

No documentation presently available indicates that the Estimate was a response to Gen. Cabell's July 27 request for an evaluation. Nor does any documentation show that Cabell was even aware of the Estimate.

Instead, the only available documentation indicates that Cabell was not aware of the AMC opinion until after he asked for it in a November 3 letter (described later), over a month after the Estimate had been rejected by Vandenberg. Perhaps Cabell knew about the Estimate but didn't allow his knowledge to be documented. On the other hand, the ATIC/Sign investigators, being in a separate chain of command from AFI, may have acted entirely on their own in creating the Estimate of the Situation and then they may have simply bypassed AFI and sent the Estimate through AMC channels to Vandenberg. (It may be that the ATIC/Sign personnel wrote and sent the Estimate simply to "test the waters," i.e., to find out if "interplanetary" was an explanation that the Top Brass would accept.)

Gen. Cabell did get a response to his July 27 request from AFI. On August 11, he was given an interim response on the methods of analysis "being utilized in the preparation of the required study and the methods suggested to Project Sign personnel at Headquarters, Air Materiel Command, for pursuing flying object phenomena to the end that positive identifications might be achieved." The final response came as an attachment to an October 11 letter written by Col. Brooke Allen, Chief of the Air Estimates Branch of AFI. It was not as bold as the Estimate, arguing only that the sightings were of real objects, and suggesting that they were of foreign (Soviet) origin. Although there is no direct evidence of this, the fact that the AFI and ATIC personnel worked quite closely on the sighting analysis makes it very likely that the AFI intelligence personnel who wrote the response to Cabell were aware of the Estimate and its rejection at the very top, and so wrote their response in a way that would not be rejected. Thus, in a sense, the following report may be the "cousin" of the Estimate. The report was sent along with the following Top Secret letter, which was not released to the public until the mid 1980s:

1. As directed by Cover Sheet, dated 27 July 1948, subject "Pattern of Flying Saucers," a study was commenced to determine the tactics of flying objects and the probability of their existence.

2. The attached study, "Analysis of Flying Object Incidents in the United States," has been compiled in an attempt to answer the questions.

3. An exhaustive study was made of all information pertinent to the subject in this Division and the Intelligence Division of Air Materiel Command. Opinions of both aeronautical engineers and well-qualified intelligence specialists have been solicited in an endeavor to consider all possible aspects of the question.

4. Because the subject matter is of such an elusive nature, this study is presented as a preliminary report to be reconsidered when information at hand warrants it.

5. Tentative conclusions have been drawn and are as follows:

    a. It must be accepted that some type of flying objects have been observed, although their identification and origin are not discernible. In the interest of national defense it would be unwise to overlook the possibility that some of these objects may be of foreign origin.

    b. Assuming that the objects might eventually be identified as foreign or foreign-sponsored devices the possible reason for their appearance over the U.S. requires consideration. Several possible explanations appear noteworthy, viz:

        1. To negate U.S. confidence in the atom bomb as the most advanced and decisive weapon in warfare.

        2. To perform photographic reconnaissance missions.

        3. To test U.S. air defenses.

        4. To conduct familiarization flights over U.S. territory.

        5. It is recommended that distribution of this study be limited to the Air Staff.

Here was an analysis of the situation that Gen. Vandenberg could accept. Although the writers of this document concluded that flying saucers are real, there is no suggestion that they might be of extraterrestrial origin. Instead, this document confines the discussion to missiles that are (add qualifier of choice: probably, maybe, possibly, or "we hope") of foreign, i.e., Soviet, origin. The formerly Top Secret document attached to the above letter, titled "Analysis of Flying Object Incidents in the U.S.", was jointly published in December 1948 by the Directorate of Intelligence of the Air Force and by the Office of Navy Intelligence as "Air Intelligence Division Study No. 203" (declassified in 1985).

Following a standard format for such documents, it established that the sightings did, indeed, pose a problem by presenting a strong case for saucer reality. The main text states that about 210 sightings were analyzed and that "among the observers reporting on such incidents are trained and experienced U.S. Weather Bureau personnel, USAF rated officers, experienced civilian pilots, technicians associated with various research projects and technicians employed by commercial airlines." In other words, the witnesses were generally above average in credibility and accuracy of reporting . . . definitely not the publicity seekers, dreamers, hoaxers, and town drunks. Two dozen unexplained sightings are summarized, including two that were investigated by the FBI: the William Rhoads sighting (his UFO photos were reprinted in the report) and the Portland police officer sighting. Other summarized sightings were by meteorologists, scientists, private pilots (including Kenneth Arnold), commercial pilots, and military pilots.

Of particular interest are the following. On November 12, 1947, the second officer of the Navy tanker *Ticonderoga*, twenty miles off the coast of Oregon, watched for forty-five seconds as "two flying disks trailing jet-like streams of fire" traveled in a "long low arc" at a speed estimated at 700–900 mph. On April 5, 1948:

> . . . three trained balloon observers of the Geophysics Laboratory Section of the Watson Laboratories, N.J. reported seeing a round, indistinct object in the vicinity of Holloman Air Force Base, New Mexico. It was very high and fast, and appeared to execute violent maneuvers at high speed. The object was under observation for approximately thirty seconds and disappeared suddenly.

Twenty-five days later, on April 30, a Navy pilot flying near Anacostia, Maryland saw "a yellow or light colored sphere, twenty-five to forty feet in diameter" that was "moving at a speed of approximately 100 miles per hour at an altitude of about 4,500 ft.." On July 1:

. . . twelve discs were reported over Rapid City Air Base by Major Hammer. These disks were oval shaped, about 100 ft. long, flying at a speed estimated to be in excess of 500 mph. Descending from 10,000 ft., these disks made a thirty-degree to forty-degree climbing turn accelerating very rapidly until out of sight.

With sighting reports such as these it is not surprising that Project Sign investigators were convinced that saucers were real and definitely not man-made.

Not mentioned in this document are six of the ten sightings claimed by Ruppelt (in his draft manuscript) to be in the ATIC/Sign Estimate. The fact that some sightings attributed by Ruppelt to the Estimate are not found in this document can be considered to be evidence that it is *not* simply a modified version of the Estimate. Unfortunately, without a copy of the Estimate we can never be certain just how dissimilar the two documents were.

According to this document, of the 210 sightings analyzed, *only eighteen* could definitely be identified. Of the eighteen explained sightings "three were hoaxes and two were from unreliable witnesses." The other explained sightings were honest misidentifications or failures of the witnesses to recognize what they were seeing. Thus the information in this report directly contradicted the public position of the Air Force that most sightings could be explained and that many sightings were from hoaxers and unreliable people. (Sounding a bit like a cover-up, perhaps?)

Meanwhile, we can imagine that back at ATIC the Project Sign investigators were trying to recover from the Estimate debacle. Although the ET spacecraft explanation for saucers was disallowed by Vandenberg's rejection, his rejection did not apply to the possibility of *spacecraft from another country on earth!* In an October 22 letter, Col. William R. Clingerman, who was at this time the Acting Chief of the Intelligence Department and one of the Project Sign investigators, proposed a special study by the Rand Corporation to determine the technical requirements for creation of space-capable vehicles. According to Clingerman's letter:

The possibility that some of the unidentified aerial objects that have been reported in the United States and in foreign

Col. William R. Clingerman,
Acting Chief of Intelligence
and Project Sign investigator.

countries may have been experimental spaceships or test vehicles for the purpose of assisting in the development of spaceships has been given consideration by this Command. If such craft have actually been sighted it is believed more likely that they represent the effort of a foreign nation rather than a product from beyond the Earth.

Although Clingerman included the obligatory qualifier, "if such craft have actually been sighted," it is clear that he was pushing the bounds of reason by suggesting that some country was advanced enough to experiment with vehicles capable of space flight. He probably did not believe that *anyone* on earth had created such vehicles. Nevertheless he was sufficiently confident that some of the flying saucers were real that he was willing to spend government money to investigate the possibility that they were man-made spaceships or spaceship test vehicles. This document by Clingerman can be considered as evidence that the spaceship hypothesis had been seriously considered by the ATIC investigators.

On November 3, 1948, after reading the Top Secret AFI report, Cabell wrote to the commanding general of AMC (now Lt. Gen. Joseph

McNarney) to point out that Project Sign had been set up under his command. Cabell went on to say that "the conclusion appears inescapable that some type of object has been observed. Identification and the origin of the objects is not discernible to this Headquarters. It is imperative, therefore, that efforts to determine whether these objects are of domestic or foreign origin must be increased until conclusive evidence is obtained. The needs of national defense require such evidence in order that appropriate counter-measures may be taken."

During the previous months, members of the press had been nosing around trying to find out what the Air Force had learned about the saucers after a year of study. One particularly insistent reporter was Sidney Shallett, a well-known writer for the very popular *Saturday Evening Post* magazine. Cabell reacted to Shallet's persistence and the general press interest by recommending, in the November 3 letter to General McNarney, that the Air Force should be "informing the public as to the status of the problem." He wrote, "To date there has been too little data to present to the public. The press, however, is about to take it into its own hands and demand to be told what we do or do not know about the situation. Silence on our part will not long be acceptable."

Cabell closed his letter by asking AMC for its "conclusions to date and recommendations as to the information to be given to the press. Your recommendation is requested also as to whether that information should be offered to the press or withheld until it is actively sought by the press." (The fact that Cabell asked for the AMC "conclusions to date" suggests that Cabell was not aware of the Estimate of the Situation.)

On November 8, Col. McCoy responded in detail to Cabell's request for the AMC opinion. As you read this, keep in mind that one or more of the men who worked for McCoy in the Project Sign office (MCIAXO-3) had written the Estimate of the Situation, so McCoy almost certainly was aware of the ET Estimate and Vandenberg's rejection. If so, he was sensitive to the fact that "extraterrestrial" had been removed from the list of acceptable explanations, leaving foreign missiles, misidentifications or misperceptions of natural phenomena, or of man-made objects, hallucinations (psychological problems), and hoaxes as the only acceptable types of explanation. What you are about to read represents the collective opinion of the Project Sign aeronautical experts:

1. In attempting to arrive at conclusions as to the nature of unidentified flying object incidents in the United States, this Command has made a study of approximately 180 incidents. Data derived from initial reports have been supplemented by further information obtained from check lists submitted by mail, from interrogations of other field agencies, and by personal investigation by personnel of this Command in the case of incidents that seem to indicate the possibility of obtaining particularly significant information.

2. The objects described fall into the following general classification groups, according to shape or physical configuration:

   a. Flat disc of circular or approximately circular shape.

   b. Torpedo or cigar-shaped aircraft, with no wings or fins visible in flight

   c. Spherical or balloon-shaped objects

   d. Balls of light with no apparent form attached.

This formerly Secret letter (declassified in 1986) says that the ATIC/Sign personnel analyzed about 180 sightings (about thirty less than the 210 analyzed by the Air Estimates Branch in the Pentagon). According to this letter, some of the round or balloon-shaped objects had been identified as upper-air balloons, some of the objects had been identified as "astrophysical" in nature, some may have had a psychological origin, some might have been hallucinations, and some might have been deliberate hoaxes. (By not specifying the exact numbers this letter makes it sound as if a sizable percentage had been explained, in contradiction to the "Analysis" document, which says that less than ten percent (eighteen out of 210) had been positively explained.)

McCoy's letter then says that ATIC was in the process of hiring a prominent astrophysicist who would study the sightings to determine which could be stars, meteors, planets, etc. (this would be Dr. J. Allen Hynek, who was the Air Force consultant in astronomy from 1948 through 1969). ATIC was also coordinating "a study of psychological problems . . . in coordination with the Aero-Medical Laboratory at this Headquarters." This study was intended to identify the sightings that could be reasonably explained as resulting from mental aberrations, or the inability of people to accurately perceive and report unexpected phenomena. McCoy's letter continues:

> 6. Although explanation of many of the incidents can be obtained from the investigations described above there remains a certain number of reports for which no reasonable every day explanation is available. So far no physical evidence of the existence of the unidentified sightings has been obtained.

Here once again, we find the conclusion that at least some of the sightings are of real, unexplainable flying objects. His statement that there is no physical evidence suggests that either he did not know of the Roswell material, that he knew but was intentionally covering it up in this letter, or else the Roswell material was not related to the saucer sightings. If the first possibility were true, then the above statement is further evidence of a cover-up at an extremely high level.

In the next paragraph, McCoy writes that the various types of observed phenomena were not related to projects *"of domestic origin"* and that, although disc-shaped aircraft could be made to fly, they would have *"poor climb, altitude and range characteristics"* with the available propulsion systems (propeller, jet). Col. McCoy then says that a more awesome possibility had been considered:

> 8. The possibility that the reported objects are vehicles from another planet has not been ignored. However, tangible evidence to support conclusions about such a possibility are completely lacking. The occurrence of incidents in relation to the approach to the Earth of the planets Mercury, Venus, and Mars have been plotted. A periodic variation in the frequency of incidents, which appears to have some relation to the planet approach curves, is noted, but it may be purely coincidence.

This letter proves that the ATIC analysts *seriously* considered the extraterrestrial hypothesis because they took the time to test the idea that the saucers might be coming from Venus or Mars in spite of the strong belief by astronomers that neither Mars nor Venus were inhabited by intelligent life. The letter also noted a periodicity in the sightings which seemed similar to the periodicity of planet approaches to the Earth, but this seeming correlation in the 1947–1948 sightings did not persist through the following years.

This letter could be called the "Ghost of the Estimate." The letter does not say that the ET hypothesis was proven false, but simply that the available evidence, being nontangible, was not sufficiently convincing for it to be accepted. The implication of this statement is that, regardless of how good the *sighting* evidence might be, the ET hypothesis could be accepted only if hard evidence—crash debris and, perhaps, alien bodies—were available.

Col. McCoy's letter presents the following conclusions:

a. In the majority of cases reported, observers have actually sighted some type of flying object which they cannot classify as an aircraft within the limits of their personal experience.

b. There is as yet no conclusive proof that unidentified flying objects, other than those which are known to be balloons, are real aircraft.

c. Although it is obvious that some types of flying objects have been sighted, the exact nature of those objects cannot be established until physical evidence, such as that which would result from a crash has been obtained.

These three paragraphs illustrate the confusion that set in when Vandenberg rejected the Estimate. In paragraphs (a) and (c) we find McCoy saying that observers actually sighted some types of flying objects; yet, in paragraph (b) he says there is no proof that these objects, other than balloons, are "real aircraft." Does this mean that the witnesses saw unreal aircraft that appeared real? Or does this mean that witnesses saw *real objects which were not aircraft (i.e., not airplanes)?*

Finally, Col. McCoy answered Gen. Cabell's question regarding what, if anything, should be said to the press:

11. It is not considered advisable to present to the press information on those objects which we cannot yet identify or
about which we cannot present any reasonable conclusions.
In the event that they insist on some kind of statement, it is
suggested that they be informed that many of the objects
sighted have been identified as weather balloons or astral
bodies, and that investigation is being pursued to determine
reasonable explanations for the others.

Evidently Col. McCoy did not think it advisable to tell the American
people the truth about the results of the saucer investigations! By advising
Gen. Cabell to tell the American people what amounts to an untruth,
McCoy was recommending that the Air Force avoid (some might say
"chicken out" from) facing up to the difficult issues that would be raised if
the Air Force admitted that many of the sightings simply could not be
explained as known objects or phenomena. Instead, McCoy recommended a format for information release that became the basis of Air
Force saucer information policy for most of the next twenty-one years: (a)
discuss openly the explained sightings, (b) formulate statements which
make it appear to the American people that most sightings can be
explained, (c) suggest that continued investigations will uncover explanations for those sightings not yet explained, and (d) do not discuss the
unexplained sightings. In later years one more element would be added to
this information release format: (e) state that the sightings that could not
be explained simply had insufficient information for an explanation.§

On November 30, 1948, Maj. Gen. Cabell again addressed the problem
of the press in a letter to Brig. Gen. E. "Dinty" Moore, Assistant for Production of the Directorate of Intelligence. The letter, titled "Publicity on
Flying Saucer Incidents" referred to the AFI conclusion "that some type
of flying objects have been observed although their identification and
origin are not yet discernible," and went on to say that "insufficient data

§ A very comprehensive study of about 3,000 sightings, carried out in 1952–1953 and
presented in Project Blue Book Special Report #14, showed that (e) was untrue: many of
the unexplained sightings had more than enough information to confirm a conventional explanation if such were possible. The Air Force continued to use (e) in public
statements anyway.

is available to date to warrant any further action except continuing attempts to determine the nature and origin of these objects." Noting the "increasing pressure on the part of the U.S. Press to publicize 'flying saucer' incidents," Cabell said that he "has attempted to dissuade the Press from publishing articles of this nature" because the articles would be "speculative in nature and would probably result in a flood of reports, making the problem of analysis and evaluation . . . increasingly difficult." He closed the letter by recommending that "inquiring agencies be informed that the Air Force is investigating carefully all valid reports . . ." and by requesting that the Secretary of Defense, James Forrestal, be asked to grant authority for the Air Force "to assist the press, upon request, in the preparation of such articles . . ."

Assist the press in writing articles? Does this mean that Cabell had a change of heart and would provide the press with "honest-to-goodness" flying saucer data? Or does it mean that by assisting the press Cabell could exert some *control over what the press reported?*

Sidney Shallett's persistence prevailed. He got approval for his flying saucer article from the Secretary of Defense, the Secretary of the Air Force, and the Chief of Staff of the Air Force (Gen. Vandenberg), who directed Air Force intelligence to assist Shallett. On January 5, 1949, Capt. Burton English, Chief of the Review and Policy Section of the Directorate of Public Relations, wrote a memo for Stephen Leo, the Director of Public Relations, regarding "Sid Shallett's 'Flying Saucers' article." Capt. English placed certain restrictions on Shallett's "use of classified documents and intelligence files":

1. No documents classified Top Secret should be made available to him.

2. He should not be permitted to copy any documents emanating from a foreign source regardless of the classification.

3. The copies made of domestic documents should be classified, as indicated on the original documents, and should not be removed from the building.

    The Air Force aggregate conclusions on various reports should not be made available to Shallett. In the event any foreign documents or information contained therefrom are used, I do not think that they should specify the area over which they were sighted, but rather that they be loosely identified as Europe or Asia, whichever the case may be.

Capt. English also stated that his Directorate would review Shallett's article before publication.

About a week later, on January 13, 1949, Stephen Leo wrote to Lt. Gen. Benjamin Chidlaw, who was the Deputy Commander of the Air Materiel Command, to alert him to the arrival of Shallett whom he referred to as "our friend Sid Shallett." (Evidently Shallett had a close relationship with the Air Force.) Leo told Chidlaw that Shallett "had the approval of the Secretary of the Air Force, Chief of Staff of the Air Force and the Secretary of Defense" and that he had spent several days talking to officials at the Pentagon before traveling to AMC. Leo wanted Chidlaw to be sure that Shallett met Col. McCoy and that "General Vandenberg wants him to be sure and talk to the staff involved on this project." Leo continued:

Shallett has already gone through the two volumes of condensed incident summaries available here, including incidents 1 through 177, and he would like to go through the third volume, which I understand your people have prepared. We would also like to have him accompany a field investigative unit if one happens to be sent out while he is there. He has indicated that he might like to contact some of the civilians who had provided information on this project and we have advised him that such contacts should be cleared through Colonel McCoy's shop.

Our intelligence people have had a telecon with McCoy's office, advising them of Sid's impending visit and, also, what material was provided here. The only restriction we have on the project is that no final, overall Air Force conclusions be revealed.

Shallett was provided the needed assistance by the Air Force, and by the end of January 1949, he had seen most or all of the sighting data.

This assistance was, no doubt, very helpful to Shallett. However a cynic might make the following observation: Air Force intelligence really wanted no publicity because they feared that the publication of saucer stories would cause, to quote Gen. Cabell's letter of April 1949, a "flurry of 'crank' reports and a consequent flooding of our investigative resources." Hence Air Force intelligence may have decided to assist Shallett in order to influence or exert some control over Shallett's conclusions and thereby to damp down the public interest in making sighting reports. Whatever the reason for providing assistance, the fact is that the article, which was published in May 1949 (and discussed further in chapter 9), was almost 100 percent *against* saucer reality.

Project Sign formally ended in the middle of January 1949, but the saucer intelligence collection and analysis project continued under a new name, Project Grudge. During the following months, many of the senior Project Sign investigators were transferred to other projects. The remaining lower-level Sign employees did little more than collect and file sightings while working on a final report that would summarize the findings of Project Sign. The quality of saucer investigations declined rapidly during Project Grudge as a strong skepticism set in at AMC. This was a reaction to Vandenberg's rejection of the logical conclusions presented in the Estimate. If the saucers weren't our projects, and if they couldn't be Russian devices and if they couldn't be extraterrestrial craft, then, as illogical as it might seem, they had to be misidentifications, errors in reporting, delusions, anything but what they really appeared to be.

Although the investigative activity at Project Sign was winding down in late 1948 and early 1949, AFI in the Pentagon was maintaining its interest in saucer activity. On February 4, 1949, Maj. Gen. Cabell issued "Air Intelligence Requirements Memorandum Number 4," titled "Unconventional Aircraft," with the purpose "to enunciate continuing Air Force requirements for information pertaining to sightings of unconventional aircraft and unidentified flying objects, including the so-called "Flying Discs," and "to establish procedures for reporting such information." This multipage document specified the methods of reporting and the exact types of information desired relative to the observation (time, date, location, weather, etc.), relative to the observed object or objects (size, shape, distance, speed, color, etc.) and relative to the observer or observers (employment, hobbies, reliability, police or FBI records, etc.). The depth of the information requested in this memorandum made it clear that AFI was very serious about investigating saucer sightings.

It is a good thing AFI was still seriously interested, because a new version of the unidentified flying object phenomenon was about to begin. On October 14, 1948, Lt. Col. W. Earle, Jr., of the Air Intelligence Requirements Division, wrote a letter to the Plans and Collection Branch of Army Intelligence. The letter says: "Research which has been conducted by the Air Materiel Command reveals that groups of sightings of flying discs and/or other unidentified aerial objects occur at periodic intervals and that the beginning of a new interval is imminent." The letter then goes on to request help from the Army in reporting "sightings of unidentified aerial objects" directly to AMC "by the fastest means." The letter also asks that Army installations "initiate investigative action with special emphasis placed on the accumulation of photographic evidence of reported sightings." On November 7, 1948, Col. R. F. Ennis, acting for the Director of Army Intelligence, wrote the following memorandum to the commanding generals of the armies stationed in the continental U.S.: "The Department of the Air Force has advised that sightings of 'Flying Discs' and/or other unidentified aerial objects occur periodically and that the beginning of a new period is imminent. It is requested that your command be particularly alerted to report sightings of any unidentified aerial objects to include, if possible, photographic evidence."

Only a month later, this AMC prediction was confirmed in an unexpected way—strange green lights were observed flying over sensitive military installations in the Southwest. These new sightings began just as the FBI was being dragged back into the saucer business.

CHAPTER 6

Protection of Vital Installations

FBI Director Hoover wanted to get out of the flying saucer business and he succeeded for about a year, during which time the Air Force grappled with the saucer mystery and tried to make it "go away." But saucers and "unidentified aerial phenomena" wouldn't just go away. Instead, they were seen in areas of strategic importance to the United States, including areas where atomic bombs were designed, tested, built, and stored.

Oak Ridge, Tennessee, was one of these areas. During the Second World War, the U.S. War Department had established at Oak Ridge a 59,000-acre restricted area in which secret experiments were carried out to obtain the material necessary for the atomic bomb. Classified nuclear experiments and bomb fuel production were still conducted there in 1949. Naturally, the government wanted Oak Ridge to be protected from communist subversion and spying, and the FBI was responsible for that protection. Hence a close watch was maintained for anything out of the ordinary.

TO: DIRECTOR FBI January 10, 1949
FROM: SAC, KNOXVILLE
SUBJECT:
"FLYING SAUCERS" OBSERVED OVER OAK RIDGE AREA
INTERNAL SECURITY - X

Thus begins a letter sent to FBI headquarters, which dragged Hoover and his agents back into the saucer fray.

The Knoxville, Tennessee, FBI agent, C. C. McSwain, sent this letter along with two photographs that appeared to show a flying saucer over Oak Ridge in July 1947. The agent had been given the photos by George Rathman, Chief Investigator of the Security Division of the Atomic Energy Commission (predecessor of the Department of Energy) at Oak Ridge.

According to the letter, Rathman had gone to the trouble of locating and retrieving about two dozen copies of the pictures that the photographer had given to his friends. He had collected the photos at the request of Col. Clyde Gasser, the resident engineer of the Nuclear Energy for the Propulsion of Aircraft (NEPA) Research Center at Oak Ridge, because Col. Gasser had become concerned about publicity regarding the photos. Gasser had also asked Rathman to advise persons who had the photos "to say nothing to anyone concerning them." (Gasser did not explain why this happened one-and-a-half years after the photos were taken.)

Rathman had then contacted the FBI to ask for an evaluation of the photos. Agent McSwain pointed out that, "In accordance with Bureau instructions, no active investigation of this matter was made." Nevertheless, Agent McSwain felt it was "advisable to interview Col. Gasser prior to submitting the photographs to the Bureau." The importance of this letter lies not in the fact that photos were submitted, but rather in what Col. Gasser told the FBI about the Air Force investigation.

In his September 1947 letter recommending a special project to study flying saucers, Gen. Twining said that several special military research projects should be kept informed about the results of saucer investigations. Project NEPA was one of these special projects and so Col. Gasser, who himself was an employee of AMC, was aware of some of the results of saucer research, but not all of it. He told Agent McSwain that "he knew nothing of an official nature concerning [saucers] other than the fact that they were believed by Air Force officials to be man-made missiles, rather than some natural phenomena." Gasser believed that "a great deal of information had been compiled concerning these missiles by Air Force intelligence and that research on the matter was being extensively done at Wright Field." He also said the Air Force was treating the matter seriously, and that "the matter was being given absolutely no dissemination by the Air Force or other military personnel, and that they had not deemed it advisable to advise him of all information pertaining to the missile." So far as he knew there were no pieces of a flying saucer available for analysis. It was his opinion that the best evidence available to the Air Force at that time was "telephoto photographs which are now in the possession of the engineers at Wright Field," but he did not know how clear these photos were. Although he had not been told of any crashed flying saucer, he had heard of a report of a collision in early 1947 of a Czechoslovakian airliner with an unidentified missile, which he thought might have been a flying saucer.

Col. Gasser said that these flying saucer "missiles" could travel "at a certain altitude above the contour of the ground" indicating some sort of "radio altimeter or radio control." (Recall the August 13, 1947, sighting by A. C. Urie, discussed previously in chapter 2, who saw a saucer following the contours of the ground as it flew through the Snake River Canyon.) Gasser was also aware of several sightings of vapor trails created by "aircraft" at extremely high altitude, which left trails across the sky. He had observed one himself, "completely unlike any vapor trail he had ever observed before in all of his experience with the Air Force. It was his judgment that whatever created the vapor trail was traveling at an unbelievably tremendous speed."

The most disturbing information provided by Col. Gasser was his conjecture that these were Soviet atomic energy missiles. He based his conjecture on conversations with investigators at Wright Field, and on reports written by intelligence agents in other countries. He pointed out that it was known "as early as four years ago that some kind of flying disc was being experimented with by the Russians. In addition . . . he stated that more recent reports . . . from representatives of the Central Intelligence Agency in southern Europe and southern Asia [indicated that] the Russians were experimenting with some kind of radical aircraft or guided missile which could be dispatched for great distances out over the sea, made to turn in flight and return to the base . . ." In comparison, in the U.S. military experiments had only gone so far as "delivering a missile to the required point of impact and no consideration has been given to [giving] the missile the ability to return." He also claimed that "all appearances . . . have usually approached the United States from a northerly direction and have been reported as returning in a northerly direction" as if they came to North America over the North Pole and returned over the North Pole. (This was incorrect information since saucers, or "missiles," had been seen traveling in all sorts of directions. However, Gasser apparently believed it to be correct and the FBI took him at his word.)

Of particular interest is the fact that Col. Gasser told the FBI that the presence of these "missiles" (saucers) had "given impetus to the research being done by the Air Force in their own program of nuclear energy for the propulsion of aircraft to develop guided missiles." (Note: The NEPA project at Oak Ridge had started in 1946. In 1948 the secret Lexington Project of the Massachusetts Institute of Technology reviewed the NEPA research and concluded that, although there was no guarantee of success, with "adequate resources and competent manpower" it might be possible to construct a nuclear-powered aircraft. The time scale for development was estimated at *fifteen years*.) Col. Gasser also told the FBI that "great efforts have been expended by the service to determine just what the nature of these missile(s) might be and . . . to decide whether or not an adequate defense can be established."

Col. Gasser's latter statements to the FBI show that *the sightings of flying saucers had actually affected the direction of Air Force research into advanced forms of propulsion and defense.* This is decidedly different from the "ho-hum" attitude the Air Force portrayed to the American people when it publicly emphasized that most sightings could be explained, that no evidence of advanced technology had been found, and that saucer sightings were unimportant.

On January 24, 1949, an Assistant Director for Security, D. M. Ladd, summarized Gasser's remarks in a two-page memorandum for J. Edgar Hoover. The memorandum made it clear that the matter of flying saucers was serious business, that AFI had compiled a lot of information on the subject and that "research on the matter was being extensively done at Wright Field." The memorandum also discussed the Air Force opinion that saucers were "man-made missiles" operated by nuclear power, and emphasized *Gasser's conjecture that they were missiles flown from Russia which had the ability to turn around and return to their point of origin.* The memorandum made it clear that the exact nature and origin of the missiles was not known and that much of what was reported was based on Gasser's own conclusions having read many intelligence reports on the sightings.

Although there is nothing in the available record to indicate Hoover's immediate reaction to this information, it must have made some impression on him. After all, the thought that a major enemy country could fly bomb-carrying missiles over our country without hindrance is frightening. The fact that the Air Force seemed to be covering this up may have been disconcerting to Hoover. Perhaps the information from Col. Gasser combined with the sudden appearance of strange lights over secure areas (see the next chapter) convinced Hoover that the American people should know more about these sightings than the Air Force was telling them. Perhaps Hoover became convinced it was necessary to break security to tell the American public that the Air Force thought Soviet missiles were overflying the United States. It's difficult to prove, but there is evidence to suggest that Hoover *did exactly this several months later!*

CHAPTER 7

Great Balls of Fire

After the practice periods La Paz assumed the weapons would be loaded with an atomic warhead.

—from an FBI memorandum, February 10, 1949

A **month before** the FBI interview with Col. Gasser, agencies responsible for security at atomic defense installations in the southwestern United States were suddenly confronted with a puzzling, and frightening, nighttime phenomenon—the repeated appearance of greenish lights moving through the sky at high speed near these installations. The lights began appearing at the end of November 1948, as if to satisfy Lt. Col. Earle, Jr.'s prediction of an imminent increase in sightings (see the conclusion to chapter 5). They were very bright green-yellow lights, somewhat like large meteors, which generally are called "fireballs." (Fireball meteors are much larger, brighter and longer-lasting than the typical meteor, which is small piece of interstellar material that makes a fleeting streak in the sky. Fireballs can be startling in their brilliance and duration, lasting sometimes up to ten seconds or more. They appear randomly all over the world, but are rarely seen more than once a year from any one location.) The greenish lights appearing near the sensitive installations would have been identified as fireball meteors if it weren't for three peculiar and disturbing characteristics: their colors were unusual, they were seen *many times per* *month* in the vicinity of the atomic defense installations in New Mexico, and *they were hardly seen anywhere else.* Even though it soon became apparent that they weren't fireballs in any ordinary sense of the word, these lights were given the name "green fireballs."

The first ones to appear in the skies over New Mexico were thought by the observers to be green military flares, and were ignored. However, a series of sightings on December 5 made the flare idea seem impossible. A *dozen* green fireballs were seen traveling generally north to south between 7:30 P.M. and 11:30 P.M. by security guards at military installations in the vicinity of Albuquerque and Las Vegas, New Mexico (east of Santa Fe). Some of the witnesses were guards at Sandia Base (now the Sandia National Laboratory, near Albuquerque) where atomic bombs were being assembled. These sightings really caught the attention of the security forces. The next day Lt. Col. Doyle Rees, Commander of the 17th District of the Air Force Office of Special Investigations (AFOSI) at Kirtland Air Force Base in Albuquerque, launched an intense investigation into the possibility that the fireballs were related to conspiracy and *sabotage.*

The AFOSI investigation had no sooner begun when there was another sighting. On December 6, at 10:55 P.M., a security guard at Sandia Base saw a green fireball traveling north to south. The next night, a security guard at Los Alamos, New Mexico, saw a fireball traveling on a north-south trajectory.*

AFOSI investigators Melvin Neef and John Stahl checked with every agency in the area that could have been launching green flares. None had. Neef and Stahl wanted to see one for themselves, so they boarded a small plane during the evening of December 8. At 6:35 P.M., while flying at an altitude of 5,000 feet near Las Vegas, NM, they saw one burst into full brilliance seemingly instantaneously. It traveled almost parallel to the horizon for about two seconds, then dimmed while suddenly dropping downward, leaving a trail of reddish-orange sparks that lasted another second. It was decidedly "un-fireball-like."

The next day Agent Neef contacted Dr. Lincoln La Paz, the Director of the Institute of Meteoritics at the University of New Mexico. Dr. La

*Los Alamos is a laboratory west of Santa Fe and north of Albuquerque that had been constructed during the Second World War as a secure area where atomic bombs were designed.

Paz had a Top Secret clearance and had worked with the Air Force during the Second World War at the White Sands Proving Ground. The sighting descriptions reported by Neef interested him and he began a nightly watch for Geminid meteors which were being seen at the time.†

In Dr. La Paz's opinion, based on years of experience observing meteors, the Geminid meteors were neither extremely bright nor green. In a letter to Doyle Rees, written on December 13, he stated that observations made between the evening of the December 9, and the morning of December 12, confirmed his opinion. He further stated that "all meteors both Geminid and non-Geminid that I have observed during periods of Geminid activity since December 1, 1926 . . . a total of 414 [for which] color was reported . . . [of these] none . . . were [described] as green or greenish."

On the night of December 12, 1948 La Paz became a witness. While riding in a car with two Air Force officers westward from Las Vegas, New Mexico, he saw a bright green light suddenly appear and travel in a horizontal trajectory north to south for about two seconds. It turned out that the same fireball was observed from Los Alamos. This allowed La Paz to locate the path of the object by triangulation. His analysis showed it traveled a distance of about twenty-five miles at an altitude of about ten miles and at a speed of eight to twelve miles per second. (Typical meteors and fireballs burn up at altitudes around fifty miles.) There was no noise, yet there should have been, according to La Paz, if it were a normal meteor. At the end of his December 13 letter to Col. Rees, he wrote, "I am now convinced the various 'green flare' incidents reported to the AFOSI are *not* meteoric in nature [emphasis underlined in the original]."

The intelligence agencies responsible for protection of the atomic installations were obviously not comforted by Dr. La Paz's opinion that the green fireballs were not normal fireball meteors. Jerry Maxwell, the FBI Special Agent in Charge at Los Alamos, asked the FBI agent at El Paso to check with White Sands Proving Ground about the possibility

---

† At several times during the year the Earth passes through regions of space where there are numerous small chunks of matter, leftovers from the "tails" of long-gone comets. The Geminid meteor shower, with meteors seeming to come from the direction of the constellation Gemini, occurs typically around December 10–12, with occasional meteors as early as December 3.

that some rockets had been test-fired during the periods of fireball observation. White Sands reported that no rockets had been fired.

Maxwell told Col. Rees, "the FBI was carrying out any undeveloped leads relating to these phenomena that were brought to their attention."

Agent Maxwell then became an active investigator. He accompanied La Paz and several AFOSI agents to a night watch in the mountains west of Los Alamos on December 19. Unfortunately they were one night too early. Had they been watching the next night they would have seen something truly amazing: a green fireball that changed direction!

The time was 8:54 P.M. on December 20. The witnesses were security guards at two locations near the Los Alamos laboratory. Dr. La Paz analyzed their sighting descriptions and on December 30, he wrote to Lt. Col. Rees:

> It is found that the fireball doubly observed by Wilson, Truett, Strang, and Skipper appeared at a height of at least 10 miles and descended at an angle of about 45 degrees to the vertical [according to Truett's estimate] to . . . an elevation of only 2.3 miles above the horizontal plane [illegible] the point from which Strang and Skipper observed. As the fireball approached . . . [the 2.3 mile altitude] its path leveled off and from [then] to its point of disappearance . . . the fireball followed a nearly horizontal path approximately 7.5 miles long, moving with a velocity of between 3.75 and 7.5 miles per second, depending upon the duration estimate adopted . . . The foreward [sic] extension of the fireball's trace on the earth as determined by the above projections, passes some six miles to the north of the town of Los Alamos. It should be noted that the descending branch of the path of the fireball was observed by Inspector Truett alone, but he was absolutely certain that his observation of this portion of the path was correct. It should also be noted that no sound was heard, although the distance from the observers to the fireball and from the fireball to the earth could only have been a few miles at most. I have no hesitancy in testifying that an object possessing the

flight path and other peculiarities observed by Wilson, Truett, Strang, and Skipper was not a falling meteorite.

The next sighting occurred December 28. Again the flight path appeared to be horizontal from northeast to southwest but the color was different; it was blue-white. Just before the object disappeared, it created a vapor trail which remained in the sky for several minutes. The witness could see this vapor trail being blown and dissipated by the wind. After reading about sightings such as these, one can easily see why La Paz was convinced the green fireballs were not normal fireball meteors.

The intelligence agencies responsible for protecting the secret military installations had a jurisdictional dispute over which agency should take the lead in the investigation of these fireballs. By the end of December, the AFOSI had taken charge and, from then on, the FBI merely "sat in" on the conferences where green fireballs were discussed. These conferences would occur over the next two years!

Were the intelligence agencies worried by these sightings near secure military installations? You bet they were, considering world events of the time, a time of spies and intrigue. In the years following the Second World War, the Soviet Union had been exerting political and military pressure on neighboring countries to join with Russia in building what became a barrier of satellite states between the Soviet Union and Western Europe. The Cold War had heated up, and it was obvious that the Soviets were on the march. Czechoslovakia had been forced to join the Communist bloc a year before. The Berlin blockade had begun the previous April (1948), and was continuing. Who knew where the Soviets would strike next, and with what weapons? The Soviet scientists were known to be working feverishly to create an atomic bomb. It was also known that the Soviets had captured German rocket scientists and missiles when they took over the eastern part of Germany. Would the next Soviet weapons be missiles with atomic bombs?

At the same time the United States was putting some teeth into its undisguised threat to use atomic weapons if war broke out with the Soviets. Two years earlier, in December 1946, President Truman had established the Atomic Energy Commission (AEC) to manage the atomic weapons program. It was Truman's intent to use the threat of "The Bomb" to keep the Soviets under control. In order to make this threat realistic, however, it was necessary that the U.S. have a supply of atomic bombs. In 1945, there were only two atomic bombs in existence . . . and they were used that summer. Bomb production resumed after the war and the production rate increased slightly, limited primarily by the availability of nuclear fissionable material. By the end of 1946, there were nine warheads. By the end of 1947, there were thirteen, and by the end of 1948, there were fifty. The bombs were designed at Los Alamos. Fissionable material was made at the Hanford nuclear facility in Washington state, and at the Savannah River nuclear plant in South Carolina. Bomb parts and the fissionable material were shipped to Sandia Base at Albuquerque (about sixty miles south of Los Alamos) for assembly. The assembled bombs were shipped to Fort Hood, Texas and stored in a special facility known as Killeen Base. These areas were prime targets for Soviet espionage and so any potentially threatening phenomenon had to be investigated.

First, the appearance of flying saucers and then the appearance of the green fireballs threw a cold chill onto the warm complacency of U.S. security agencies. Could it be that our arch-enemies had really made a "quantum jump" beyond our own rocket technology? Could the green fireballs be Soviet missiles targeted against our defense installations? No one doubted that the fireballs were being seen. But, what *were* they? A memorandum to the Director of Intelligence of the Fourth Army at Fort Sam Houston, Texas, from Army Col. Eustis Poland, dated January 13, 1949, demonstrated the level of concern and listed several theories:

> Agencies in New Mexico are greatly concerned over these phenomena. They are of the opinion that some foreign power is making "sensing shots" with some super-stratosphere devise [sic] designed to be self-disentergrating [sic]. They also believe that when the devise [sic] is perfected for accuracy, the disentegrating [sic] factor will be eliminated in favor of a warhead.
>
> Another theory advanced as possibly acceptable lies in the belief that the phenomena are the result of radiological

warfare experiments by a foreign power, further, that the rays may be lethal or might be attributed to the cause of some of the plane crashes that have occurred recently.

Still another belief that is advanced is that, it is highly probable that the United States may be carrying on some top-secret experiments.

This memorandum ends by proposing that "a scientific board be sent to this locality to study the situation" because "these incidents are of such great importance, especially as they are occurring in the vicinity of sensitive installations.

Then the "big one" occurred. A green fireball was seen by over a hundred people in West Texas, New Mexico, and Colorado during the night of January 30, 1949. According to a Confidential Priority message from the Commanding Officer at Kirtland Air Force Base to the Air Force Director of Special Investigations (copy to the FBI), "Estimate at least 100 total sightings. AEC [Atomic Energy Commission], AFSWP [Air Force Special Weapons Project—in charge of nuclear weapons], Fourth Army local commanders are perturbed by implications of phenomena."

Perturbed, indeed, because they could not prove that these were *not* Soviet missiles that were being tested for bombardment of the very installations where our atomic bombs were designed and built.

The next day, the Special FBI Agent in Charge at San Antonio, Texas, wrote a letter to inform FBI headquarters of what had been going on:

```
TO: DIRECTOR, FBI Jan. 31, 1949
FROM: SAC, San Antonio
SUBJECT: PROTECTION OF VITAL INSTALLATIONS
```

At recent Weekly Intelligence Conferences of G-2 [Army Intelligence], ONI [Office of Naval Intelligence], OSI [Air Force Office of Special Investigations] and FBI in the Fourth Army Area, Officers of G-2, Fourth army have discussed the matter of "Unidentified Aircraft" or "Unidentified Aerial Phenomena" otherwise known as "Flying Discs," "Flying

Saucers," and "Balls of Fire." *This matter is considered Top Secret by Intelligence Officers of both the Army and Air Forces* [emphasis is underlined in the original].

Thus begins a two-page letter to FBI headquarters describing the onset of the green fireball phenomenon, which military intelligence considered to be Top Secret. The SAC briefly summarized the previous history:

> It is well known that there have been during the past two years reports from various parts of the country of the sighting of unidentified aerial objects which have been called in newspaper parlance "flying discs" and "flying saucers." The first such sightings were reported from Sweden‡ and it was thought that the objects, the nature of which was unknown, might have originated in Russia.

The agent then described the Chiles-Whitted sighting of July 24, 1948 of a "rocket ship" that appeared "out of a thunderhead ahead of the Eastern Airlines plane and immediately disappeared in another cloud, narrowly missing a collision with the Eastern Airlines plane," (discussed in chapter 5) before proceeding to the main subject of his letter:

> During the past two months various sightings of unexplained phenomena have been reported in the vicinity of the A.E.C. Installation at Los Alamos, New Mexico, where these phenomena now appear to be concentrated. During December, 1948 on the 5th, 6th, 7th, 8th, 11th, 13th, 14th, 20th, and 28th sightings of unexplained phenomena were made near Los Alamos by Special Agents of the Office of Special Investigation, airline pilots, military pilots, Los Alamos Security

---

‡ The reference to sightings in Sweden concerns objects termed "ghost rockets" that were reported by numerous witnesses in 1946, and were thought by the Swedish military to be Soviet missiles. An investigation of these sightings by Swedish and U.S. military scientists failed to find hard evidence to prove that these "rockets" were Soviet devices. Nevertheless some of the sightings were so well witnessed that the sightings could not be attributed to war nerves or psychosis. Many of the sighted objects were lights of various colors, sometimes trailing sparks and trails as they flew through the sky. No final explanation was ever publicized, if, indeed, one was found.

Inspectors and private citizens. On January 6, 1949 another similar object was sighted in the same area.

Dr. Lincoln La Paz, a Meteorologist [sic; should be *meteoricist*] of some note, has been generally in charge of the observations near Los Alamos, attempting to learn characteristics of the unexplained phenomena. Up to this time little concrete information has been obtained.

There have been daytime sightings which are tentatively considered to possibly resemble the exhaust of some type of jet propelled object. Night-time sightings have taken the form of lights usually described as brilliant green, similar to a green traffic signal or green neon light. Some reports indicated that the light began and ended with red or orange flash. Other reports have given the color as red, white, blue-white and yellowish green. Trailing lights sometimes observed are said to be red. The spectrum analysis of one light indicates that it may be a copper compound of the type known to be used in rocket experiments and which completely disintegrates upon explosion, leaving no debris. It is noted that no debris has ever been known to be located anywhere resulting from the unexplained phenomena.

The agent then described the travel paths and speeds of the fireballs and made a statement which may have shocked Hoover:

Their reported course indicates that they travel on an east-west line with probability that they approach from the Northern Quadrant, which would be the last stage of the great circle route if they originated in Russia . . .

As if this weren't scary enough, being consistent with Col. Gasser's opinion that the saucers had been launched from Russia, the agent went on to say that Dr. La Paz listed half a dozen reasons why "the phenomena observed are not due to meteorites" and that,

. . . the only conclusions reached thus far are that they are either hitherto unobserved natural phenomena or that they

are man-made. No scientific experiments are known to exist
in this country which could give rise to such phenomena.

Hoover's reaction to learning about the fireballs is not contained
within the available FBI records. However, one might guess that, after
comparing this information with what Gasser said, Hoover reached the
logical conclusion that *atomic powered missiles from Russia were being
targeted at our atomic installations.*

On February 7, Col. Eustis Poland wrote again to the Director of
Army Intelligence about the "'unusual lights' that have been observed for
some time past in the vicinity of Los Alamos." The memorandum says
that, "Due to the inexplicability of this phenomena, it has become a matter of some concern to this Headquarters as well as the USAEC and the
OSI." Therefore, the Security Division of Los Alamos had recommended
that "representatives of the three interested services" (Army, AEC,
AFOSI) "hold a joint conference to include eminent scientists appointed
for the purpose." The conference was scheduled for February 16.

Apparently the Director of Army Intelligence was not worried, inasmuch as he responded by indicating that the "inexplicability" resulted
only from a lack of data and that "it is not believed that any 'unnatural'
or hostile basis exists for these occurrences or that they are due to
'unconventional aircraft.'" ("Unconventional aircraft" in this context
meant "flying saucers.") Another Army memorandum from the office of
the Director of Army Intelligence indicates that the AEC was not worried either: "(a) check with AEC discloses that they will not officially
approve such a meeting, as they do not think the phenomena justifies
such action."

On February 10, FBI headquarters received a letter from SAC El Paso,
Texas, which summarized Dr. La Paz's frightening hypothesis:

> Dr. La Paz advanced the theory . . . that the objects were
> controlled missiles traveling around the earth at an altitude
> of approximately 25 miles and at a speed of approximately
> 15 miles per second. The missile was probably controlled by
> agents stationed at various intervals who are able to bring the

missile down over a designated area and explode it . . . Dr. La Paz added that he believed the Russians or some other country was practicing with these weapons which carried no warhead and were being exploded at an altitude of approximately 10 miles. After the practice periods La Paz assumed the weapons would be loaded with an atomic warhead.

Dr. La Paz, a top meteor expert, said these fireballs were not natural phenomena. However, Army intelligence couldn't accept La Paz's alternative Russian missile theory because the Army and Air Force were certain that the United States was at least even with, if not well ahead of, the Soviet Union in the development of nuclear energy and long-range missiles. Furthermore, they did not believe that the Soviet Union would actually test their missiles *over* the U.S. (By carrying out such tests they would risk losing their technological advantage because one of the missiles might malfunction and crash, thereby handing us their secret technology. Certainly we would never do the same.) Therefore, in spite of Dr. La Paz's opinion, many intelligence officers believed these fireballs would turn out to be unusual but natural phenomena.

The fireball sightings attracted the interest of Theodore von Karman, a famous mathematician who was the chairman of the Air Force Science Advisory Board. (Recall that Col. McCoy of AMC/ATIC, in March 1948, told the AFSAB about Project Sign and the saucer investigation, see chapter 5.) On February 11, 1949, he wrote a letter to Gen. Cabell indicating that, although he was extremely skeptical about flying discs and other unidentified flying objects, he was impressed by the quality of the fireball observations, and by La Paz's analysis. He therefore recommended that the Air Force take a scientific approach and attempt to obtain objective measurements of the fireballs. An aide to Gen. Cabell, in responding to von Karman's letter, stated that AMC/ATIC had already contacted Dr. La Paz and offered him the job of acting as an astrophysical consultant to Project Grudge. However, La Paz, living in New Mexico, was too far away from Dayton, Ohio, to be able to work closely with the AMC personnel, so he recommended Dr. J. Allen Hynek, who was a professor of astronomy at Ohio State University. It

Dr. J. Allen Hynek, professor of astronomy at Ohio State University. He later became consultant to Project Grudge and Project Blue Book.

was Hynek's job to supply astronomical explanations whenever possible for sightings of unconventional objects, including green fireballs.§

The aide to Cabell also wrote that twenty percent of the 210 incidents had been explained, mostly as weather balloons. (That would mean roughly forty sightings had been explained. The "Analysis of Flying Object Incidents in the U.S.," discussed in chapter 5, indicated that only eighteen had been explained.) With regard to the remainder, there was no tangible evidence which proved the objects to be from a foreign nation, even for the sightings outside the United States. Furthermore, "the possibility of foreign devices becomes more remote in the case of domestic incidents, and would represent achievements which defy many well defined limits in aeronautical science." Cabell's aide did not respond directly to von Karman's recommendation for objective measurements. Instead the aide responded by saying that AMC/ATIC was analyzing the sightings and attempting to explain them.

§ Hynek, who died in 1986, was the Air Force astronomy consultant from 1948 through the closing of Project Blue Book in 1969. Although initially very skeptical, by the 1960's he had begun to realize that saucers or Unidentified Flying Objects, were real phenomena that deserved investigation. In 1973 he founded the Center for UFO Studies (CUFOS) to collect and analyze UFO sightings and related phenomena. The Center still exists in Chicago.

Dr. Edward Teller,
physicist and "Father
of the H-bomb."

On February 16, a meeting was held at Los Alamos to attempt to arrive at a conclusion regarding the fireballs. Present were representatives of the Fourth Army, the Air Force Special Weapons Project, the FBI (Agent Maxwell), the AEC, and the University of California (which "ran" Los Alamos under contract to the Defense Department and the Atomic Energy Commission). The best-known scientist at the meeting was Dr. Edward Teller. The director of Los Alamos laboratory, Dr. Norris Bradbury, was also there. Dr. La Paz, as the meteor expert, essentially ran the meeting. He began by discussing the characteristics of ordinary meteors, and then describing how these differed from the fireballs sighted, listing half-a-dozen peculiarities, including the color and, essentially, the horizontal path. The meeting went on for several hours and numerous related subjects were discussed. Perhaps one of the most puzzling facts was this: whereas meteor reports for most of the U.S. were average for the months of December, January, and February, no green fireballs had been reported in areas other than the Los Alamos, Las Vegas (New Mexico), and west Texas areas. Another aspect which confounded the experts, including Dr. Teller, was that no noise had ever been reported, even though shockwaves would have been expected for material objects moving through the atmosphere at speeds of several miles per second. (Note: Lack of sound

despite high speed has been a consistent characteristic of "flying saucers.")
Teller suggested the lights might be nonmaterial, perhaps optical phenomena of some sort. The meeting concluded with more questions raised, and no answers.

A further report on the green fireball mystery came to FBI headquarters on March 22, from SAC San Antonio. According to his report, at the weekly Intelligence Conferences there were discussions about the green fireballs that were "considered secret by Intelligence Officers of both the Army and Air Force." He learned from the Army intelligence that the "above matter is now termed 'Unconventional Aircraft' and investigations concerning such matters have been given the name 'Project Grudge.'" This was a reference to the fact that Project Sign had been terminated in January 1949. Recall that a new name, Grudge, had been given to the continuation of the Project Sign intelligence collection effort. The new project was intended to handle both flying disc and green fireball investigations.

In the March 22 letter, SAC San Antonio mentioned the previously discussed February 16 conference at Los Alamos, and then said he had been told by Army intelligence that,

> . . . as of November 1, 1948 information had been received from higher Military authorities that the Air Force had advised that such sightings occur periodically and that another period of sightings was then imminent. Further, on February 14, 1949, higher Military authorities advised that it was believed that ultimately it would be found that the phenomena in question would have a natural explanation.

There was no reason given why "higher Military authorities" believed the green fireballs would "have a natural explanation" in contradiction to Dr. La Paz's opinion that they weren't meteors. Perhaps it was wishful thinking on the part of the higher authorities. Perhaps they stated this opinion in order to avoid the very difficult political situation that would ensue if they admitted that the fireballs were *not* natural phenomena.

What the agent reported next in the same letter was not at all reassuring. In fact, it must have appeared to the security agencies that things were really getting out of hand because there had been several incidents of "flares" seen,

> . . . north of Killeen Base in the area of the Vital Installation at Camp Hood, Texas . . . It has been concluded that the flares seen near Killeen are probably similar to the phenomena previously noted in the Los Alamos, Sandia base area . . .

In other words, the luminous nighttime phenomena that had first been seen around the areas where atomic bombs were designed (Los Alamos) and built (Sandia Base) were now being seen *where the bombs were stored!* Recall that these sightings were unique to the American Southwest. There were no similar concentrations of fireball sightings anywhere else. It may have seemed to some of the intelligence agents that the green fireballs were following the atomic bombs. According to the agent's letter,

> There appears to be reason to believe that the above-mentioned phenomena may be connected with secret experiments being conducted by some U.S. government agency, as it is believed that the United States is farther advanced in guided missile development than any foreign power.

The SAC letter of March 22 illustrates just how confused the security officers and intelligence agents were by the green fireball sightings. They accepted the fact that the fireballs were real objects or phenomena, and were trying to determine the most likely, or the *least unlikely,* explanation for the sightings. They rejected the Soviet missile theory in spite of La Paz's analysis. The suggestion by "higher Military authorities" that the fireballs were natural phenomena did not convince them because Dr. La Paz had rejected the "natural" theory. Furthermore, they were fully aware that, in spite of having Top Secret clearances, *they didn't know about every Top Secret test program of the United States military.* Therefore, the only remaining possible explanation, since the "extraterrestrial explanation" had been ruled out by the Air Force (Gen. Vandenberg), was that these objects were secret test devices of the United States.

About this time, while Hoover's FBI was digesting Col. Gasser's Soviet missile theory and learning of the green "fireballs" over the nuclear weapon areas in the Southwest, the FBI received fifty copies of Gen. Cabell's Requirements Memorandum #4, dated February 15, 1949 (mentioned at the end of chapter 5). It must have appeared to the FBI that the "high brass" of the Air Force were desperate for information about "unconventional aircraft" and green fireballs.

This veritable deluge of unsettling information caused the FBI to modify its policy on saucer sightings. An assistant to D. M. Ladd wrote a memorandum recommending that the FBI issue a new directive to the FBI agents throughout the country. The memorandum includes the following paragraph, which emphasizes the source of concern for the FBI:

> [Col. Gasser] . . . has recently and confidentially advised the Bureau that flying discs are believed by the Air Force to be man-made missiles rather than some natural phenomenon, and that as much as four years go it was learned that some type of flying discs were being experimented upon by the Russians. It was further determined from Col. Gasser that most all of the flying discs seen by persons in the United States approached this country from a northerly direction and returned in the same direction, indicating the strong possibility that they are coming from Russia.

The memorandum referred to the recent receipt of "a sufficient number of copies of a memorandum dated February 15, 1949, captioned 'Unconventional Aircraft' which can be furnished to our field offices." (The FBI knew that AFI was serious because the AFI had taken the time to type all fifty copies rather than forcing the FBI to use its own secretaries to make copies.) The memorandum ended by pointing out that the matter of flying discs was "of sufficient importance to the internal security of the country that our field offices should secure as much information as possible from complainants in order to assist the Department of Air Force." (Here "complainants" means persons who voluntarily submit flying disc information to the FBI.) On March 25, the FBI issued "SAC letter No. 38, series 1949" which reads:

> Your attention is directed to Bureau Bulletin #57, Series 1947, dated October 1, 1947, relating to the discontinuance of investigation by this Bureau in matters concerning flying discs.
>
> For your confidential information, a reliable and confidential source has advised the Bureau that flying discs are believed to be man-made missiles rather than natural phenomenon. It has also been determined that for approximately the past four years the USSR has been engaged in experimentation on an unknown type of flying disc.
>
> The Department of the Air Force has furnished to the Bureau the attached memorandum classified "restricted" dated February 15, 1949, entitled "Unconventional Aircraft." This memorandum is being furnished to you in order that all agents assigned to your office can be informed of the type of information desired by the Air Force in this matter.
>
> As set forth in Bureau Bulletin #57, referred to above, no investigation should be conducted by your office relative to flying discs, however the attached memorandum should be referred to in securing data from persons who desire to voluntarily furnish information to your office relating to flying discs.

The situation regarding fireballs and flying discs must have appeared to the FBI to be quite confusing. On the one hand, the AFI desired information on sightings of unconventional aircraft (flying saucers) and green fireballs. The AFI clearly considered these to be real objects. Some elements of the Air Force believed they were Soviet missiles being tested over the United States. At the same time, other elements of the Air Force couldn't believe that the Soviets would test missiles over the U.S. and were suggesting that these were secret U.S. devices. But why would the Air Force want sighting information on our own secret projects? And if that weren't confusing enough, "higher Military authorities" were saying the green fireballs would turn out to be natural phenomena, presumably meteors, in contradiction to Dr. La Paz's claim that they couldn't be meteoric in origin.

With all this contradictory information, what was a poor FBI agent to think?

CHAPTER 8

An Unimpeachable Source

On **April 4,** the agent in San Antonio, Texas, further updated the situation in a letter to headquarters:

> Lights of unknown origin were observed on March 6, 7, 8,
> and 17, 1949, by military personnel of the alert force sta-
> tioned approximately 1,000 yards east of the fences which
> surround the Killeen Base.

Many months later, Project Grudge personnel who tried to explain *all* saucer and fireball sightings, decided that the lights of March 6, 7, and 8 must have been meteors. However, the March 17 sighting at 7:52 P.M. was too much for them. It remains unidentified. The witnesses were guards at the Second Armored Division who, for an hour, watched eight large red, green, and white flare-like objects fly around, generally in straight lines.

On March 31, at 11:50 P.M. another witness saw a lighted object, which was described as being different from what had been seen before. It was so unusual the FBI agent described it:

... [the] lighted object about the size of a basketball, reddish white in color, followed by a fire trail, was observed southwest of Killeen Base adjacent to Camp Hood, Texas. The observation was made by Lt. Frederick Davis who was in charge of a platoon, Company C, 12 armored Infantry Battalion, which is assigned as part of an alert force [called Force Abel] from Camp Hood, whose function is to protect the installation at Killeen Base.

Davis advised that the object was at an altitude estimated at 6,000 ft., was traveling parallel to the ground and passed directly over him at a rapid rate of speed. It was in view ten to fifteen seconds and suddenly disappeared high in the sky without having ascended. No sound or odor was detected. The night was clear and visibility good. The object passed almost directly over the airstrip at Killeen Base.

When Davis attempted to advise his headquarters by telephone immediately after the sighting, he heard static or electrical interference on the telephone line, which he stated might be possible radio interference.

This is case number 326 in the master list of about 13,000 sightings collected by Projects Sign, Grudge, and Blue Book. Recall that after Vandenberg rejected the ET explanation there were only two other explanations available to the investigators at ATIC/Grudge: natural phenomena or man-made missiles, where man-made meant "of foreign origin," i.e., Soviet missiles. However, in this case they couldn't believe a Soviet missile was flying over Killeen Base. Therefore it *had* to be a natural phenomenon. They identified it as a meteor, in spite of the low altitude and lack of sound.

In the same letter, the SAC San Antonio called the attention of FBI headquarters to a radio broadcast by respected newsman Walter Winchell:

It is noted that Mr. Walter Winchell, on his Sunday evening broadcast, April 3, 1949, stated that "flying discs" seen in this country definitely emanated from Russia.

Newsman Walter Winchell.
The Fourth Army wanted
Winchell interviewed by the
FBI regarding his statement
that "flying discs" came
from the Soviet Union.

Evidently this caught the attention of the agencies that were aware of the green fireball threat to vital installations, because an intelligence officer of the Fourth Army contacted the FBI at San Antonio for more information:

> On April 4, 1949, G-2, 4th Army, contacted this office, inquiring as to whether we had any information that would substantiate or discredit the statements made by Walter Winchell.
>
> In view of the interest and concern of the 4th Army military authorities who have the duty of protecting the vital installations at Los Alamos, NM, Sandia Base, NM in the El Paso division, and the Camp Hood area in the San Antonio Division, it is suggested that the Bureau may desire to arrange to have Mr. Winchell interviewed concerning the source of his information that "flying discs" emanated from Russia.

Hoover's response to the agent's suggestion came on April 26:

```
SAC - San Antonio
Director - FBI
FLYING DISKS
INTERNAL SECURITY - R
```

In regard to your request for information that would substantiate or discredit the statements made by Walter Winchell
on his broadcast of April 3, 1949, your attention is directed
to SAC Letter No. 38 dated March 25, 1949, captioned "Flying Discs."

For your strictly confidential information, the data contained in SAC Letter No. 38 was obtained in confidence from
a colonel in the United States Air Materiel Command, who
obtained his information from persons actively engaged in
the investigation of this subject.

No interview with Walter Winchell will be made by the
Bureau concerning the source of his statements referred to in
your letter.

Why didn't Hoover want to find out the source of Winchell's information? After all, Winchell was perhaps the most influential news com-
mentator of his day. He wouldn't be expected to make such an important statement without some supporting evidence or at least *an
unimpeachable source!* And certainly any evidence Winchell had that
proved the Russians were sending missiles over the United States would
be valuable to the FBI because it would have important political ramifi-
cations, affecting everyone up to the President. One can imagine the
furor if the FBI had presented President Truman with undeniable evidence that the Russians were testing missiles over the U.S. and the Air
Force couldn't do anything about it!

Now, years later, we can guess why Hoover didn't want Winchell
interviewed: *Hoover was Winchell's unimpeachable source!*

Preposterous? Consider this. Winchell and Hoover had been very well
acquainted for many years. Winchell had closely followed Hoover's
exploits in the 1930s when Hoover was chasing the mobsters of that era.

Consider also the information that Winchell conveyed: saucers are missiles from the Soviet Union. That is not what the Air Force was saying publicly, but it is what Col. Gasser had confidentially told the FBI several months before. Hoover, of course, knew this. He also knew of Dr. La Paz's theory that the green fireballs were Soviet missiles. Hence Hoover had the information Winchell reported.

Of course, it is possible that Winchell had gotten the information from an Air Force official. However, I think this unlikely. If that were the case, Hoover wouldn't have known who had leaked the information and so he might have wanted to have Winchell interviewed. On the other hand, if Hoover had told Winchell, he would have known the source. Furthermore, Hoover wouldn't want some FBI agent to find out that he had leaked this important, classified information to Winchell.

Why would Hoover tell Winchell? Perhaps he was disturbed by the failure of the top generals and the President to react seriously to what was clearly a perceived by the people closest to the problem as a continuing real threat to our most "vital installations." Perhaps Hoover decided to use the press to try to create pressure on the government to react . . . *to do something!*

However, the government did not react to Winchell's announcement. Why not? Weren't the President, et al., *worried* about the Soviet threat? Of course they were. And one can imagine that if verified Soviet missiles had been spotted flying toward the U.S. there would have been harsh words, if not all-out war.

Of course, if the Top Brass and the President knew that the strange lights were *something else* . . . perhaps something that *couldn't be defended against* . . . perhaps *something related to extraterrestrial intelligence* . . . they wouldn't have been worried about a Russian threat. Instead they would have tried to *downplay the importance of the sightings by publicly claiming that they all could be explained as natural events.*

And that's what exactly what they did. There was heightened press activity for a few days after Winchell's announcement, as the news media attempted to confirm his statement. Of course the Air Force and government officials denied that saucers were Russian missiles and assured everyone there was nothing to worry about. Then, three weeks later, two very "convenient" events happened (convenient for the Air Force in its attempt to decrease public interest in saucers): the report of Project Sign was released and three days later Sidney Shallet's *Saturday Evening Post* article on the Air Force's saucer investigation was published. Neither of these publications was favorable toward the possibility of flying saucers having an extraterrestrial origin.

Once again, public pressure on the Air Force ended.

But the saucer sightings didn't.

CHAPTER 9

Air Force: "They Don't Exist."
UFOs: "We're Baaack!"

It was at this time that the security agencies were getting an extreme case of the jitters over saucers and fireballs, and the Air Force was disparaging Winchell's statement, that a highly credible, yet unexplainable, *daytime* sighting occurred near one of the restricted military test areas.

The sighting by Charles Moore and four Navy enlisted men at Arrey, New Mexico, not far from the White Sands Proving Ground and Alamogordo, New Mexico, convinced many people that, not only were flying saucers real, but they were highly advanced technological devices— *advanced beyond anything human beings could create.*

On April 24, at about 10:30 A.M. local time, Moore, a graduate engineer, aerologist, and member of the Navy's high-altitude balloon project team, was tracking a balloon that had been launched ten minutes earlier when he and the other Navy men noticed another object moving through the sky, nearly in the direction of the balloon. The object was large and bright enough that it could be seen with the naked eye. He tracked it with the theodolite (a type of telescope) they had been using to follow the balloon. Through the telescope it appeared to have an elliptical shape with about a 2.5 to 1 ratio of the maximum to minimum dimensions. The object traveled in a large arc through the sky, appearing first in the southwest at about 210 degrees azimuth and forty-five degrees elevation. It then traveled rapidly eastward passing through 127 degrees azimuth and sixty degrees elevation (the approximate location of the sun), and then turned northward. It traveled to the north-north-east at about twenty degrees azimuth and stayed at that azimuth while it *climbed* from a twenty-five degrees elevation to about twenty-nine degrees. Evidently it traveled almost directly away from the observers at a high speed. It had been visible for about a minute.

During the first portion of observation, Moore estimated that it traveled at an angular rate of about five degrees per second and he estimated its angular size at 0.02 degrees. Moore thought that the altitude was as high as 300,000 ft. (sixty miles), which would make its length about 100 ft. and its speed about 18,000 mph, but it may have been lower, in which case the speed and size would be smaller. (Since only the angular size and angular speed were measured the calculated size and speed are proportional to the assumed distance.) For example, if it had been at 100,000 ft. it would have been about thirty feet in size and traveling about 6,000 mph. Moore launched another balloon which, after about an hour and a half, burst at an altitude of about 93,000 ft., having traveled only about thirteen miles horizontal distance from the launch site. Hence there were no high-speed winds at any altitude to 93,000 ft. Moore filed a report with the Navy Special Devices Center, where it attracted a lot of interest. The report also turned up in the flying saucer file of the CIA as well as in the Project Blue Book file, where it is officially unexplained (it is not in the FBI file).

Dr. Moore's sighting was known to only a few people when, three days later, on April 27, 1949, the director of AFI briefed the Deputy Chief of Air Force Operations on the status of the UFO project. The Director of AFI also sent to the Joint Intelligence Committee (JIC) a formal report, "On Unidentified Aerial Objects."* This report summarized the results of Project Sign with an interpretation or "slant" that was

---

* The JIC was composed of representatives from the several armed services plus the State Department, CIA, and FBI. There is no mention of this report in the FBI record, however.

biased by the new policy of skepticism toward UFO reports. The important summary of results was in the appendix of the report, which states:

1. As of March 10, 1949, a total of 256 incidents involving unidentified aerial objects had been recorded under Project Sign. The majority of these were domestic observations, but there were many reports from foreign sources. In each incident the observers have been interrogated by investigators and the results have been analyzed by technical personnel.

2. Condensed summaries have been prepared on each incident to provide basic information to individuals and agencies having a responsibility or interest in the project.

3. The extreme lack of accurate observed details and unpredictable occurrence of incidents have made positive identification extremely difficult. Data on unidentified aerial objects has grouped the incidents as follows:

    13.3% discs; 43% spherical or eliptical [sic] shape (including balls of fire); 6% cylindrical shape; 2.5% winged objects; 32.2% shapes other than those above.

According to the report, graphical methods were used to relate sightings to shape, location, direction of flight, missile test areas, airfields and airports, radio beacons, radar stations, meteorological stations, balloon releases, celestial phenomena, and known flight paths of birds. A preliminary psychological analysis of reports by the Aero-Medical Laboratory of AMC indicated that "a considerable number of incidents can be explained as ordinary occurrences that have been misinterpreted, as a result of human errors." The Air Weather Service had studied the first 172 sightings and reported that twenty-four of them could be correlated with releases of weather balloons. The report states that "Professor Hynek, Ohio State University astrophysicist and head of the University Observatory . . . indicates that thirty percent of the first 200 reports are positively attributable to astronomical phenomena, and forty-five percent could be explained on the basis of such phenomena or the sighting or weather balloons or other objects." Even though this indicated that at least seventy-five percent of the sightings could be explained, the possibility that some sightings might be "space ships or satellite vehicles" caused them hire the Rand Corporation to carry out "a special study . . . to provide analysis from this standpoint" and also to "provide fundamental information, pertaining to the basic design and performance characteristics that might distinguish a possible 'space ship.'" However, the scientists at Rand, after analyzing all the reports, concluded "there is nothing in any reported incidents which would go against a rational explanation." The AFI report to the JIC briefly discussed the possibility that "ball lightning" might account for some sightings but "it appears that the subject of 'ball lightning' occupies an undetermined status and authorities are not at all convinced that such a phenomenon actually exists." The report mentioned the green fireball sightings and the belief of Dr. von Karman that this problem "is more properly in the field of upper atmosphere research than the field of intelligence." The report also says that "credible unexplained incidents which might involve the use of atomic powered craft of [un]usual design should be considered jointly by the Atomic Energy Commission and highly competent aerodynamicists to determine the necessity for further consideration of such incidents by the National Defense Intelligence Agencies." The report concludes:

17. The majority of reported incidents are [sic] reliable to the extent that they have involved the sighting of some object or light phenomenon.

18. In spite of the lack of accurate data provided by witnesses, the majority of reported incidents have been caused by mis-identifications of weather balloons, high altitude balloons with lights and/or electronic equipment, meteors, bolides, and the planet Venus.

19. There are numerous reports from reliable and competent observers for which a conclusive explanation has not been made. Some of these involve descriptions which would place them in the category of new manifestations of probable natural phenomena but others involve configurations and described performance which might conceivably represent an advanced aerodynamical development. A few unexplained incidents surpass these limits of credibility.

20. It is unlikely that a foreign power would expose a superior aerial weapon by a prolonged ineffectual penetration of the United States.

The last comment indicates that the writers of this report rejected the Soviet saucer hypothesis, as had the AFI and ATIC/Sign analysts in the past. They did admit that there were numerous unsolved sightings, some of which *"surpass these limits of credibility"* by which they meant that the descriptions were so accurate and the objects were so unlike man-made craft as to be *incredible!*

Two days later, the Air Force publicly announced the results of its first saucer investigation. The Office of Public Relations of the National Military Establishment issued a memorandum, for immediate release to the press, which was described as "a digest of preliminary studies made by the Air Materiel Command, Wright Field, in Dayton, Ohio, on 'Flying Saucers.'" The title of the memorandum was "Project Saucer." It was a sanitized version of the final report of Project Sign, which had been completed in February after Project Grudge had formally "taken over" the saucer and fireball investigations. Because the project names Sign and Grudge were classified, the public version was called Project Saucer.

The Project Saucer report, like the JIC report discussed above, pointed out that there were unsolved sightings, and left the door open for the possibility that some UFO sightings might represent something new. It therefore may be considered the "last gasp" of the investigators who ran Project Sign in the heady days of September 1948, when they tried to convince Gen. Vandenberg that saucers were interplanetary craft. On the other hand, the report also tried to make it appear as if the unsolved sightings would be solved eventually. Hence the national military establishment may have thought that it would provide a sort of technical backup to the previously mentioned article that was prepared by Sidney Shallett.

Was it merely coincidence that Shallet's article appeared in the *Saturday Evening Post* only three days later? In a letter dated April 25, 1949, from Gen. Cabell to the Director of Public Relations, Cabell pointed out that although Shallett was "urged not to attempt his article" he wrote it anyway and "presumably others also will be so inclined." Shallett had been given access to AMC/ATIC material on saucers and Cabell could "see no grounds for denial of a similar (access) to other correspondents." He goes on to say, referring to a draft of the Project Saucer report as "the attached article":

> Since the attached article includes essentially the same material made available to Shallett, there do not appear to be any grounds for denying this material to others, similarly interested and equally responsible. On the other hand, it is certain that the release of this article on any broad basis would result in a flurry of "crank" reports and a consequent flooding of our investigative resources. The end result would be a disservice to our effectiveness in eliminating the presently remaining question marks. Our efforts must be based upon reports by other than "cranks" who will make their reports without the spur of widespread press speculation.

Gen. Cabell concluded his letter by saying he did not object to the release of the Project Saucer report but that he thought, in order to "reduce its use on a broad scale," it should be made available at the public relations office rather than distributed widely as a press release. Evidently the national military establishment thought otherwise. The memorandum was widely distributed.

According to the "Saucer" report, since the "birthday" of Project Saucer on January 22, 1948, the Air Force had studied more than 240 domestic and 30 foreign sightings. After spending a year studying these sightings,

> . . . with the assistance from several other government and private agencies, and with the entire facilities of the Wright Field laboratories at their disposal, Project 'Saucer' personnel have already come up with identification of about 30 percent of the sightings studied thus far as conventional aerial objects. It is expected that further probing of incidents in relation to weather balloon locations, etc., will provide commonplace answers to at least an equal number of the sky riddles.

Answers have been—and will be—drawn from factors such as guided missile research activities, weather and other atmospheric sounding balloons, astronomical phenomena, commercial and military aircraft flights, flights of migratory birds, shots from flare guns, practical jokers, victims of optical illusion, the phenomena of mass hallucination, etc.

However, the Air Force admitted that "there are still question marks in the 'Saucer Story.'" The Air Force considered it "highly improbable" that any foreign country had created flying saucers and "visitations from Mars, Venus, or other distant planets attached to other star systems is looked upon as an almost complete impossibility."

So what were the unidentifiable saucers?

[Whereas] . . . no definite and conclusive evidence is yet available to either prove or disprove the existence of at least some of the remaining unidentified objects as real aircraft of unknown and unconventional configuration, exhaustive investigations have turned up no alarming probabilities.

The twenty-two-page report described several sightings, discussed the methods of investigation and the potential explanations, and then concluded:

The "saucers" are not a joke. Neither are they cause for alarm to the population. Many of the incidents already have answers: meteors, balloons, falling stars, birds in flight, testing devices, etc. Some of them still have question marks. It is the mission of the AMC Technical Intelligence Division's Project "Saucer" to supply the periods.

In other words, there was no real conclusion. Instead, the Air Force said this about the unexplained sightings: *don't worry, we're working on it! The answers will come soon.* The Air Force wanted the public to believe that everything was under control. However, if the national military establishment thought that the Project Saucer report, when combined with Shallett's article, would put a damper on saucer interest, it was wrong. By admitting that a large fraction of the sightings were unexplained and by not positively ruling out interplanetary vehicles, the Air Force left open the door for the "unworldly" to enter public discussion. Astute investigative reporters realized this. One author in particular made it the cornerstone of his proof that saucers were extraterrestrial visitors. This particular author, Donald Keyhoe, discussed in chapter 13, would become the most vocal critic of Air Force saucer policy in years to come.

The release of the Project Saucer report may have made the press and the general public feel good but it didn't impress security guards around Fort Hood and Killeen Base. On the same day as the JIC briefing, and two days before the release of Project Saucer, they saw unexplained phenomena four times between 9:20 to 9:40 P.M. local time and then, the next day, *nine* times between 8:30 and 9:30 P.M. These guards may have thought that the saucers and fireballs had decided to retaliate against the authors of the Project Saucer report. The sightings are summarized below to illustrate the varying types of phenomena reported.

APRIL 27
#1: 9:20 P.M.; small; dull violet; first seen stationary, 6–7 feet above ground and 10–12 feet from 2 witnesses; then departed to the west; seen for 60 seconds; no sound, no odor; passed through branches of a tree, thereby establishing conclusively its location and approximate size; level flight.

#2: 9:25 P.M.; size of baseball; bright white; round; no glare; first seen 6–7 feet above ground, 200 yards away; level flight in a semicircular path around witnesses; light was round but "had a point shaped apparatus extending two to four inches behind it; the point of the cone was to the rear."

#3: 9:37 P.M.; size of a silver dollar; "rustless white" in color no glare; first seen 100 feet from 4 observers; 6–8 feet above the ground; approached 4 observers in a zig-zag path going on and off; no sound; no odor; no trail.

#4: [time not given]; similar to #3.

APRIL 28

#1: 8:30–8:50 P.M.; 1 observer; 4 objects seen individually at 5 minute intervals; each in sight 3–5 minutes; moving slowly, rising slightly, then falling; size of a tennis ball at arm's length [roughly 10 ft. in diameter if 100 ft. away; proportionally larger or smaller if the distance were larger or smaller]; white turning to red and then to green.

#2: 8:30 P.M.; 1 observer; 1 object seen intermittently at 5 minute intervals over 1 1/2 hours; horizontal flight toward the south at 3 mph; appeared to be about 10 [in.] in diameter; white, then turned red.

#3: 8:37 P.M.; 4 observers; 8 or 10 lights occurring at intervals of 5 minutes; each in sight for about 5 minutes; moved in southerly direction at low speed; constant elevation; made a turn; size of softball at arm's length [about 10 ft. if 100 ft. away]; one appeared to have a cone-shaped rear end tapering to a point; white, turned to red, and then to green.

#4: 8:40 P.M.; 1 observer; one light; just above treetops; about the size of a baseball at arm's length; slow speed; white light with red blinking light.

#5: 9:00 P.M.; 1 observer; four lights, no pattern; size of tennis ball at arm's length; 5 mph toward the south; first light was white, then red and then green; the other three lights were white only.

#6: 9:10 P.M.; 1 observer; one object; about the size of a baseball at arm's length; about 300 yards away [corresponding to roughly 90 feet in diameter if 900 feet away]; observed for 8–10 minutes; stationary [color not reported].

#7: 9:10 P.M.: 1 observer; one object; size of baseball at arm's length; white; moved northward; in sight for about 2 seconds; estimated speed, 75 mph; described as being like a 75 watt bulb at 50–75 ft.

#8: 9:30 P.M.; 2 observers; one light; 10–15 inches long; observed for 5–6 minutes; moved in southerly direction;

speed estimated at 10–15 mph; color changed from white to red to green.

#9: 9:30 P.M.; 1 observer; one light appeared three times for 3, 2 and then 1 minute [approximately] durations; moving toward the west; speed about 5 mph; round; about the size of a baseball at arm's length; bright white, then turned to red.

The Project Saucer press release implied that the Air Force would eventually discover explanations for all the sightings. This put the Project Grudge personnel under pressure to explain all the sightings. Hence, for each sighting they tried to find a few descriptive details which, when considered alone and ignoring other details if necessary, might suggest plausible explanations. The sightings by the security guards were assumed not to be hallucinations, so the explanations had to involve real objects or phenomena. The Project Grudge personnel therefore claimed the April 27 lights were *birds* and the April 28 lights were *flares or fireworks*.

Another sighting on the day following the release of the Project Saucer report was a real challenge to the Project Grudge investigators. It did not appear near a military installation, but it was important because it was a daytime sighting. It occurred at Tucson, Arizona, at 5:45 P.M. Several witnesses saw a sausage- or cigar-shaped object travel from the northeast to the southwest over a period of approximately twelve minutes. The object was shiny metallic and it reflected the sun. It appeared to be revolving as it moved "like the slow roll of an airplane." There was no noise, nor was there exhaust or a vapor trail. There were no wings or engines or "protuberances of any sort." It appeared to be traveling at 300–600 mph. The Project Grudge personnel had no other choice than to leave this one unexplained.

The Project Saucer press release was written in a way that implied all the unexplained sightings could be simply unusual natural phenomena. The Air Force hoped that this would allay any fears the public might have that the Air Force had lost control of the saucer situation, and that it would dampen public interest in the subject. However, as pointed out previously, the report did not absolutely rule out the possibility that some sightings might be truly "revolutionary" in nature. A couple of days later Sidney Shallett's flying saucer article in the *Saturday Evening Post* magazine seemed to squash that possibility.

The first part of the article was published on April 30, three days after the release of the Project Saucer report. The second part was published a week later. In the first article, entitled "What You Can Believe About Flying Saucers," Shallett was very critical of saucer sightings, which he referred to as the "great Flying Saucer Scare." He used phrases such as "fearsome freaks" and "full-blown screwiness." He said that the Air Force had *reluctantly* been dragged into investigation of saucer sightings because of the public furor in the summer of 1947.† Shallet also said that, based on what he had been shown by the Air Force, there was not a "scrap of bona fide evidence" that saucers represented either a technological development of the human race, or visitors from another planet. In other words, according to Shalett all saucer sighting reports belonged to the following three general categories: misidentifications and failures to identify natural and man-made phenomena, delusions and mental aberrations, or publicity seekers and hoaxers. Shallet's second article supported the viewpoint in his first article by demonstrating how experienced observers such as pilots could be fooled. The bottom line: saucer sightings are basically mistakes, they are certainly nothing to worry about, and the Air Force has everything under control so *don't worry, be happy!*

The Project Saucer report stated that saucer sightings were "no joke" and indicated that the ATIC investigators believed, but *could not prove,* that all the unexplained sightings were natural phenomena. This left the door open a crack for the possibility that some unexplained sightings *might not be natural phenomena.* The Shallett articles, on the other hand, presented a more positive attitude toward explanation, an attitude that more accurately portrayed the beliefs of the Project Grudge personnel (colonels and below) at the time. They were quite certain that, because saucers couldn't be *ours* and couldn't be *theirs* (Soviets) and couldn't be *extraterrestrials,* then they *must* be natural phenomena, hoaxes, or delusions, and therefore *of little importance to*

---

† This was wrong. The available Air Force records clearly show it was sightings by Air Force pilots and not public furor that attracted the interest of the Air Force.

the Air Force. This was *not* the belief of Gen. Cabell and other high brass, as will be seen.

After Shallet's article was published, the Project Grudge investigative activities steadily declined, with the project virtually shutting down in August 1949. However, the analysis of the previously received unexplained sightings referred to in the Project Saucer report continued because the Grudge personnel knew that sooner or later they would have to supply explanations for all of them.

To the skeptical world, the decreased Air Force interest in saucers probably appeared logical because saucer sightings were nothing to worry about, so why investigate? However, to the FBI, with its connection to the insiders at the Air Force and its knowledge of the green fireball reports, this may have looked precisely like a *cover-up.*

CHAPTER 10

Observers of
Unquestioned Reliability

The "unimportant," yet still unexplained, phenomena seen in the American Southwest had established quite a track record by this time, and they were still being seen. According to a summary of observations written by Lt. Col. Doyle Rees in May 1950, by the end of April 1949, the total number of sightings in the vicinity of the previously mentioned areas in New Mexico and at Camp Hood totalled about fifty. Of these, a dozen were labeled as "'Disk' or variation," indicating that there were flying saucer or "flying machine" aspects to some of the sightings. According to Rees, the witnesses in these sightings were "scientists, Special Agents of the Office of Special Investigations (IG) USAF, airline pilots, military pilots, Los Alamos Security Inspectors, military personnel, and many other persons of various occupations whose reliability is not questioned."

Rees' list included Charles Moore's sighting (rated as very reliable), but did not include another more important sighting that occurred a month later because it did not occur within the area of Rees' investigative jurisdiction. Instead, it occurred many hundreds of miles away at the mouth of the Rogue River in Oregon. This sighting is important because of the quality of the observations by the several observers, and because the witnesses reported the sighting *only* to their local security agency, and to the AFOSI.

During the afternoon of May 24, 1950, five people, three men and two women, were fishing in a boat near the mouth of Oregon's Rogue River. At about 5:00 P.M., they were scanning the river with 8x Navy binoculars looking for signs of jumping fish, when they first noticed a strange circular object approaching from the northeast. They watched it for about two-and-a-half minutes as it hovered east of them before it departed at high speed in a southward direction. The sky was clear and the afternoon sun was at their backs. To the naked eye, it appeared shiny and shaped like a coin with the flat surface parallel to the ground. At its closest it seemed to be only a couple of miles away and about a mile high. They heard no noise.

Two of the witnesses, a draftsman and a wind-tunnel mechanic, were employees of the Ames Research Laboratory at Moffett Field, south of San Francisco.* These two men shared the binoculars. Each man had about a minute to look at the object through the binoculars. The men observed that the object was *circular and thin relative to its diameter, with a shape similar to that of a pancake,* and with some sort of a vertical fin on the upper surface at the trailing edge. They could see no wings, no antenna, no lights, no propellers, and no jet engines. According to the AFOSI report:

> [The] object appeared round and shiny, something like a fifty-cent piece, viewed from below and to one side. Object's color was silvery and it appeared round in plan view . . . Just before Mr. [name censored in the publicly available copy of the original Air Force document] handed the glasses to Mr. ————, the object made a turn on its vertical axis with no tilting or banking . . . The trailing edge of the object as it traveled appeared somewhat wrinkled and dirty looking.

* The Ames Research Laboratory carries out research on jet engines, among other things. Employees have Secret or Top Secret security clearances.

The trailing edge looked "wrinkled and dirty," but there were no exhaust ports. Then they saw it speed off in a southeasterly direction, "accelerating to the approximate speed of a jet plane" in a few seconds without making any noise. About three weeks later the Ames employees reported their sighting to the security office at Moffett Field. The security office then requested that AFOSI agents investigate the sighting.

In 1952, Project Blue Book hired the Battelle Memorial Institute of Columbus, Ohio, to carry out a statistical study of flying saucer reports that occurred between 1947 and the end of 1952. The main intent of the study, called Project Stork, was to determine whether or not there were consistent differences between sighting reports that were explained and those which could not be explained as mundane phenomena. To carry out this study, the Battelle scientists, working along with the Air Force personnel at ATIC, first analyzed each sighting to determine whether or not it could be identified. The scientists were able to do much better in explaining sightings than the Air Force had done in 1948 and 1949; they were able to explain about seventy percent of the 3,201 sightings they studied. About ten percent of the sightings had too little information for a positive identification. However, about twenty percent had sufficient information for identification, yet resisted explanation. Of these they found a dozen they considered the most descriptive of the sighted phenomena. The Rogue River sighting is the best of that dozen. The two main witnesses were technically trained and, as nearly as can be determined from the case file, thoroughly reliable. In the final report of the study, called Project Blue Book Special Report Number 14, the scientists included two rough sketches, based on the verbal descriptions of the Ames employees, showing two views of a circular object with a thickness much less than its diameter, no wings, no tail, and no engine, but a "wrinkled" outer edge.

The object's description by the witnesses is very clear: it was *neither an ordinary aircraft nor a hallucination*. It either was a hoax or *the real thing—a flying saucer*. Could it have been a hoax? I would say unequivocally "no," because the two Ames employees reported their sighting to *the security officer at Moffett Field*. A hoaxer might report a sighting to the press, radio, or TV, but no person of reasonable intelligence whose job depended upon holding a security clearance would try to hoax the security officer at his place of employment. Furthermore, there is no evidence that this sighting was ever mentioned in the popular literature. Apparently these witnesses reported the sighting to no one but the Ames security officer. The security officer then requested an investigation by the AFOSI. The AFOSI investigators interviewed all of the witnesses once, and interviewed the Ames employees a second time. The interviews established the high degree of credibility of this sighting.†

The Project Blue Book microfilm at the National Archives is supposed to contain all the records collected by the Air Force. In that microfilm two sightings are listed for May 24, 1949. One sighting, case number 402, is explained as "aircraft." The second sighting, not numbered, is explained as "kites." The second sighting is not numbered because, according to a handwritten note, the "cards" are missing. This means that the copy of the AFOSI investigation report, which originally was sent to Project Grudge, *had been removed from the sighting file by someone* many years before the file was microfilmed and released in 1975. Fortunately, the original AFOSI investigation report was not kept at Blue Book headquarters, but rather at the headquarters of AFOSI, so when the Air Force released the *combined* AFOSI and Blue Book records to the National Archives, I was able to find the record of this case investigation in the AFOSI section of the microfilm.

How did Project Grudge personnel explain this multiple witness sighting, you may ask? First, accidentally (or intentionally?) they divided it into two parts and treated each separately. The sighting numbered 402 in the master case list contains the interview of one of the two women. According to the AFOSI report, this woman was interviewed on August 8 (the last of the witnesses to be interviewed). The report, in part, read:

> . . . at approximately 1700 hours, 24 May 1949, she and four other persons, while fishing on the Rogue River near Elephant Rock, approximately 1½ miles above the highway bridge near Gold Beach, Oregon, sighted an object described

† Note: The names of the witnesses are unknown since they were expunged from the AFOSI records before the records were released to the National Archives in 1975.

as being round in shape, silver in color, and about the size of a C-47 aircraft. When first brought to Mrs. [name censored] attention by one of the other witnesses, the object appeared to be three or four miles away. It was coming from the east but later turned to the southwest. It appeared to be traveling at the same rate as a C-47. It made no noise, left no exhaust trail, and made no maneuvers. The interviewee stated that she was not familiar with aircraft; therefore she could not estimate with any accuracy the speed or altitude at which the object was traveling. Mrs. ———— made the comparison between the object and a C-47 because she is familiar with that type of aircraft. Her son has pointed out C-47s to her as they flew over the Gold Beach.

Based on this verbal evidence the Project Grudge personnel identified the object as an "aircraft" because, "No data [were] presented to indicate object could NOT have been an aircraft [capitalization in the original]." The Grudge personnel were able to "get away with" that explanation only because they (1) ignored her claim that the object was circular, and (2) treated her description separately from the descriptions by the other witnesses.

In order to explain the sighting by the other four witnesses, the Grudge personnel used information provided by the AFOSI investigator. This man checked airport records for air traffic or anything else that could conceivably have been in the area at that time. There were no known aircraft in the area. However, the agent learned that radar kites, which are balloons supporting thin metallic radar reflectors, were launched twice a day from military radar installations near San Francisco. He wrote in his report:

These devices are of aluminum sheet, approximately five feet on a side, roughly diamond shaped and containing a double set of triangular fins on the top side. These are carried aloft by gas-filled balloons approximately two feet in diameter when they leave the earth. When these devices reach high enough altitude, the expanding gases cause the balloon to burst and the devices known as "kites" fold and drift earthward. It is possible that one of these devices from one of these radar installations may have been blown as far north as Gold Beach, Oregon, on 24 May 1949.

This is where the official *"kites"* explanation comes from. (I don't know why the explanation is plural.) Based on this information it is immediately obvious to the most casual observer that what they saw was a radar kite, *right?*

Think again. The description given above is sufficient to make it clear that a radar kite is not pancake shaped. Furthermore, such a kite, if traveling through the air, would be supported by one or more balloons which would have been obvious to the witnesses since the balloons are about the same size as the kite, and it could have moved no faster than the wind. If the kite were falling because the balloons had deflated, the witnesses would have seen it fall rather than accelerate to a high speed and disappear in the distance.

As illogical as it may seem, the Project Grudge and Blue Book analysts, acting on the behalf of the U.S. Air Force, *have officially accepted "kites" as the explanation for the sighting.*

However, the Battelle scientists knew better. They did not accept the Air Force explanation. Neither do I.

I have found another reason to reject the Air Force explanation. An errant radar kite launched from the San Francisco area would have had to be carried north-northwestward a distance of about 300 miles. About thirty years after the AFOSI closed their investigation of this case, *I reopened it and completed it* by obtaining the weather records for the coast of northern California and Oregon. These records show that the winds at all altitudes for the day of the sighting and the day preceding were blowing from the *west to the east,* and *could not* have carried a balloon from San Francisco *northward* to the Rogue River. The AFOSI agent who conducted the investigation of this case could have discovered that for himself in 1949. Apparently he decided to end the investigation once he had found a "possible" explanation.

The fact that this explanation was accepted as "official" is clear evidence that the Project Grudge personnel applied the policy of explaining sightings any way possible, following the Vandenberg rejection of the Estimate.

CHAPTER 11

Don't Worry, Be Happy

On May 5, 1949, only five days after the Project Saucer report told everyone that flying saucers and related phenomena were nothing to worry about (so be happy!), and about two-and-a-half weeks before the previously described Rogue River sighting, there was a secret meeting at Camp Hood, Texas. The meeting was a discussion of the continuing phenomenon of "unusual lights." Why? Because by this time there had been so many sightings that the people responsible for security of Killeen Base were not happy, *they were very worried.* According to an AFOSI report, at the previous weekly intelligence conferences in April, the AFOSI, FBI, ONI, the Army Special Weapons Project (ASWP, at the Killeen Base), and the Fourth Army representatives had disputed over which agency had the investigative jurisdiction over these sightings (recall that there had been a similar dispute in December, 1948, over the Los Alamos area sightings). It was decided that the AFOSI, the ASWP, and Fourth Army investigate sightings within the various areas of Camp Hood where they were in control. The FBI had no part in this, inasmuch as the FBI was authorized only to investigate civilian sabotage or subversion.

Of more importance than the dispute is the fact that the main subject of discussion was the repeated sightings of strange lights. According to the AFOSI report, the participants discussed the possibility that the observers might have failed to identify fireflies or other natural causes due to lack of training. The participants agreed that a "more exact and comprehensive system of observing was necessary." The representatives of the Fourth Army and the ONI "expressed great concern about the unknown phenomena as they believed some of the sightings to be valid, and even after all questionable sightings were discounted, that there remained a sufficient number of unknown manifestations to cause grave concern." On the other hand, the Special Weapons Project representatives were not worried because they believed that they had adequate security measures. They believed that "a logical natural explanation could be found for the strange lights." The FBI representatives were noncommittal. The Fourth Army, in order to resolve the questions, proposed that a special observation team made up of "trained Artillery observers" should be stationed around the base every night.

Over the next two weeks the special observing plan was put in force by the Fourth Army. It was a very meticulous plan, which began with the reason for its existence:

TO: All members of the Artillery Training Force

1. You are familiar with the fact that there have been numerous reports within the past year of a phenomena [sic] appearing in several parts of the United States commonly called "flying discs" or "flying saucers." Sufficiently authentic reports of this condition have been received by the Department of the Army to justify a detailed study.

2. In the past several weeks, this condition has been reported as occurring, intermittently, over the southern portion of the Camp Hood Military reservation. You have been designated as part of a force to determine accurately the following information.

   a) Does this condition exist and, if so, to what extent?
   b) A description of the phenomenon.
   c) Its location, altitude and duration.

d) If it is produced by any individual or machine on the ground, to apprehend such individuals.

3. This entire project has been classified as "Confidential" and, as such, you will not discuss any phase of the operation, or your work in connection with it, with anyone except as is required by your work.

The plan was to have observers at several locations in communication with a command post at all times. Whenever a "phenomenon" would appear, the first to see it would alert the others and then they would all watch while recording exact directions and angular elevations. The resulting data would allow for triangulation and size estimates.

During the weekly meeting on May 19 the Fourth Army announced the preliminary results and all the attendees agreed that the "new observation system instituted by the Fourth Army provided precise results and definitely indicated that the unknown phenomena in the Camp Hood area could not be attributed to natural causes."

Project Grudge personnel were not involved in these observations.* The conclusion of Projects Sign and Grudge that the unexplained sightings could be explained as natural phenomena and certainly were nothing to worry about had already been publicized in the Project Saucer report. They assumed they didn't need any more sighting data. Only a few weeks later, an explicit investigation by the Army had shown that the strange lights were *not natural phenomena*. Did this result bother the AMC/ATIC personnel? Not a bit, as the FBI was to find out in the latter part of May.

For the FBI, these Army experiments may have once again cleared up the controversy: the objects *were* Soviet missiles! Perhaps Hoover felt justified in breaking security over a month earlier in order to alert the American public, through Walter Winchell, that we were virtually under attack from the Russians.

Then Walter Winchell came back into the picture in a way that muddied the waters once again.

According to a May 26 office memorandum written by one of the FBI agents, Hoover received a telegram from Winchell. This was a telegram

---

* They may not even have been aware of the Army's efforts to do what Dr. von Karman had recommended to the Air Force; that is, to get more precise observational data.

that had been sent to Winchell in early May by none other than Robert Ripley of "Believe It Or Not" fame. Apparently Ripley believed that he had located "the only authentic Japanese flying saucer in this country." Winchell wanted the FBI to confirm or deny that there could be such a thing. One of the FBI agents contacted someone in the Intelligence Division of the Army (G-2) and was told that they had "no information concerning any Japanese flying saucer ever having been recovered in the United States."

The FBI file does not indicate what ultimately became of Ripley's "Japanese saucer" (it subsequently turned out to be one of the "fire balloons" that was launched by the Japanese during the Second World War to "bomb" the West Coast of the United States). However, the file does say what the FBI's information source was told by the ATIC personnel about the continued saucer sightings:

> This matter was discussed with Colonel [name censored] OSI-USAF, who advised on April 27, 1949 that he had interested himself in the flying saucers and related subjects and that in so far as could be determined by him through his sources in the Air Force, which are excellent, there is no authentic information available concerning the phenomenon of flying saucers. He advised he would check with the authorities at Wright Field to determined if any information is available concerning the recovery of a Japanese flying saucer.
>
> Colonel ——— has now [the latter part of May] advised that there is no information available in any arm of the Air Force to the effect that any flying saucers of any kind have been recovered in the United States. Colonel ——— stated delay had been encountered in determining this fact inasmuch as inquiries had been directed through individuals known to him and trusted by him and not through the usual channels from which he possibly would receive a stock answer.

Well now, this is a "Don't Worry, Be Happy" answer if ever there was one. *"No flying saucers of any kind have been recovered . . ."* So, what did you expect? The documentary record indicates that ATIC personnel (colonels and below) didn't know about any crashed saucer debris or—if they did—they certainly weren't going to tell someone who didn't have clearance for that sort of information.

What about the colonel's statement that there was *"no authentic information available . . ."*? On the face of it, this implies that the Air Force had no proof that flying saucers were real, unexplainable objects. This statement must have puzzled the FBI because only about four months earlier, in January, Col. Gasser had said that there *was* authentic information suggesting the objects were Russian missiles. Then there were all the indisputable reports of strange "green fireball" phenomena in the vicinity of "vital installations," and Dr. La Paz's Russian missile theory. And finally, there were the recent Army observations that proved the phenomena *did not* have a natural origin. With all this observational evidence, how could the ATIC personnel say that there was no authentic information? (The FBI must have been totally confused.)

The ATIC personnel were able to say "with a straight face" that there was no authentic information because they didn't believe the sightings were valid. At this time, in the late spring of 1949, Project Grudge was operating on the assumption that all sightings could be explained as mistakes, natural phenomena, delusions, and hoaxes, because they didn't believe the objects or phenomena were our secret experimental devices, they didn't believe the objects or phenomena were Russian (or other foreign) devices, and they couldn't, because of Gen. Vandenberg's rejection of the Estimate, seriously consider the extraterrestrial possibility.

At least one person who believed the green fireballs were natural phenomena was Dr. Joseph Kaplan, a professor of physics at the Institute of Geophysics at the University of California, a member of the Air Force Scientific Advisory Board, and formerly of the Operational Analysis branch of AMC. At this time, he was acting as a consultant to AMC. Kaplan first heard of the green fireballs in February 1949 and he alerted Dr. von Karman to the fireball sightings, and the work of Dr. La Paz. Von Karman then sent a letter to Gen. Cabell recommending that the Air Force investigate these sightings more fully (see chapter 7). Cabell then asked Kaplan to continue to study the problem. In early July, Cabell wrote to Kaplan to ask about the status of the fireball investigation. Kaplan responded that he had been very impressed with the sightings by the security guards and that he was particularly interested in their descriptions of the unusual green color. Kaplan pointed out that green is the color of aurora afterglow.† He therefore suggested that perhaps the green fireballs were actually some new form of aurora occurring at low altitude and low latitudes. He admitted, however, that this proposal could not explain the observed trajectories nor the geographical localization over New Mexico and western Texas. Kaplan mentioned that Dr. Norris Bradbury, the director of the laboratory at Los Alamos, proposed to hold a conference in September to discuss the sightings, and said that he planned to attend the conference to present his aurora hypothesis as a potential explanation for the fireballs.

On August 16, 1949, the FBI agent in San Antonio again mentioned the sightings around the military installations:

> I am attaching hereto a number of copies of reports being received in great numbers in this office concerning the so-called flying disks or unnatural phenomena being frequently observed around Camp Hood, Texas. This is, of course, a primary concern of the Air Corps. Consequently, this office is following the practice of reviewing the data and destroying them in the event there appears to be nothing of FBI interest therein. It is pointed out that the filing of these would result in the rapid accumulation of very bulky files. Unless the Bureau believes this is unwise, this practice will continue.

The FBI file does not contain a response to the above letter, nor does it contain the reports sent by SAC, San Antonio.

Fortunately, the AFOSI file *does* contain the reports. The sighting catalogue by Lt. Col. Doyle Rees, mentioned before, lists Camp Hood/Killeen Base (CH/KB) sightings on May 6, 7, 8; July 11, 28 (three sightings), 30 (two), August 10 (eight), 11, 12 (two), 14, and 20. Thus there were files on twenty-two sightings just in those months. No

---

† The aurora is a greenish glow in the upper atmosphere that is created when electrons hit oxygen atoms. It is often seen near the poles of the Earth where magnetic lines of force "funnel" electrons downward into the thin upper atmosphere.

wonder the SAC San Antonio was worried about the accumulation of paper! (Previously there had been about ten sightings in March, but none in April.)

It is a matter of interest that there are *no further* listings of sightings at Fort Hood in Col. Rees' catalogue, which runs to May 1950. (Had the "fireballers" completed their activities in the area of Fort Hood?) The same catalogue shows that sightings in the Los Alamos-Sandia Base area continued. In May 1949 there were five sightings, in June there were five, none in July, and in August there were ten. Furthermore, sightings in the Los Alamos-Sandia Base area continued at a rate of several per month through the next year, and caused the Air Force to set up an observing project that provided *photographic proof of the existence of flying saucers*—proof that was later *suppressed!*

CHAPTER 12

Twinkle, Twinkle, Little Fireball

Between May 1, 1949 and the end of that year, the FBI had very little UFO "action." FBI headquarters received a copy of a sighting by a Navy pilot and a couple of reports from civilian witnesses. During the same time period, according to the Project Blue Book master list file at the National Archives, Project Grudge received about 250 reports, a couple of which are discussed below.

One of the reports received by the FBI is published here, for the first time, because it illustrates a class of unidentified objects reported numerous times over the years, but which receives very little "press interest" because the objects are small. The witness's name was removed from the FBI document when it was released to the public. He wrote:

> An incident happened this afternoon which after consideration I felt I should report. I most certainly do not want this incident disclosed, as I do not want any publicity concerning it. If you regard it of no special interest to the FBI please disregard this correspondence.

121

I was flying from Clark Field to Parkersburg, W. Va. this afternoon and about four miles airline, southwest of Parkersburg I suddenly noticed a bright yellow object coming directly toward me. It came at me with such speed, added to my 100 mph forward speed, that it startled me and had passed by in a matter of a couple of seconds. But it passed by about 100 feet under my ship and about 50 feet to my right, and because of the dark green background of forests below I was able to get very clear outline of the object and what I believe is a very accurate description.

Color — bright canary yellow; Length — 15 to 18 inches.

Diameter — about 4 inches at the largest part.

It resembled a rocket, in fact was about the same shape and proportions as the fuselage of a Lockheed Air Force X-90.

No wings but vertical and horizontal fins on rear $1/3$ of the rocket.

No visible means of propulsion such as a propeller, vapor trail, smoke or exhaust.

The front of the rocket was very sharp with a needle nose, the needle looked about 6 [in.] long and was the size of a lead pencil. The rear end was blunt similar to the rear end of a jet fuselage.

It appeared to have spent its force and seemed to be dropping slightly as it passed by, or had been fired or launched from a higher altitude than I was flying.

It happened at 2:45 on September 25, 1949.

I was flying at an altitude of 3450 ft. above sea level.

I was flying a course of 60 degrees (E.–NE.) and the rocket was traveling almost west at 240 degrees.

The visibility was exceptionally good (30 miles).

The letter also described the type of aircraft the witness was flying in (a Luscombe 8A, NC 1440K) and the exact location of the sighting. The FBI retyped the letter and sent it to the Director, Office of Special Investigations of the Inspector General of the Air Force at the Pentagon. However, it does not appear in the file of reports collected by Project Grudge.

Col. Harold Watson,
director of Air Technical
Intelligence Command.

Meanwhile, back at the "vital installations," Army intelligence and the AFI continued to monitor sightings. ATIC/Grudge was not investigating sightings and, in spite of the Army's request, never did send a trained observer team to Camp Hood. Moreover, the new director of ATIC intelligence, Col. Harold Watson, who took over in July 1949, was strongly "anti-UFO." Under his direction, Project Grudge only analyzed previous sightings. His goal was to be able to explain each one in order to justify the public statements released in the Project Saucer report. These efforts were to prove valuable in December 1949, when the first major challenge to the Air Force was published.

Because ATIC/Grudge did not participate in the Army observation "experiments" no ATIC observer was present to witness the success of these experiments during the nights of May 4, 6, 7, 8, and 23. Nor did Grudge personnel participate in the triangulation (localization) of a UFO! This occurred on the night of June 6, when observers at two locations at Camp Hood saw a hovering orange light. They determined that it was about three miles away from one of the observation posts and four-and-a-half miles from the other and about a mile high. The estimated size based on the distance and measured angular size of the light was thirty to seventy feet. After hovering, it started to move in level flight and then burst into small particles. It had been visible for almost three minutes. Months later, Project Grudge personnel, in their attempts to explain everything, identified this as a "balloon."

Dr. La Paz continued to monitor sightings of the "fireballs." On August 17, 1949, he wrote another report to Lt. Col. Rees. He went into great detail about attempts to detect copper dust in the atmosphere after two green fireball sightings. He pointed out that such dust had, in fact, been detected but that there was no conclusive evidence that the dust was not from some terrestrial source. He emphasized that a greater measurement effort was needed because if it could be proven that green fireballs created copper dust, then this would be strong confirming evidence that the fireballs were not meteors. He also summarized the results of investigations into sightings in June, July, and early August, and pointed out that in most reports the fireballs were described as falling vertically downward rather than traveling horizontally as in previous months. He pointed out that perfectly vertical falls were as extraordinary as perfectly horizontal trajectories. He also suggested that the Institute of Meteoritics should publicize its interest in receiving reports of meteors and sky phenomena in order to collect more reports.

The Army and Air Force had tried to keep a lid on the sightings around the New Mexico area, but news leaked out anyway. The August 30 issue of the *Los Angeles Times* carried a story about saucers seen at the White Sands Proving Ground, where advanced rockets were tested. According to the story, technicians in the area had seen strange objects flying over the grounds during normal operations. In one case an object seemed to travel along with a rocket. The story even summarized the sighting by Charles Moore discussed previously in chapter 9. The appearance of the *Times* article caused Army intelligence, responsible for security around White Sands, to try to determine the source of the leaked information. The source turned out to a Navy rocket scientist, Comm. Robert McLaughlin. Although Army Capt. Edward Detchmendy, the Army Public Information Officer, was angry at the leak, Comm. McLaughlin was not reprimanded for a breach of security, and about six months later he wrote a magazine article about these events!

In early September 1949, a new discovery seemed to confirm the suggestion that fireballs and saucers could be Soviet atomic-powered missiles: especially instrumented aircraft flying over the northern Pacific detected a cloud of nuclear radiation. Over the next few days the cloud was tracked and analyzed. The conclusion: *the Russians now had atomic bombs!* No one knew just how advanced the Soviet delivery systems might be. Could they really fly an atomic bomb over the southwestern United States?

A month later, the theory that flying saucers used nuclear fuel got a further boost from sightings around Mt. Palomar. During October, high-speed objects were seen flying past the observatory where the Office of Naval Research had placed a cosmic ray monitoring station with Geiger counters and chart recorders. On October 14, at 1:14 P.M., a witness saw a dozen-and-a-half objects fly past. The silvery objects had no wings or tails, they seemed to be about a mile up, and they emitted a strange noise. A technician happened to check the Geiger counters a few hours later and found that at the time of the sighting, the recorder pen had gone wild. Several days later, at 7:20 A.M. on October 17, a staff member of Palomar Observatory, while checking on the Geiger counters, saw a small black dot zip by beneath the 7,000 ft. cloud ceiling. At the same time the recorder pen went off scale. The Navy and Air Force were immediately informed. A third sighting near Palomar, of a single, high-speed object with no wings or tail on October 21, did not affect the Geiger counters. There was a dispute over whether or not there had been electrical malfunctions during the October 14 and 17 sightings.

The technicians who designed the equipment were sure that the high scale readings were not electrical malfunctions. The Navy took an interest in these sightings, and went so far as to carry out a test in which they had Navy aircraft fly past Mt. Palomar to find out whether or not the passage of ordinary aircraft would affect the Geiger counters. As expected, there was no effect. Some more people now believed in atomic-powered saucers. Several months later the equipment was removed from Mt. Palomar for a detailed study and it was found that there was a loose fuse clip. When jiggled it caused the pen to move erratically. The technicians were not able to determine whether or not this explained the coincidence of anomalous readings with the saucer sightings.

The continued sightings of unusual phenomena in the New Mexico skies were the subject of a joint intelligence meeting during the afternoon of October 14 at the Los Alamos National Laboratory. This was the meeting, originally planned for September, which Dr. Kaplan had mentioned in his July letter to Gen. Cabell meeting (see chapter 11). The meeting was held at the request of Dr. Norris Bradbury, the Director of the laboratory. A month before, Kaplan had met with personnel from the Geophysical Sciences Branch of Air Force Research and Development and convinced them of the seriousness of the matter. With their help, Kaplan succeeded in getting some action. A month before the meeting, on September 14, under the authority of Gen. Hoyt Vandenberg (the man who had rejected the Estimate the year before!), the Geophysical Sciences Branch of Air Force Research and Development ordered the new AMC commander, Lt. Gen. Benjamin Chidlaw, to begin an investigation of the unusual phenomena. The investigation would be carried out at the AMC's Air Force Cambridge Research Laboratory (AFCRL) in Boston. Furthermore, AFCRL was directed to send representatives to the Los Alamos meeting.

Several of the attendees were the illuminati of the military science community, Dr. Edward Teller, "Father of the H-Bomb" (recall that he had attended the first green fireball conference in February 1949), Stanislaw Ulam (who worked with Teller on the hydrogen bomb), and George Gamow, astrophysicist (famous for his "Big Bang" theory and nucleosynthesis of elements). Dr. Lincoln La Paz (who had analyzed dozens of green fireball sightings by this time), and, of course, Dr. Bradbury, were also present, as were two other physicists from Los Alamos and the intelligence contingent: Lt. Col. Doyle Rees and Capt. Melvin Neef of the 17th District, AFOSI; Major L. C. Hill of the Fourth Army; Major Frederic Oder, Director of the Geophysical Research Division of the USAF (the Cambridge representative); Major K. Kolster, AFSWP, Sandia Base; Sidney Newberger, Chief of Security at Los Alamos; and, of course, the ever-present FBI, represented by SAC Albuquerque (Phil Claridge) and SAC Los Alamos (Jerry Maxwell). It was Dr. Kaplan's intention to have La Paz outline the fireball problem for these people and to enlist their support for setting up a research project.

As is usual for a classified meeting, the security instructions were outlined and it was pointed out that the subject matter was classified Secret under the "code name Grudge" even though Grudge personnel were not present (recall that the investigative activities of Project Grudge had ended several months before). Then Dr. La Paz reviewed previous observations in the Sandia-Los Alamos area and the main elements of his presentation at the February meeting. His discussion contrasted two possibilities: natural versus man-made phenomena. The scientists did not reject Dr. La Paz's "man-made hypothesis," but they did reject Dr. Kaplan's auroral hypothesis for the very reasons listed by Kaplan in his letter to Cabell: auroras are not localized, they are generally seen much farther north, and auroras do not travel along horizontal paths.

Although Dr. Kaplan was not successful in convincing the attendees that fireballs were some new form of aurora, he was successful in enlisting their support for obtaining better observational data. The attendees recommended "that a project be set up at the earliest date in order to make photographic, sound, and mathematical observations on a continuing basis."

Finally, after *ten months* of continual green fireball reports, some important people were pushing for an investigation. Dr. von Karman asked Dr. Kaplan to make a special report on fireballs during the AFSAB meeting on November 3, 1949. At that meeting Dr. Kaplan presented a brief history of the fireball sightings and summarized the analytical work by Dr. La Paz. He made a strong case that the fireballs were real objects, as opposed to misidentified meteors or psychological aberrations. He further stated that he had written a report on the fireballs. This report had been sent to Gen. Cabell who, in turn, had sent it to the Geophysical Directorate at AFCRL where they were "setting up the necessary observational program to obtain pictures and spectra." Kaplan did not present his auroral hypothesis at the AFSAB meeting. Instead, he merely said that he believed the fireballs were some new type of natural phenomenon.

On November 7, Maj. Oder, Director of AFCRL, wrote his report on the Los Alamos meeting to the Commanding General (CG), AMC (Chidlaw). Here is a shortened version of the report (Note: The Chief of Staff, USAF, was Gen. Vandenberg.):

> In accordance with instructions in classified letter from Chief of Staff, USAF, to CG, AMC, subject "Light Phenomena," . . . the undersigned attended a conference at Los Alamos on the subject of a phenomena [sic] observed in the northern New

Mexico area. The phenomena has the appearance of a green fireball and because of the fact that it had been observed only (as far as can be determined) in the northern New Mexico area and only since the year 1947, has caused a high degree of apprehension among security agencies in the area. In view of the fact that the phenomena has been observed by independent and trained observers there is little doubt that something was actually observed.

The first part of the conference was devoted to a summary presentation of all collected and organized observational information regarding green fireballs . . .

The second part of the conference was a discussion by the scientists present of various possible explanations and hypotheses concerning the phenomena. Little success was had.

It was the conclusion of the group present at the meeting that the present information on the phenomena was not sufficiently quantitative and objective to allow any profitable scientific consideration. Instrumental observations (especially photographs, triangulation and spectroscopic) were considered essential.

Dr. Joseph Kaplan . . . [will recommend to the next meeting of the Scientific Advisory Board] that the USAF provide a suitable investigation of the phenomena using the Geophysical Research Directorate, AFCRL, AMC as the agency for the project.

It is the opinion of this office that . . . AFCRL is capable of performing the required investigation . . . provided that necessary funds, personnel authorizations and equipment are provided. Inasmuch as the phenomena appears to be atmospheric in nature, such an assignment is considered appropriate.

(Note: By the time Major Oder got around to writing this letter, Dr. Kaplan had already presented his fireball report to the Science Advisory Board.)

The combined actions of Dr. Kaplan and Maj. Oder were successful. On December 9, a deputy to Lt. Gen. Chidlaw wrote a letter of recommendation for continued research under the Air Force Geophysical Research program, and requested that the Research and Development Board approve the necessary funds. On December 20, 1949, Col. Benjamin Holzman, in the office of Maj. Gen. Donald Putt, the Air Force Director of Research and Development (who was also the Military Director of the AFSAB), wrote a letter of concurrence which pointed out that "prior to approval of the Research and Development Board . . . it will be necessary for you to prepare a project plan," and a budget.

Everything was a "go" for the first instrumented "search" for unidentified phenomena (fireballs and saucers). Unfortunately things proceeded slowly and there was a budget crunch. Nevertheless, according to a May 1950 letter to Gen. Putt, AMC stated that it had been able to "initiate subject project on a limited basis utilizing personnel and equipment which have become available at Holloman Air Force Base." The letter mentions in particular the use of "Askania phototheodolites in order to provide trajectory data and photo records," spectrographic cameras, and radio-spectrum analyzers.

This was the beginning of the project with the delightful name of Project Twinkle. It was during the time of this project that one of these Askania phototheodolites got the *proof of the existence of "flying saucers."* It was also during this project that the *proof was ignored or covered up.*

CHAPTER 13

Project Grudge vs.
the ET Hypothesis

SIX **days after** Maj. Gen. Putt approved Project Twinkle, a very important event in UFO history occurred. A magazine article claimed that information collected by the Air Force proved that *flying saucers were extraterrestrial craft.* This astounding statement, published in the January issue of *True* magazine, was given credibility by the fact that it had been written by a retired Marine Corps aviator, Maj. Donald Keyhoe, an independent reporter who was to become the most consistent critic of the Air Force policy toward UFO sightings. In his article, "The Flying Saucers Are Real," Keyhoe claimed he had reached his conclusion after studying the Project Saucer report, the available sighting reports, and after talking with witnesses and Air Force representatives. He further claimed that saucers were spaceships of several types, and had been visiting the earth for at least over a hundred years.

True magazine hit the stands a day after Christmas 1949, and immediately the news media were on a roll. The story made front-page news throughout the United States. (*True* magazine later stated that that particular issue of *True* contained the most widely read and discussed

Maj. Donald Keyhoe, retired
Marine Corps aviator and
author of *The Flying Saucers
Are Real.*

magazine article ever up to that time.) The very next day the press fury
increased as the Air Force exercised its *preplanned retaliation.*

The release of Project Saucer in the April 1949, and the publication of
Sidney Shallet's articles, had not quieted down the public interest in
saucer reports. A few reporters knew that the Air Force had not been
dragged reluctantly into saucer investigation by civilian saucer sightings,
as claimed by Shallet, but rather had become interested because Air Force
personnel were also witnesses. These reporters thought the Project
Saucer report was really intended to divert attention from the real story,
whatever that was. Because the Project Saucer report had not flatly stated
that all sightings had been explained, and because it said the investigation
was continuing, it had left open the door for three possibilities, the latter
two of which were potentially quite frightening: one, that the United
States government had developed a technology so secret that the Air
Force could not refer to it publicly and, in fact, had to deny its existence
to cover it up (similar to the secrecy surrounding the Stealth bomber in
more recent times); two, the Russians had developed a totally new and
superior weapon system with potentially disastrous consequences for the
free world; and three, intelligent beings from outer space were visiting
Earth. Because of these possibilities, reporters began to pester AFI and

ATIC to learn about the latest on the Air Force investigation. They realized that the story behind any one of these possibilities would be the news scoop of the year. The only response they got from the Air Force was that the investigation was ongoing. The late August 1949 article about saucers being seen at White Sands increased the press interest. Some reporters, including Keyhoe, began to do their own investigations. They traveled around the country and talked to witnesses who, they discovered, were generally credible people who had seen and reported incredible objects.

Of course, the Air Force was aware of all these press activities and expected a big story to come out eventually. The only questions were who would write it and when would it be published.

During the spring of 1949, ATIC personnel had stopped the careful study of new sightings. Instead, they concentrated their activities on analyzing old sightings so that they could prepare the final "Grudge Report." This report would be needed to close out the project in a manner consistent with the official Air Force policy, as implied in the Project Saucer report, that all sightings could be explained. The ATIC personnel pushed to get the Grudge report finished as soon as possible. They finished it in August and then waited until it would be needed. Shortly before Keyhoe's article was published, according to Ruppelt in *The Report on Unidentified Flying Objects,* ATIC formulated a plan for a response to whatever would be the first article to hit the newsstands. When the *True* magazine article appeared, the Air Force was ready.

On December 27, 1949, the day after Keyhoe's big "coming out party," the Air Force rained on his parade by executing the first part of the plan—it held a press conference that featured a general saying everything was hoaxes, hallucinations, and misidentifications of known objects. The general also made the following announcement:

> The Air Force has discontinued its special project investigating and evaluating reported flying saucers on the basis that there is no evidence the reports are not the result of natural phenomena. Discontinuance of the project, which was carried out by the Air Force, was concurred in by [sic] the Department of the Army and Navy.

The Air Force Materiel Command has been working very closely with intelligence on the whole matter of flying saucers.

We probably have the most complete file on the saucers anywhere, but there is nothing new or startling to indicate that the saucers are interplanetary visitors.

Continuance of the project is unwarranted since additional incidents now are simply confirming findings already reached.

The Air Force then carried out the second part of the plan: the Air Force announced that the secret Grudge report *would be declassified and made available in a few days.* Apparently the top Air Force officials believed that the release of the Project Grudge report would be enough to kill the saucer stories forever. They were wrong.

Whereas Keyhoe's work was impressive, the 400-page Grudge report was unconvincing. There were too many poor or just plain wrong explanations. Instead of making the saucer problem go away, it merely increased the confusion over what really was going on.

According to the report, Project Grudge had studied 228 sightings out of the 244 available for analysis. This was forty-two fewer than Project Saucer (i.e., Project Sign, which had studied 240 domestic and thirty foreign sightings for a total of 270), although by August 1949, there were "approximately 375 incidents on record." The reason that analyses of the other 131 sightings did not appear in the final report is simply that the Grudge personnel felt it to be a waste of time because the newer reports were similar to the older ones. The Grudge report also did not mention the approximately seventy sightings between August and December. The reporters did not know the content of the new sightings, of course, since this information was not released until years later.

The Air Force had told the press that all sightings could be explained, and proclaimed that the Grudge report would prove it. Although on the face of it, the final report *did* seem to support this claim, astute reporters were not convinced. The report showed that, with the help of Dr. Hynek, the consultant in astronomy (see chapter 7), they had been able identify thirty-two percent as astronomical. (Many of the green fireball reports were claimed to be meteors despite Dr. La Paz's arguments against that identification.) With the help of experts at the Air Force Weather Service and Air Force Cambridge Research Laboratory, the Grudge personnel identified twelve percent as sightings of weather balloons or high-altitude Skyhook balloons. The Grudge personnel and the expert consultants further concluded that about seventy-two percent of the 228 could be explained and thirteen percent had insufficient information for evaluation. *That meant that the expert consultants could not offer explanations for fifteen percent of the sightings (thirty-four out of the 228).* This did not stop the Project Grudge analysts, however. The last appendix to the Grudge report contained a discussion of tentative explanations for the unexplained sightings.

This appendix created a big problem for the Air Force because members of the press who read it were not convinced. The explanations seemed, at the very least, strained, and in some cases simply wrong. Ruppelt, in *The Report on Unidentified Flying Objects,* cited one good example of the approach to explaining these reports. In a November 1948 report, which was analyzed by Dr. Hynek and the Air Weather Service, an Air Force pilot had reported seeing a glowing white light over Andrews Air Force Base, near Washington, D.C. He chased it for ten minutes as it went through some turning maneuvers before it finally "headed for the coast." He did manage to get a glimpse of a dark oval object smaller than his airplane. "I couldn't tell if the light was on the object or if the whole object had been glowing," he reported. Witnesses on the ground concurred with the pilot's report: *they had seen the light and the airplane chasing it.* Hynek reported it was not astronomical, and the Air Weather service reported that it was not a balloon. This didn't stop the Project Grudge personnel. The official explanation was—*a balloon!*

Ruppelt illustrated the press reaction to the Grudge explanations by referring to a conversation he had several years later with one of the reporters who had gotten a copy of the report. "He said the report had been quite impressive, but only in its ambiguousness, illogical reasoning and very apparent effort to write off all UFO reports at any cost. He personally thought that it was a poor attempt to put out a 'fake' report full of misleading information, to cover up the real story." (Note what this reporter said, to "cover up the real story"!)

Because the Grudge report included an explanation for each sighting, it was able to present the following conclusion:

1. ... unidentified flying objects constitute no direct threat to the national security of the United States.
2. Reports of unidentified flying objects are the result of:
   (a) A mild form of mass hysteria or "war nerves."
   (b) Individuals who fabricate such reports to perpetuate a hoax or seek publicity.
   (c) psychopathological persons.
   (d) misidentification of various conventional objects.

So, there you have it. After two-and-a-half years of investigating, starting in the summer of 1947, the Air Force publicly concluded that there was nothing to flying saucers and related unusual phenomena. The sightings were of such little importance that the analysis project was being closed. (The Air Force did not tell the public that the project had virtually died six months before.) So the outside world, along with most of the people who worked for the Armed Forces, ATIC, AFI, AFOSI, and the FBI may have wondered whether the Air Force had really lost interest in UFOs— *or whether it had taken its interest underground.*

Fact: AMC claimed that the closing of Grudge was the end of Air Force saucer investigations.

Fact: AMC lied.

Fact: A year and a half later Maj. Gen. Cabell admitted that the Grudge Report was "unscientific worthless tripe."

Fact: Only about two weeks later government investigative organizations were asked to be on the alert for saucer sighting reports. On January 12, 1950, Cabell circulated to intelligence agencies a *new* memorandum regarding the reporting of "Unconventional Aircraft." According to the memorandum, "In the future any information obtained on this subject should be accorded the same consideration as that given to intelligence information on other subjects."

Saucer investigations did not end, and the most convincing were yet to come.

CHAPTER 14
A Knight in Grudging Armor

In spite of protestations by the Air Force, reports of flying saucers and related phenomena would not go away. In spite of the continued sightings Project Grudge presented the "party line" as stated in December 1949, at each opportunity: UFOs are not extraterrestrial craft because Project Grudge proved that all sightings had been explained. Of course, Grudge had proved no such thing. Nevertheless, even the FBI was not immune to this "party line."

In late March 1950, FBI headquarters received a memorandum from Guy Hottel, the SAC for Washington state, which stated that "an investigator for the Air Forces" had told Mr. Hottel that three crashed saucers had been recovered in New Mexico, along with nine bodies of three-foot-tall aliens. It turned out that this report was based on a hoax, but the FBI didn't know that at the time. The importance of the report is what it caused J. Edgar Hoover to do. He asked Special Assistant D. M. Ladd to ask the Air Force "just what are the facts re: 'flying saucers?'" Hoover wanted, "A short memo as to whether it is true or just what the Air Force, etc., think of them." In other words, it appears that Hoover was completely, and justifiably, confused by the conflicting pronouncements by the Air Force.

The FBI-Air Force liaison, Agent S. W. Reynolds, who had been contacted by Gen. Schulgen almost three years before at the very beginning of the saucer controversy, met with AFI representatives, Maj. Boggs and Lt. Col. J. V. Hearn, and was told the following:

> The Air Force discontinued their intelligence project to determine what flying saucers are the latter part of last year. They publicly announced to the press in December 1949, that the project had been discontinued. They advised that the press release had been concurred in by the Army and Navy. The reason for the discontinuance, according to Major Boggs and Lieutenant Colonel Hearn, was that after two years of investigating over three-fourths of the incidents regarding flying saucers proved to be misidentifications of a wide variety of conventional items such as lighted weather balloons and other air-borne objects.
>
> Colonel Hearn pointed out that the Commanders of the various areas are charged with the security of those areas. Reports concerning flying saucers received at this time will be investigated by the Area Commander and his report submitted to the Air Force Intelligence Division as an intelligence item.
>
> Major Boggs and Lieutenant Colonel Hearn made the observation that many of the reported sightings of flying saucers at this time appear to be an outgrowth of recent magazine articles. They reiterated that the Air Force is conducting no active investigation to determine whether flying saucers exist or what they might be.

This waffling answer was clearly intended to imply that the Air Force didn't think much of flying saucers. They admitted that reports were still coming in, but they weren't being analyzed by any central group because most of the previous sightings had been explained, and Project Grudge had been closed. Any sighting analysis had to be done at the location of the sighting and information forwarded as ordinary intelligence. Hearn and Boggs did not give the FBI any impression of what

ATIC might be doing with the collected sighting reports. Whether or not this "non-answer" satisfied Hoover is not reflected in the record.

Another article in *True* magazine provided a direct contradiction to the official Air Force policy as stated by Boggs and Hearn. The March 1950 issue contained an article by Comm. Robert McLaughlin, who had been the Chief of the Navy missile test activities at the super-secret White Sands Proving Ground test and development area. Recall that he had been the source of information about White Sands sightings that had leaked to the press during the previous summer (see chapter 12). In the *True* article, "How Scientists Tracked the Flying Saucers," he discussed the tracking of a saucer during a missile test. He reported that several times during 1948 and 1949 his crew at White Sands had observed UFOs. One of the sightings mentioned was that of Charles Moore, which has already been described. By referring to calculations based on measurements by the White Sands instruments, he concluded that the saucers were not a natural phenomenon and voiced his opinion that saucers were "space ships" operated by "intelligent beings." When queried about McLaughlin's ET conclusion, the Air Force referred to the Project Grudge report, and stated that there is no evidence that saucers are other than hallucinations, hoaxes, and errors in identification.

The controversy over saucer reality again became a hot press item in early April in response to a surge in sightings the previous month (the Air Force received over three dozen reports in March). The *New York Times* of April 4, 1950 carried an article saying that saucers were real, and were secret U.S. warplanes. The controversy over whether or not the saucers were secret weapons elicited a response directly from the White House. According to the *New York Times* of April 5, White House Press Secretary Charles Ross, "seemed to demolish the element of reality that had been creeping into current reports of flying saucers" when he stated that "no one . . . knows anything about them including the President." Ross admitted that the Navy had experimented with a disc-shaped craft (the Navy's XF-5-U circular, propeller-driven "flying pancake") but that this aircraft could not be the source of saucer reports. Ross also indicated that no other country was operating flying saucers over the United States. Four days later, the *Times* carried another story about President Truman's reaction: "The President said he was just as puzzled as the next fellow by the latest flurry of reports about weird and wonderful sights in the sky." According to the article, "If the Air Force thought that its official report (the Grudge report) would put an end to speculation, it was underestimating the public curiosity and imagination. If anything the theories have multiplied . . ." The article publicly discussed theories such as: (a) U.S. secret weapons; (b) foreign (Russian) secret weapons; (c) weather balloons; (d) planets and meteors; (e) optical illusions; and (f) interplanetary visitors. The Air Force vehemently denied that saucer sightings were (a), (b) or (f), but obviously the press and the general public were not convinced by the denials.

Two weeks later, on May 22, the FBI received a Confidential document that was a clear statement of the official Project Grudge opinion of flying saucers. It was written as an "insider's response" to public comments by Capt. Eddie Rickenbacker, a famous pilot, who was quoted in the press: "There must be something to them for too many reliable persons have made reports about them. . . . However, if they are real you can rest assured that they are ours." The response shows just how cynical the ATIC personnel were about the flying saucer reports. It begins with a brief discussion of ancient sightings of strange aerial phenomena and mentions the Swedish "ghost rocket" sightings in 1946. It then discusses the present sightings and the Air Force response to them:

> The USAF for a long time conducted a thorough investigation of each of the hundreds of incidents involved. It found that approximately seventy-five percent of the reports could be related to known causes such as meteorological balloons, aircraft, meteors, and other common phenomena. A public statement was issued debunking the entire existence of flying disks or saucers. This did little to cut down the flood of reports. It only resulted in convincing a large number of people that the National Military Establishment was trying to cover up our own experiments with new weapons.
>
> Many theories have been advanced to explain these reports of aerial phenomena over the U.S. These include space ships, Soviet guided missiles or aircraft—probably

atomic-powered, U.S. experiments with new weapons, natural phenomena, and mass hysteria or other psychological causes. While it is not possible to categorically rule out the space ship theory, it is very easy to do so on reasonable grounds. The existence of any form of life on other planets is extremely tenuous and debatable. The level of technical achievement required to launch piloted or unmanned missiles from one planet to another and return is several orders of magnitude beyond that existing on earth today and probably would have resulted in some firm contact prior to this, either through deliberate landings or unscheduled crashes. (Even these have been reported in the press—complete with descriptions of men only eighteen inches tall! Such reports are sheer fabrication.)

The document then rejects the Soviet missile hypothesis *("There is absolutely no evidence . . .)* and the secret U.S. missile hypothesis. The document concludes as follows:

The continued reporting of aerial phenomena must then be attributed to a mass hysteria caused by the present tenseness in the international situation; the public belief in the ability of science to accomplish miracles; and to statements by "name" individuals hinting at the existence of a new weapon. Such statements, of the type attributed to Rickenbacker, often solicited in the most sensational form by news reporters in order to make a good story, make people watch the sky and any object they cannot immediately recognize is called a "flying saucer." This helps to maintain the "chain reaction" of such reports.

Since this document accurately expressed the opinion of the personnel at ATIC, it is not surprising that investigative activity had virtually ended.

During the spring and summer of 1950, the FBI received only a few reports. Then, in late August, FBI agent A. M. Belmont provided a summary of the fireball situation which showed—are you surprised?—that the Air Force had not stopped investigating the sightings:

Information Concerning Phenomena in New Mexico
Aug. 23, 1950

1. The OSI has expressed concern in connection with the continued appearance of unexplained phenomena described as green fireballs, discs and meteors in the vicinity of sensitive installations in New Mexico.

2. Dr. La Paz, meteor expert of the University of New Mexico, reported that the phenomena does not appear to be of meteoric origin.

3. OSI has contracted with Land-Air, Inc., Alamogordo, New Mexico, to make scientific study of the unexplained phenomena.

Observations of aerial phenomena occurring within the vicinity of sensitive installations have been recorded by the Air Force since December 1948. The phenomena have been classified into three general types which are identified as follows:

1. Green fireballs, objects moving at high speed in shapes resembling half moons, circles and discs emitting green light.

2. Discs, round flat shaped objects or phenomena moving at fast velocity and emitting a brilliant white light or reflected light.

3. Meteors, aerial phenomena resembling meteoric material moving at high velocity and varying in color.

The above phenomena have been reported to vary in color from brilliant white to amber, red and green.

Since 1948 approximately 150 observations of aerial phenomena referred to above have been recorded in the vicinity of installations in New Mexico. A number of observations have been reported by different reliable individuals at approximately the same time.

Dr. Lincoln La Paz, Institute of Meteoritics, University of New Mexico, submitted an analysis of the various observations on May 23, 1950. He concluded, as a result of his investigation, that approximately half of the phenomena recorded were of meteoric origin. The other phenomena commonly referred to as green fireballs or discs he believed to be U.S. guided missiles being tested in the neighborhood of the installations. Dr. La Paz pointed out that if he were wrong in interpreting the phenomena as originating with U.S. guided missiles that a systematic investigation of the observations should be made immediately. Dr. La Paz pointed out that missiles moving with the velocities of the order of those found for the green fireballs and discs could travel from the Ural region of the USSR to New Mexico in less than fifteen minutes. He suggested that the observations might be of guided missiles launched from bases in the Urals.

On the basis of the investigations made by Dr. La Paz and the Air Force it was concluded that the occurrence of the unexplained phenomena in the vicinity of sensitive installations was a cause for concern. The Air Force entered into a contract with Land-Air, Incorporated, Alamogordo, New Mexico, for the purpose of making scientific studies of the green fireballs and discs. It was pointed out in the summary furnished by OSI on July 19, 1950, that the unexplained green fireballs and discs are still observed in the vicinity of sensitive military installations.

The Air Force together with Land-Air, Incorporated, have established a number of observation posts in the vicinity of Vaughn, New Mexico, for the purpose of photographing and determining the speed, height and nature of the unusual phenomena referred to as green fireballs and discs. On May 24, 1950, personnel of Land-Air, Incorporated, sighted eight to ten objects of aerial phenomena. A 24-hour day watch is being maintained and has been designated as "Project Twinkle."

The Albuquerque Office, in a letter dated August 10, 1950, advised that there have been no new developments in connection with the efforts to ascertain the identity of the strange aerial phenomena referred to as green fireballs and discs. The Albuquerque Office advised that [name removed from FOIA document], Project Engineer, had been informed of the Bureau's jurisdiction relative to espionage and sabotage and arrangements have been made so that the Bureau will be promptly advised in the event additional information relative to this project indicates any jurisdiction on the part of the Bureau.

One can imagine that this news must have come as a surprise to J. Edgar and the FBI after being told *officially,* only five months earlier, by Maj. Boggs and Lt. Col. Hearn of ATIC, that the Air Force was "out of it . . . no longer investigating . . ." and "[saucers, etc. are] believed to be natural phenomena."

What the FBI hadn't been told by Boggs and Hearn, perhaps because they didn't know, was that the continued sightings had kept AFI and AFOSI interest alive during the latter half of 1949 and the first half of 1950 even though ATIC was no longer "officially" interested in sightings. However, ATIC interest in saucers was regenerated three months after Boggs and Hearn spoke to the FBI by a memorandum from Brig. Gen. Ernest Moore of Air Force Intelligence, which was supported by an official directive from Maj. Gen. Cabell. Gen. Moore's memorandum reads:

```
1 July 1950
MEMORANDUM FOR: CHIEF, Evaluation Division
CHIEF, Air Targets Division
CHIEF, Air Estimates Division
SUBJECT: UNIDENTIFIED OBJECTS
```

The continued reports of sightings of unidentified aerial objects require that cognizance of the activity be a continuing function. When Project "Grudge" was abolished, it was not intended that this function should be ignored as a possibility of foreign activity. Consequently, the Evaluation Division should continue to monitor these reports and handle each incident in accordance with the evaluation of the relative importance in each case.

General Moore's memorandum indicates that although Grudge was abolished, just as the press release in December 1949 stated, it was the intent of AFI that ATIC personnel should continue to analyze sightings in the event that a saucer or UFO should turn out to be some foreign (that is, Soviet) aircraft. Six days later, Maj. Gen. Cabell sent a directive to Col. Harold Watson, who was in charge of Project Grudge:

July 7, 1950

I am sending this by Major Pianitza hoping to save the bother of an officially coordinated directive. Gen. Cabell's views regarding the "Flying Saucer" project are in substance as follows:

(a) He feels that it probably was a mistake to abandon the [Grudge] project and to publicly announce that we are no longer interested. However, the decision having been made, he feels that it was incumbant [sic] upon him not to over-rule, at least for the time being.

(b) Our instructions, which rescinded a long list of letters to numerous agencies, were published in an unnumbered HQS, USAF letter, File AFOIR-CO 7 dated 12 January 1950, Subject : "Reporting of Information on Unconventional Air-craft." The last paragraph of this letter requested all recipi-ents to continue to treat information and observations received as intelligence information and to continue the pro-cessing in a normal manner. We have continued to receive from many USAF sources a number of reports of this nature.

(c) Gen. Cabell's views are that we should reinstate, if it has been abandoned, a continuing analysis of reports received and he expects AMC to do this as part of their obligation to produce air technical intelligence. He specifically desires that the project, as it existed before, be *not* fully re-implemented with special technical teams travelling around the country interviewing observers etc., and he is particularly desirous that there be *no* fanfare or publicity over the fact that the

USAF is still interested in "flying saucers"[emphasis under-lined in the original].

(d) Gen. Cabell desires that we place ourselves in a posi-tion that, if circumstances require an all-out effort in this regard at some future time, we will be able to announce that we have continued quietly our analysis of reports without interruption.

(e) Under this philosophy, then, we will continue to receive from USAF sources reports of "flying saucers" and we will immediately transmit these reports to AMC. You will be at liberty to query, through AFOIC-CC normal channels, the USAF source for more information. We will also be scanning State, CIA, Army and Navy incoming reports for pertinent information which will be relayed to AMC . . .

(f) Ordinary newspaper reports should be analyzed with-out initiating specific inquiry. Information received direct from non-USAF individuals may be acknowledged and interrogated through correspondence. Where geographically convenient, specific sightings may be investigated quietly at your discretion, by AMC depot personnel and requests for investigation may be filed with your local OSI office.

(g) Queries from news agencies as to whether USAF is still interested in "flying saucers" may be given a general answer to the effect that AMC is interested in any information that will enable it to produce air technical intelligence—and just as much interested in "flying saucer" information as it would be in any other significant information. Work in the "flying saucer" field is not receiving "special" emphasis because emphasis is being placed on all technical intelligence fields.

The foregoing is probably in more detail than is necessary. If, after reading this you are still uncertain as to what to do, give me a call. If this clarifies your questions, go ahead under AMC's general directive to produce air technical intelligence.

Wow! No mincing of words here. The top AFI guy was not happy with the way AMC was handling the saucer situation. One may imagine that the colonels and captains jumped out of their chairs and saluted briskly as they received their direct orders to *do something for a change!*

Two months later, in September, Gen. Cabell requested a slight modification to this directive. Referring to (c) above, he indicated that he *did* want to have investigative teams available and that "it will be AMC responsibility to send such teams as they consider necessary."

Not only did Cabell order AMC to revitalize Grudge, he also issued yet another intelligence collection memorandum. On September 25, this was received by the Director of the FBI as well as by numerous Air Force and Army Commanding Generals, Navy Intelligence, the State Department, and the CIA. The memorandum asked for the usual details about any sighting, asked for the information to be sent as quickly as possible by electronic means with a follow-up written report, and made one further request: "It is desired that no publicity be given this reporting or analysis activity." In other words, this is important stuff and we are interested, but let's not tell anybody who doesn't need to know—such as the American people.

Gen. Cabell was a "Knight in Shining Armor," come to rescue flying saucer sightings from the dungeon of Project Grudge. Unfortunately he was not entirely successful, as he found out a year later. Col. Watson and the Grudge staff were basically "anti-UFO." They did not carefully study the sighting reports that AFI sent to them. All they did was invent plausible explanations for the sightings and send these explanations to AFI. The reports were seldom filed. A year later, when Capt. Edward Ruppelt took over the project, he found that many reports had been packed into boxes, and others were simply lost.

Cabell's displeasure at the lack of ATIC activity is not surprising, considering the number and quality of sighting reports being received by AFI and passed on to ATIC for analysis. Reports for 1950 began on January 2. There were about a dozen sightings in January and again in February, and over three dozen in March. After that, they continued at a rate of one to two dozen every month for a total of about 240 sightings for the year. By far the largest proportion were from the United States, but there were some from other countries as far away as Japan, Cyprus, and Chile. In fact, in retrospect it appears that a worldwide flap of sightings occurred.

The reader can probably imagine the confusion in the press that resulted from the contrast between the large number of reports by scientists and pilots who believed they had seen something truly unusual, and the publicly expressed Air Force attitude that there was no evidence of something unusual. To add to the confusion, there were also fake "crashed saucer" reports.

How to separate the wheat from the chaff? That was the problem, and it could only be solved by good investigation, good data, and good analysis.

Good data, that was what Project Twinkle was intended to supply. And it did. Too bad the data were ignored—*or suppressed!*

CHAPTER 15

Twinkle, Twinkle, Little *Craft*

. . . no information was gained.

—Dr. L. Elterman

. . . objects sighted in some number.

—from a report to Dr. Mirarchi

The efforts of Dr. Kaplan and Maj. Oder to start a fireball research project came to fruition in the spring of 1950. A $20,000 half-year contract was signed with the Land-Air Corporation, which operated the phototheodolites at White Sands Proving Ground. Land-Air was to set up a 24-hour watch at a location in New Mexico to be specified by the Air Force, and the phototheodolite operators at White Sands were to film any unusual objects that happened to fly past.

The investigation began on March 24, 1950. By this time there had been many sightings in the Southwest according to the sighting catalogue compiled by Lt. Col. Rees of the 17th District OSI at Kirtland AFB, many of them around Holloman AFB. His catalogue shows the following data for New Mexico in 1949: the area of Sandia Base (Albuquerque) had seventeen sightings, mostly in the latter half of the year; Los Alamos area twenty-six sightings spread throughout the year; Vaughn area (none); Holloman AFB/Alamogordo/White Sands area (12); other areas in southwest New Mexico (20); total (75). For the same areas in the first three months of 1950 there were: Sandia (6—all in February); Los

Alamos (7); Vaughn (1); Holloman AFB/Alamogordo/White Sands (6); others (6); total (26). With all these sightings, the scientists were quite confident that they could "catch" a fireball or a saucer.

On February 21, an observation post was set up at Holloman manned by two people with a theodolite, telescope, and camera. The post was manned only from sunrise to sunset. The observers saw nothing unusual during a month of operation. Then the scientists decided to begin a constant 24-hour watch on the first of April that would last for six months, with Land-Air personnel operating cinetheodolites (theodolites with movie cameras), and with Holloman AFB personnel manning spectrographic cameras and radio frequency receivers. Thus began Project Twinkle with the high hopes of solving the fireball/saucer mystery.

A year and a half later, in November 1951, Dr. Louis Elterman, the Director of Project Twinkle, who worked at the Atmospheric Physics Laboratory (APL) of the Geophysical Research Division (GRD) of the Air Force Cambridge Research Laboratory (AFCRL), wrote the final report. According to Dr. Elterman's report, Project Twinkle was a dismal failure: "*no information was gained.*" He recommended it be discontinued. His recommendation was accepted.

But was it a failure? Was there really no information gained? Recall the FBI report presented in the last chapter, which states that on May 24, 1950, personnel of Land-Air saw eight to ten unidentified objects. Isn't this "information?" Let us look more carefully at Project Twinkle.

According to Dr. Elterman, before Twinkle began there had been "an abnormal number of reports" from Vaughn, New Mexico, so it was decided to place a lookout post there. Why this place was chosen is a mystery to me. It is about 120 air miles from Los Alamos, about ninety miles from Sandia Base and nearly 150 from Alamogordo/Holloman AFB. I have listed above the sighting statistics for the various New Mexico areas, being careful to list the sightings around Vaughn separately. Note that Vaughn had only one sighting in the whole previous year. So why did they "waste" a lookout post at Vaughn? Why didn't they put one at Los Alamos, or at White Sands? Did they think that they could triangulate over a *very* large baseline distance with the lookout post at Holloman AFB *or were they actually trying to avoid sightings?* These are questions that must forever remain unanswered.

Anyway, it was a mistake. After Project Twinkle began, the sighting rate dropped precipitously. The Blue Book sighting list shows one sighting in April, one in May, and one in August in the Holloman area. There were also fewer sightings in the other areas. In fact, for the period from April 1 to October 1 covered by the first Land-Air contract there were only about eight sightings in the whole of New Mexico as compared with the roughly thirty sightings during the previous six months.

The effect of this sudden decrease in sighting rate is reflected in the Twinkle Final Report, which says that there were very few observations. However, of more importance is what is *not* reflected in the report— what is ignored or *covered up* in the report: the fact that *Twinkle was successful.*

Just so the reader can understand where the writer of the Project Twinkle report was dishonest, here is one part of it, verbatim. Commenting on the "first contractual period, 1 April 1950 to 15 September 1950," Dr. Elterman wrote:

> Some photographic activity occurred on 27 April and 24 May, but simultaneous sightings by both cameras were not made, so that no information was gained. On 30 August 1950, during a Bell aircraft missile launching, aerial phenomena were observed over Holloman Air Force Base by several individuals; however, neither Land-Air nor Project personnel were notified and, therefore, no results were acquired. On 31 August 1950, the phenomena were again observed after a V-2 launching. Although much film was expended, proper triangulation was not effected, so that again no information was acquired.

During the second contractual period, October 1, 1950 to March 31, 1951 there were *no* sightings. It was as if the phenomenon had reacted to the setting up of observation posts by moving elsewhere. There were continuing sightings in other parts of the country and even a few in the other parts of New Mexico, but none near Holloman AFB. The lack of sightings was enough to end the contract. After the contract ended there were discussions about what to do with the data and whether or not to continue observations at some low level of effort. In the late spring of

1951, it was decided not to continue the special effort. Elterman, writing in November 1951, recommended "no further expenditure" of time and effort . . . and there was none.

But, what about the sightings during the first half of the contract, the sightings at Holloman Air Force base in April and May 1950? According to Eltermann, no information was gained. Was Elterman justified in making such a comment?

No! Certainly information "is gained" when a number of qualified observers simultaneously view unidentified objects from various locations. And more information is gained if some of these observers film these objects through cinetheodolite telescopes. There is useful information even if a "proper triangulation" is not accomplished. And there is even more information gained if a proper triangulation is accomplished—*and one was accomplished,* only Eltermann didn't mention it!

Farther on in the report, Dr. Elterman indicates a serious deficiency in the operational plan for Project Twinkle. The project scientists knew that they might have some film to analyze, but according Elterman *there were insufficient funds built into the contract to analyze the film.* After a discussion with Mr. Warren Kott, who was in charge of the Land-Air operations, Elterman estimated that it would take thirty man-days to analyze the film and do a time correlation study which "would assure that these records did not contain significant material." According to Elterman, "no provisions are contained in the contract" for this analysis.

One reads this previous statement with some astonishment. *They set up a photographically instrumented search for unknown objects and then failed to provide for the film analysis if they were lucky enough to get film.* What sort of a scientific project is that? Did they want to succeed or *did they want to fail?*

Furthermore, Elterman's statement that a time correlation study should be done to *assure* that the records contained *no significant material* sounds as if Elterman had already concluded that there was no worthwhile evidence in the film. Does this sound like an *unbiased* investigation?

Near the end of the report, Elterman supported his statement that "no information was gained" by offering explanations for the sightings: "Many of the sightings are attributable to natural phenomena such as flights of birds, planets, meteors, and possibly cloudiness."

The typical reader of the Project Twinkle Final Report would accept Dr. Elterman's opinion as the final word on the subject. Only the perceptive person would realize that Dr. Elterman *had not actually proven his statement to be true, even though he presumably had access to the photographic evidence which would prove it, if it were true.*

Dr. Anthony Mirarchi was not the average scientist. He was skeptical, all right, but he was skeptical of the glib explanations. In 1950, he was the Chief of the Air Composition Branch at GRD/AFCRL. Project Twinkle began as Dr. Mirachi's project. However, he retired from AFCRL in October 1950, so he was not involved with Twinkle when Dr. Elterman wrote the final report a year later. In fact, Dr. Mirarchi may never have seen that report.

Dr. Mirarchi visited Holloman Air Force Base in late May 1950, and requested a brief report on the April 27 and May 24 sightings which Elterman mentioned (see above). Fortunately for "the truth," the brief report to Mirarchi survived in the National Archives microfilm record where it was found in the late 1970s long after the Twinkle report had had its (intended?) debunking effect on the green fireball sightings. As you will see, this document refutes Elterman:

1. Per request of Dr. A. O. Mirarchi, during a recent visit to this base, the following information is submitted.

2. Sightings were made on 27 April and 24 May 1950 of aerial phenomena during morning daylight hours at this station. The sightings were made by Land-Air, Inc., personnel while engaged in tracking regular projects with Askania Phototheodolites. It has been reported that objects are sighted in some number; as many as eight have been visible at one time. The individuals making these sightings are professional observers. Therefore I would rate their reliability superior. In both cases photos were taken with Askanias.

3. The Holloman AF Base Data Reduction Unit analyzed the 27 April pictures and made a report, a copy of which I am enclosing with the film for your information. It was believed that triangulation could be effected from pictures taken on 24 May because pictures were taken from two stations. The

films were rapidly processed and examined by Data Reduction. However, it was determined that sightings were made on two different objects and triangulation could not be effected. A report from Data Reduction and the films from the sighting are enclosed.

4. There is nothing further to report at this time.

The writer of this letter is not known (no signature). The Data Reduction report attached to the letter reads as follows:

Objects observed following MX776A test of 27 April 1950
2nd Lt. [name censored] EHOSIR 15 May 50

1. According to conversation between Col. Baynes and Capt. Bryant, the following information is submitted directly to Lt. Albert.

2. Film from station P10 was read, resulting in azimuth and elevation angles being recorded on four objects. In addition, size of image on film was recorded.

3. From this information, together with a single azimuth angle from station M7, the following conclusions were drawn:

   a. The objects were at an altitude of approximately 150,000 ft.

   b. The objects were over the Holloman range between the base and Tularosa Peak.

   c. The objects were approximately 30 feet in diameter

   d. The objects were traveling at an undeterminable, yet high speed.

[signed]
Wilbur L. Mitchell
Mathematician
Data Reduction Unit

So, there you have it, four unidentified objects—UFOs—were flying at 150,000 feet near the White Sands Proving Ground. Each was roughly thirty feet in size. The sighting was similar to that of Charles Moore's a year earlier. Could Mitchell and the Askania operators have made a mistake? Not likely. Their business was tracking fast-moving objects (rockets) and calculating the trajectories of the rockets. As the writer of the above letter stated, "The individuals making these sightings are professional observers. Therefore I would rate their reliability superior."

Human beings had made no objects that could fly at 150,000 feet in the spring of 1950. What, then, were they? *Whose were they?*

Compare the above letter with the first paragraph of Elterman's statement where he says "simultaneous sightings by both cameras were not made so that no information was gained." It seems that Elterman got his information on these sightings from this report to Dr. Mirarchi. Yet he did not even give a hint of the existence of the most important result of Project Twinkle: the April 27 *triangulation that yielded information on altitude and size.* Could it be that he didn't know about the Data Reduction Unit report? Or did he know and choose to *purposely ignore or withhold the information?*

Ruppelt, in *The Report on Unidentified Flying Objects,* described the April 27 event in more detail. A guided missile had just been tracked and the cinethodolite crews were starting to unload their cameras when someone spotted objects moving through the sky. The camera stations were linked by a telephone network, so that person alerted the others. Unfortunately all but one camera had been unloaded and the UFOs had departed before the other cameras could be reloaded. According to Ruppelt, "The photos from the one station showed only a smudgy dark object. About all the film proved was that something was in the air and, whatever it was, it was moving." Evidently, Ruppelt didn't know that a triangulation had been accomplished.

Ruppelt also discussed the May 24 event and its failure at triangulation due to the fact that the two cameras were looking at different objects. Ruppelt wrote that in February 1951, when he first learned of these sightings (this was about nine months before he became the director of Project Grudge and over a year before the name was changed to Blue Book), "The records at AMC didn't contain the analysis of these films but they did mention the Data Reduction Group at White Sands. So, when I later took over the UFO investigation I made several calls in an effort to run down the actual film and analysis." Unfortunately, he was not successful even though he did manage to contact, through a "major who was very cooperative," two men who had analyzed what was either the May 24, or the August 31, film, or both (see Elterman's statement above regarding the August 31 sighting). Ruppelt writes:

> [The major's] report . . . was what I had expected—nothing concrete except that the UFOs were unknowns. He did say that by putting a correction factor in the data gathered by the two cameras they were able to arrive at a rough estimate of speed, altitude and size. The UFO was "higher than 40,000 feet, traveling over 2,000 miles per hour, and it was over 300 feet in diameter." He cautioned me that these figures were only estimates, based on the possibly erroneous correction factor; therefore they weren't proof of anything—except that something was in the air.

Obviously Ruppelt *underplayed* the importance of this report by suggesting that the films didn't prove anything. So what, if the size, distance, and speed estimates might be wrong—*something was there, obviously large, fast, and unusual* or the camera crews wouldn't have bothered to film it! Since Ruppelt apparently was not aware that a triangulation had been accomplished for the April 27 sighting, one wonders if he would have tried to downplay that film, also, as not "proof of anything."

At the bottom of the report to Dr. Mirachi is a list of enclosures, which shows that two reports (Data Red Report #1 and Data Red Report #2) and three films (P-10 and P-8 of May 24 and P-10 of April 27) were sent to Mirarchi along with a map of the Holloman range showing, I presume, the locations of the cameras. There is a handwritten note "Film on repository with AFCRL," and a few other undecipherable scribbles. Recent attempts to locate these films have failed.

Incidentally, the Project Blue Book master sighting list indicates that all four of the sightings listed by Elterman had "insufficient information" for evaluation.

The sighting rate in New Mexico dropped nearly to zero in the latter part of 1950 and remained low in 1951. During 1951, there were about a dozen sightings in New Mexico, most of which occurred away from Holloman AFB. The most important of these occurred on January 16, at Artesia, while Project Twinkle was still ongoing, but Project Twinkle personnel were not involved. During the early morning, two Navy balloon project engineers launched a giant Skyhook balloon near Artesia. Near the end of the day it caused a rash of sightings over western Texas. But the important events occurred in the morning while the balloon was still in the vicinity of Artesia airport.

At about 9:30 A.M., the project engineers were observing the balloon which, by this time, was at its maximum altitude of about 110,000 ft. and its maximum diameter of about 110 feet, and was drifting in an easterly direction at about five mph. They noted another round object that had appeared in the clear sky not far from, but seemingly above, the balloon. This unidentified object appeared to be dull white in color and considerably larger than the balloon. This object went out of sight, in the distance. These engineers then traveled several miles westward to the Artesia airport to view the balloon from another location. While again watching the balloon high overhead, this time in the company of the airport manager and several other individuals, they and the others saw two dull gray objects at a very high altitude, which came from the northeast toward the balloon, made an arc (a turn) of about 300 degrees around the balloon and then departed in a northerly direction. The objects seemed to be the same size, relative to the balloon, as the object seen earlier. They were separated by a distance about seven times the diameter of either one and, when they made the sharp turn, seemingly around the balloon, they appeared to tilt on edge and could not be seen until they apparently levelled out again. The objects traveled at high speed and, after passing around the balloon, disappeared in the distance in several seconds. In the Blue Book master list this case is listed as having insufficient information, apparently because Project Grudge did not learn of this sighting until over a year later (January 1952) and so did not carry out an investigation. (Project Twinkle was still going on, but Twinkle personnel were not involved in the sighting, so it does not appear in the Twinkle report.)

Although Dr. Mirarchi retired in October 1950 and had no part in writing the final Twinkle report that was completed over a year later, his involvement with the green fireballs and saucers did not end when he retired. Four months later he returned to "action" in a public way and his actions nearly got him into serious trouble three years afterward.

In the middle of February 1951, *Time* magazine published an article that featured a well-known scientist, Dr. Urner Liddel of the Naval Research Laboratory near Washington, D.C. In the article, Dr. Liddel stated that he had studied approximately 2,000 saucer reports and, in his opinion, the only credible saucer sightings were actually sightings of misidentified Skyhook balloons, balloons that had been kept secret by the armed services. Apparently Dr. Liddel wasn't aware of the several sightings by balloon project scientists.

Evidently Dr. Mirarchi felt it was his civic duty to repudiate Liddel's claims because two weeks later he responded publicly. According to a United Press story filed on February 26, 1951 Mirarchi said that, after investigating 300 reports of flying saucers, he believed that the saucers were missiles from Russia that had photographed our atomic bomb test sites. According to the United Press article, the forty-year-old scientist who "for more than a year conducted a top secret investigation into the weird phenomena, said that he had worked with balloons and balloons did not leave an exhaust trail." Another reason given against the balloon explanation was that balloons could not be seen at night. Mirachi explained how "scientists had picked up dust particles containing copper which could have come from no other source than the saucer motive plants (the engines)."*

Mirarchi went on to explain that the "flying saucers or 'fireballs'" as he terms them, were regularly observed near Los Alamos until he set up a system of phototheodolites to measure their speed, size, and distance away . . . but the fireballs mysteriously ceased appearing before the theodolites could go to work. Dr. Mirarchi concludes that spies must have tipped off the saucers' home base." Mirarchi referred to two sightings for which there was photographic evidence: a single photo of a

* This was a reference to efforts by Dr. La Paz to have air samples taken after a green fireball sighting to see if there were any small particles of copper or copper compounds in the air. Such compounds "burn green" or give off a characteristic green color when heated, so La Paz had conjectured that the green color could be attributed to burning copper compounds associated with the fireballs. In one case there was success in detecting such particles, although La Paz was not completely convinced that the particles were from the fireball.

round glowing object and a motion picture which "showed one streaking across the sky for one and a half minutes." Mirarchi went on to say that he was aware that some sightings were actually sightings of balloons, but that "there was too much evidence in favor of saucers to say they could have all been balloons. 'I was conducting the main investigation. The government had to depend on me or my branch for information.' He said he did not see how the Navy [i.e., Dr. Liddel] could say that there had been no concrete evidence on the existence of the phenomena."

Mirarchi concluded by accusing the government of committing "suicide by secrecy" for not admitting that the saucers were real and probably missiles from Russia.

Strong words! So strong they nearly got Mirarchi in trouble more than two years later. According to an Air Force document released in 1991, in 1953, during a time of espionage and spy hunting (the Rosenbergs, atomic weapons spies, were executed in 1953) the FBI queried the Air Force as to whether or not Mirarchi should be investigated for breaking security. Lt. Col. Frederick Oder, who had been instrumental in getting Project Twinkle started (see chapter 12), responded by writing that, because Mirarchi had released to the newspaper some information that was classified Confidential or Secret it "could cause serious harm to the internal security of the country . . . if it were to fall into unfriendly hands . . . both from the point of view of the prestige of our Government and the point of view of revealing our interest in certain classified projects." Brig. Gen. W. M. Garland, who was in charge of AMC in 1953, decided not to pursue Dr. Mirarchi because, in his opinion, the information was not that important. Furthermore, in Gen. Garland's opinion, the facts about saucers being missiles, as stated in the newspaper article, had been "disproved or are, at best, personal opinions, and are not considered classified data." In other words, Gen. Garland apparently believed that the green fireball and saucer sightings were not Russian missiles, although he did not say what he thought they were.

Perhaps Gen. Garland let Mirarchi off the hook because he recalled that there had been a recommendation to declassify and release the results of Project Twinkle in December 1951, a month after the final report was written. However, he could find no record of declassification in the files of AMC. Evidently he was not aware of the recommendation *against* declassification contained in a February 1952 letter to the Directorate of Intelligence from the Directorate of Research and Development, which states:

> The Scientific Advisory Board Secretariat has suggested that this project not be declassified for a variety of reasons, chief among which is that no scientific explanation for any of the "fireballs" and other phenomena was revealed by the [Project Twinkle] report and that some reputable scientists still believe that the observed phenomena are man-made.

Another letter, this time from the Directorate of Intelligence to the Research Division of the Directorate of Research and Development, dated March 11, 1952, adds another reason for withholding the information from the public:

> It is believed that a release of the information to the public in its present condition would cause undue speculation and give rise to unwarranted fears among the populace such as occurred in previous releases on unidentified flying objects. This results from releases when there has been no real solution.

In other words, Air Force Intelligence had realized that the public could see through the smoke screen of previous explanations and wanted real answers; so, if they couldn't come up with real answers, it was better to say nothing.

Over a year after Mirarchi responded to Liddel, *Life* magazine published an article on flying saucers (discussed in chapter 19). In that article, the authors described some of the sightings that caused the Air Force to start Project Twinkle. One of the hundreds of letters the magazine received in response to that article was from Capt. Daniel McGovern, who wrote, "I was very closely associated with Projects 'Twinkle' and 'Grudge' at Alamogordo, New Mexico, where I was chief of the technical photographic facility at Holloman Air Force Base. I have seen several of these objects myself, and they are everything you say they are as to shape, size, and speed."†

The green fireballs, or something like them, have been seen occasionally in various places in the years since Project Twinkle, but not in anything like the southwestern concentration of the 1948–1950 sightings. No one at the time could figure out what they were.

We *still* don't know.

† *Life* magazine, April 28, 1952.

CHAPTER 16

Saucers Over Oak Ridge

The summer and fall of 1950 was an important time in the history of UFO phenomena. The first book devoted to flying saucers, Donald Keyhoe's *Flying Saucers are Real* (Fawcett, New York, 1950), was published in June. The book expanded on his *True* magazine article of six months before. Keyhoe argued that the Air Force was covering up evidence that proved saucers were extraterrestrial craft because the Air Force was worried about an Orson Welles "War of the Worlds" type of panic if this information became public. Nevertheless, there had been some information leaked, such as the article by Commander McLaughlin about sightings at White Sands. Keyhoe suspected that such leaks were intended to prepare humanity for the eventual news. Furthermore, he suspected that the arrival of the saucers was related to our detonations of atomic (fission) bombs, which were first tested at White Sands. He suggested that perhaps the aliens wanted to prevent us from destroying the Earth with hydrogen (fusion) bombs.

During the time between the publication of Keyhoe's magazine article and the publication of his book, there were important national and international political and military developments that affected the FBI

163

perception of the flying saucer problem. The Cold War was hot. The Berlin blockade had been successfully overcome, but the Russians had successfully taken over the satellite countries of East Germany, Poland, Czechoslovakia, Hungary, and Yugoslavia. Then, on June 25, North Korea marched about 60,000 men into South Korea, and thus began the Korean War. Both the Soviet Union and China aided North Korea. The South Korean Army, not fully prepared, collapsed under the weight of the attack and, two days later, President Truman ordered U.S. troops to South Korea. The next day Seoul fell to the North, and Gen. MacArthur reported that the South Korean army was too demoralized to mount an effective resistance. Two days after that, Truman ordered U.S. ground forces to Korea. The first post-WWII armed conflict had begun.

Meanwhile, at the end of January 1950, President Truman announced that work would begin on the hydrogen "fusion" bomb. The race for the "Super Bomb" was on. (The Soviet Union would win this race in 1953.) Suddenly spies were being caught everywhere. In February, Klaus Fuchs was arrested for passing secrets of the atomic (fission) bomb to the Soviets. (Fuch's spy activities were in large part the cause of the Soviet Union's successful detonation of a fission bomb in August 1949.) FBI Director Hoover made a personal report to President Truman on Fuchs' capture and subsequent confession in Great Britain. A few days later, Sen. Joe McCarthy announced that there were over two hundred Communist Party members working for the Department of State. Five months later, about the time that the Korean War began, Harry Gold and David Greenglass were caught and provided information about a spy ring directed by the Rosenbergs, which had provided atomic secrets to the Soviets during the Second World War. All of this espionage activity may have affected the FBI view of the UFO phenomenon because the Air Force was clearly worried about the green fireball and disc phenomena seen near the nuclear installations (could they be related to communist subversion?), and because Col. Gasser had indicated that the saucers were man-made missiles—but not made by the United States!

Soon after the publication of Keyhoe's book, and at a time when the Air Force was publicly disparaging the subject, the first highly credible motion picture of saucers was taken at Great Falls, Montana, on August 5, 1950. The Air Force wanted to look at it but didn't want to give the owner, Nicolas Mariana, any hint of their particular interest in the subject. According to an AFOSI document, the agent contacting Mariana was to "exercise every caution so as not to unduly excite his curiousity [sic] or interest or in anywise conclude that the Air Force may have reversed its policy from that previously announced with regard to the existence or non-existence of such unconventional objects."

In later years, this film would cause a great controversy as the Air Force claimed that the two objects in the film were Air Force jets. However, the objects certainly didn't look like jets to Mariana and his secretary. When first sighted, the objects were quite close and appeared to be round and rotating. Unfortunately by the time Mariana had obtained his camera, they were considerably farther away, so the film images appear as small, bright oval dots. The images do not look like jets, and a scientific test performed years later indicated that jets filmed under similar circumstances would have been identified as such. The Air Force nevertheless claimed the objects were jets, even though the investigation turned up evidence that the only pair of jets that passed through the area of the sighting did so ten days *after* the film was shot!

All this time, the FBI was quietly monitoring the fireball and saucer situation. Recall that in late August 1950 (see chapter 14) Agent A. H. Belmont had written a memorandum to Special Assistant D. M. Ladd summarizing recent developments regarding green fireballs and saucers. On October 9, Ladd wrote a memorandum for Hoover providing an update on Project Twinkle. The memorandum states that, "To date the Air Force has not advised us of any new developments in connection with this project." Evidently, the Air Force had not told the FBI about the multiple witness sightings and filming of multiple objects on August 30 and 31. Ladd also made an explicit comparison between saucer sighting reports (referred to as "complaints") and the war in Korea, which to this point had been going poorly, but at least the North Korean army had not (yet) succeeded in pushing the United Nations and United States forces into the sea:

> According to Bureau files, an average of approximately three
> or four complaints have been received per month from June
> through September. These complaints were brought to the

attention of OSI. A review of Bureau files does not indicate that there has been any increase in sightings of these phenomena during or as a result of the war in Korea.

Hoover was probably glad to see that there were so few complaints, and that there was no apparent connection with the Korean conflict. However, there still was the major question of the origin of the phenomena seen near the vital installations, and the secondary question of just what the Air Force was doing about it. Ladd provided the following comments on these subjects:

> The Bureau has been advised in the past by OSI that many of the sightings reported to them were determined by investigation to have been of weather balloons, falling stars, meteorological phenomena and other air-borne objects.
>
> Bureau liaison determined on the morning of October 9, 1950 from OSI headquarters that the investigation of these aerial phenomena are being handled by OSI, Wright Field, Ohio. Their investigation of these phenomena fails to indicate that the sightings involved spaceships or missiles from any other planet or country.
>
> According to OSI, the complaints received by them have failed to indicate any definite pattern of activity. OSI further advised they are closely following the investigation of the captioned matters and they will advise this Bureau of any matters of interest.

Once again the FBI was told that the Air Force was sufficiently worried about these phenomena to continue secretly investigating them, even though many sightings could be explained. Since the Air Force was once again ruling out the interplanetary and "foreign country" explanations, the FBI could only presume that all saucer sightings resulted from misidentifications, delusions, and hoaxes.

Then the saucer controversy suddenly heated up again in early September with the publication of the second flying saucer book, *Behind the Flying Saucers* by Frank Scully (Henry Holt, New York, 1950). Whereas

Keyhoe had based his book on official sources and sightings, Scully based his book on a crashed saucer report. According to Scully, a total of three flying saucers had crashed and had been analyzed by government scientists. (Note: There was no connection between Scully's crash story and the Roswell crash story.) The analysis of the saucers showed that they were fantastic devices and were piloted by small humanlike creatures. Scully's book claimed that the story was first told during a lecture by oilman Silas Newton at the University of Denver on March 8, 1950 and that he had researched the story.*

It turned out later that the source for Scully's story was a con man by the name of Silas Newton who claimed he had gotten the details from another man who, in turn, claimed to be one of the government scientists who analyzed the saucers. Scully apparently did not realize the story was fraudulent (it was proven a hoax many years later).

Scully's book made quite a splash, and regenerated the public saucer controversy, claiming as it did that a mysterious government scientist had verified the facts of the crash. Furthermore, Scully severely criticized the Air Force and all government authority, arguing that there had been extreme incompetence, a "double standard of morality," and official censorship. Scully's story was so fantastic that it was almost uniformly panned by the media. On the other hand, Keyhoe's more rational approach was not as flashy, but it convinced more people.

Keeping in mind that these books came at a time of "Cold War paranoia," it is not surprising to see that Hoover took a particular interest in Scully's book. Ever on the alert for communist subversion, Hoover sent an urgent teletype message on October 13 to SAC Los Angeles:

```
FLYING SAUCERS. YOU ARE INSTRUCTED TO
DISCREETLY DETERMINE THROUGH APPROPRIATE
SOURCES OF YOUR OFFICE WHETHER FRANK
SCULLY AUTHOR OF THE BOOK QUOTE BEHIND
THE FLYING SAUCERS UNQUOTE IS IDENTICAL
TO THE FRANK SCULLY WHO HAS BEEN ACTIVELY
```

* Recall it was on March 22, 1950 that Guy Hottel, SAC Washington, wrote to Hoover about three crashed saucers, a message that prompted Hoover to ask "what are the facts re: flying saucers." See chapter 14.

ENGAGED IN COMMUNIST ACTIVITIES SINCE THE
LATE NINETEEN THIRTIES IN THE TERRITORY
OF YOUR OFFICE.

Evidently SAC Los Angeles didn't respond immediately because Hoover sent another request on October 17, and yet another on October 18. There is no document in the "Flying Disc" file that indicates whether or not SAC Los Angeles answered Hoover, or whether Frank Scully, the author, was indeed a communist sympathizer.

On the same day that Hoover initiated the investigation of Frank Scully, the FBI received the first information on strange happenings at yet another "vital installation," Oak Ridge National Laboratory in Tennessee. William Gray, SAC Knoxville, reported that radar had detected unidentified objects over Oak Ridge, the home of Project NEPA, the project to develop atomic-powered aircraft—Col. Gasser's project!

On October 19, before the FBI was fully aware of what was taking place at Oak Ridge, Hoover received from Ladd more information about Air Force activities:

> The matter of flying saucers was discussed by Special Agent [name censored] . . . with Major General Joseph F. Carroll of OSI on October 16, 1950, at which time General Carroll advised that insofar as he has been able to determine the Air Force is not working on any type of "flying saucer" or "flying disc." General Carroll stated that the Air Force is working on high altitude rockets and jet aircraft. He stated these experiments may account for some of the reports concerning flying saucers but that the air Force is not apparently working on anything which is the cause of the many flying saucers reports. He stated that the Air Force program for investigating reports concerning flying saucers, etc., has been reinstituted at Wright Field and that any pertinent information of interest coming to his attention will be furnished to the Bureau.

Recall that Maj. Gen. Cabell, Director of AFI, had requested that AMC reinstate the investigation and analysis at ATIC. On September 25, 1950, the Bureau received from Cabell a copy of an intelligence collection memorandum titled: "Reporting of Information on Unconventional Aircraft." This was yet another request to provide sighting information with the added request that "no publicity be given this reporting or analysis activity." The memorandum to Ladd, quoted above, reflected this new activity at ATIC. Once again, in private, the Air Force was contradicting its public stance that saucer sightings were not worthy of attention. In private, the Air Force and the FBI found out that sightings about to occur at Oak Ridge were worthy of attention—a lot of attention.

Recall that in January 1949, Col. Gasser had reported to the FBI that two photos of a UFO had been taken near Oak Ridge in the summer of 1947. That was the *first* Oak Ridge sighting. The second occurred at about noon on May 25, 1949. It was a multiple-witness sighting of a strange flat metallic object passing over the area while making a cracking noise. The third occurred at 7:00 P.M., June 20, 1949. Several people observed three objects, two rectangular in shape and one circular, flying over Oak Ridge. After that, there were no unusual observations until March 1, 1950. At 11:15 P.M., Stuart Adcock, a Knoxville radio amateur with experience in radar technology, called the local FBI agent, Mr. Robey, to report that he had detected an object using a surplus military radar set. The object was circling at an altitude of about 40,000 feet over Oak Ridge. Adcock reported another detection the next day at 11:15 A.M. This time the object was about 100,000 feet up. The Army Counter Intelligence Corps (CIC) and the AFOSI sent representatives to Adcock's house the night of March 2, and at about midnight, they saw radar returns indicating an object at high altitude.

Over the next several days, Adcock's radar occasionally indicated the presence of an object. The local CIC and OSI agents were not radar experts, but it appeared to them that the radar set was not particularly reliable. (To help in the investigation a radar expert was requested, but he didn't arrive until March 8, two days after Adcock had left town.) The local Navy Training Center radar equipment did not detect anything in the area where Adcock reported a radar target, but it was not adapted to detect objects at such a high altitude. A joint experiment was carried out using both Adcock's and the Navy's radar sets. They both detected two aircraft flying at 2,000 feet, indicating that Adcock's radar was working correctly. Adcock's last high-altitude radar detection occurred during the morning of March 6, after which he left town (the reason is unknown). The local OSI agent attempted to contact Adcock, but was not able to and the investigation ended on March 8. There was no conclusion to what, if anything, Adcock had detected. SAC Robey reported to FBI headquarters that the most impressive thing to him had been the "lack of any agency actually taking responsibility for the situation and taking any action to verify or disprove the threat." He also pointed out that it was many hours after the initial detection or "threat" was reported that any action at all was taken. Evidently Oak Ridge was not as well protected against a threat of sabotage as the security agencies had hoped!

Seven months later, at 11:25 P.M. on October 12, a military radar unit at Knoxville Airport suddenly detected eleven, "and possibly more," unidentified targets moving over the restricted flight zone at Oak Ridge. This time action was taken. At 11:30, the radar station commander scrambled an F-82 fighter. Nine minutes later it was in the air. The fighter was vectored toward two targets and, according to the radar, closed with the targets, but the pilot reportedly saw nothing. Ground observations also failed to detect anything in the sky. No unusual objects were seen visually, or on radar, for the next two days. Then, "the dam broke."

On October 15, at 3:25 P.M., three Oak Ridge security guards and a caretaker saw an exceedingly strange object, described as looking like a card with a long thin tail, moving through the atmosphere in the vicinity of the restricted zone. It appeared to carry out controlled maneuvers. The Knoxville radar screen showed some strange targets at the same time as the visual sightings. Again, an aircraft was scrambled and saw nothing. The Project Blue Book master list shows that ATIC could not explain the visual sighting.

The next day, at about 1:30 P.M., John Isabell, a security guard with the Oak Ridge Patrol Force, saw a silver-white spherical object traveling at high altitude from the southwest to the northeast, and passing over the K-25 restricted area. The second sighting on that day occurred at "exactly 2:55 P.M." Isabell and two other members of the patrol force saw the same round object approaching from the northeast at a lower altitude and speed. The object, while spinning about an axis, traveled in a wide circle toward the southwest, and then disappeared. In a couple of minutes, it reappeared in the southwest at a very high altitude and headed northeast at a high rate of speed. The guard phoned the information on the sighting immediately to headquarters where radar picked up an indistinct target every third or fourth sweep over the K-25 area. An F-82 was scrambled. The ground witnesses reported that the fighter plane arrived about fifteen minutes after the object had disappeared. (The ATIC sighting analysts subsequently decided that this object was a balloon in spite of the description of spinning, and the odd flight path.) Later on, during the evening, some of the security guards heard strange, loud noises.

That same day, October 16, the CIC agent decided it was time to review the situation. He wrote a report mentioning the 1947 and 1949 sightings, and discussed the recent sightings. The CIC took these sightings very seriously and thoroughly checked the backgrounds of the witnesses by using employment records and FBI reports in order "to ascertain their reliability, integrity and loyalty to the United States government." There was no reason found to discredit these witnesses, many of whom were professional security guards.

The CIC and the other security agencies discussed the situation and attempted to arrive at some conclusions. The CIC report of these discussions make for amusing reading in view of the concerted attempt later on by ATIC to explain the sightings in any way possible. One gets the impression from the following document that, when it came to explaining UFO sightings as mundane phenomena, the security officials who were involved in the investigations had "been there, done that" and now they were looking for something new and convincing to explain these sightings:

> The opinions of the officials of the Security Division, AEC, Oak Ridge; Security Branch, NEPA Division, Oak Ridge; AEC Security Patrol, Oak Ridge; FBI Knoxville; Air Force Radar and Fighter Squadrons, Knoxville; and the OSI, Knoxville, Tennessee, fail to evolve an adequate explanation for OBJECTS SIGHTED OVER OAK RIDGE, however the

possibilities of practical jokers, mass hysteria, balloons of any description, flights of birds (with or without cobwebs or other objects attached), falling leaves, insect swarms, peculiar weather conditions, reflections, flying kites, objects thrown from the ground, windblown objects, insanity, and many other natural happenings have been rejected because of the simultaneous witnessing of the objects with the reported radar sightings; because of the reliability of the witnesses; because of the detailed, similar description of the objects seen by different persons; and because of impossibility.

Because of "impossibility"? What was that supposed to mean? It meant that all the suggested explanations had been rejected because, in view of the high quality of the witnesses and the descriptive details, these explanations were *impossible*. So, having rejected mundane explanations, what were these objects? The CIC agent continued:

The trend of opinions seem to follow three patterns of thought. The first is that the objects are a physical phenomenon which have a scientific explanation; the second is that the objects are experimental objects [from an undetermined source] guided by electronics and the third is similar to the second except that an intended demoralization or harassment is involved. The fantastic is generally rejected.

These objects have apparently followed only two patterns. The first is that they were sighted at the same hour on two consecutive days and the second is that the time of flight is either to or from the Northeast and Southwest, which directions [are] parallel the terrain ridges in the locality.

The fantastic is generally rejected?
It is not too surprising that "the fantastic" would not be in an official report. However, the fact that it was rejected means that they at least *thought* about "the fantastic." They also showed a healthy degree of skepticism regarding the ATIC treatment of such sightings because they

questioned the ATIC "identification" of the image in the 1947 photographs as a photographic flaw:

> Attention is invited to the 1947 photograph of a flying object. Atomic Energy Commission officials advise that the Air Force Laboratory at Wright Field, Ohio, indicate that the object is a water spot on the photograph. Because this object does not resemble other water spots of the photograph and because the object in the second photograph is following the dim trail left by the first object, some officials at [the] Atomic Energy Commission question the veracity of this statement. They also believe it is significant that the Air Force did not return the negative of this print.

The security agencies were quite correct to be skeptical of the ATIC treatment of these sightings. The Project Blue Book record shows that the radar sightings were identified as "radar peculiarities"; the first October 16 sighting was identified as an aircraft, and the second as a balloon (even though the description of the object was the same for both sightings!). Only the October 15 sighting discussed above was listed as *Unidentified.*

Copies of the reports by the CIC agents were made available to the FBI. When he saw them, Hoover may have wondered if the saucers had now transferred their activities from the West, where atomic bombs were designed, built and stored, to Oak Ridge where the uranium isotope U-235 was being extracted for use in atomic bombs and where nuclear energy was being studied as a possible source for aircraft propulsive power.

Strange noises were also part of the phenomena reported. Maj. Ronniger, a senior instructor at Oak Ridge, reported that at 3:00 P.M. on October 15 he heard a sound like the blast of a jet engine. He and another person searched the sky for an aircraft, but could find none. The next day, several security guards reported that around 8:00 P.M. they heard what sounded like the blast of a jet several times. Each time the noise lasted about three-and-a-half seconds. "The sounds seemed to leave the vicinity making an ascent almost vertical. None of the guards could see an object in the sky."

By October 16, things were already hot at Oak Ridge, but that was only the beginning. Four days later, at 4:55 P.M. on October 20, Larry Riordan, the Superintendent of Security for the X-10 control zone, became a witness. While driving to a residential area, he saw an object he at first thought was a balloon that had lost its "basket." It was generally round, appeared to "come together at the bottom in wrinkles (rather indistinct and something was hanging below." It appeared to be eight to ten feet long and lead or "gun-metal" colored. It didn't seem to be moving but, since he was traveling and only saw it for a number of seconds, he couldn't be sure. He was sure it wasn't a weather balloon, although he thought it might have been a gas-bag balloon launched by the nearby University of Tennessee Agricultural Research Farm. On the same day, at 3:27 P.M., the radar unit at the Knoxville airport detected radar targets near the area of Riordan's sighting, and scrambled a fighter plane. The pilot searched the area for about an hour and a half, which included the time of Riordan's sighting, and found nothing.

Three days later, October 23, at 4:30 P.M., Francis Miller, an Oak Ridge laboratory employee, while driving along a road in Oak Ridge, saw an object that appeared to be less than half a mile away, and between 1,000 and 2,000 feet up. It appeared as an "aluminum flash" that was traveling in a south-southeast direction. He only saw it for a few seconds. Subsequently it was discovered that a nuclear radiation detection station (a Geiger counter) in the vicinity of the sighting registered a burst of alpha and beta radiation. The purpose of this station was to detect any leaks of radiation from the Oak Ridge laboratory. There was no leakage of radiation, however. An expert from the Health and Research Division analyzed the readings from the Geiger counter and pronounced them unexplained. This association between radiation detection and a UFO sighting was similar to that at Mt. Palomar, mentioned in chapter 13. Whether the reading of the Geiger counter was actually a result of nuclear radiation or whether the presence of the UFO induced a transient electrical fault in the counter, or whether there was some other explanation, is not known. This case does not appear in the Project Blue Book file.

During the evening of October 24, there was a "light in the sky" sighting by two witnesses who were at widely separated locations. The first to see it was Mr. William Fry, the Assistant Chief of Security for Project NEPA. He was at a drive-in theater with his family at about 6:45 P.M. waiting for the movie to begin, when he saw the lighted object in the southwest while casually looking around the sky. He reported later to the CIC investigator:

> . . . I observed what I at first thought to be an unusually bright star. The exceptional brilliance caused me to continue to observe it when it suddenly seemed to change color rapidly from a reddish hue to a bright orange and again to a brilliant light blue. [His wife and son also saw it.] . . . A few moments later I heard a plane directly overhead making passes over the Oak Ridge area, which was later identified as one of the F-82 fighter planes from the Air Force unit stationed at McGhee-Tyson Airport . . .
>
> [At this point Fry went to a phone and called someone to look, but the person could not see it because of the hills and trees.] While returning to my car I met a friend . . . who stated he had been observing the object. I continued to observe the object with my wife but it seemed to be in a more northerly position which caused me to select a fixed point to determine whether or not the object was changing in either direction or altitude. There seemed to be a deviation from north to south for approximately five to ten degrees. The changing colors were still very evident but the object seemed to be continually getting smaller and smaller as though it was becoming more distant. At approximately 7:18 by my watch it disappeared from view entirely. During these observations my wife continued to report to me the identical things that I was observing. During the entire time the F-82 airplane continued to make passes over the area until approximately 7:15. The weather conditions were excellent; the air was calm; and the sky was cloudless with the exception of a very slight haze over the distant horizon.

The following morning, upon reporting to work I confided my story to [name censored] stationed at Oak Ridge with the NEPA project, but I hesitated to go on record as having observed such an unidentified object.

Fry did go on record because he learned that he was not the only witness. Air Force Maj. Lawrence Ballweg also saw the light. Maj. Ballweg reported:

On the evening of 24 October 1950 at approximately 1855 [6:55 P.M.] I heard a plane fly over my home in the Woodland area. Being a curious individual I went outdoors to watch it with my binoculars. While looking for the plane I saw an object in the western sky which appeared at first to be a star but upon closer observation I noticed that it was rapidly changing colors from red to blue to white. When first seen, it appeared to be moving very slowly in a northwest direction. It was moving relative to the other stars. The object was too small to be able to see any details even with the glasses. It disappeared from sight about 1920 [7:20 P.M.]. During this period of time, my wife also observed the object.

Fry then learned that the radar unit had also detected something. He was told that an unidentified object appeared at 6:30 P.M. at an altitude of approximately 5,000 feet in the same general vicinity as the object he saw. The radar target disappeared at 7:20 P.M. The complete radar report to the CIC investigator says that targets appeared at 6:23 P.M. moving over the restricted flight zone, and at 6:26 a fighter was scrambled to the target area, but failed to see anything.

Considering that the atmosphere can make a star or planet within a few degrees of the horizon appear to change color and move very slightly or twinkle, one might be tempted to identify the light as the bright planet Venus, or a very bright star seen in the west an hour after sunset, which was at about 6:00 P.M. local daylight savings time. However, two elements of the description reject this explanation. First, the light was described by

Maj. Ballweg as moving relative to the stars. Since Ballweg used binoculars to view the light, it is likely that his description of motion is accurate. Furthermore, it must have been quite large because Fry, not using binoculars, also detected motion. Second, Ballweg said that the light appeared over a telephone pole that was about 100 yards away. That would make the angular elevation greater than five degrees. According to the CIC investigator, Fry indicated that the elevation from his location was thirty to forty degrees above horizontal. Hence, it was so high in angular elevation that atmospheric effects would not make it appear to change color and there would be no noticeable effects other than the normal twinkling, which affects stars at any angular elevation. The final reason for rejecting Venus or a bright star is that Venus was below the horizon at the time and there were no excessively bright stars in that sector of the sky at the time. The disappearance of the radar target at the same time as the light suggests that the UFO was a some kind of metallic unknown object hovering in the vicinity of Oak Ridge. This is another Oak Ridge sighting that is not in the Blue Book file, nor are the following October events.

About six hours later, between 2:00 A.M. and 3:00 A.M., October 25, the radar unit reported several slowly moving objects such as had been seen previously. On October 26 at 5:00 A.M. Col. Edwin Thompson heard an intermittent noise, like the blast of a jet, similar to what had been reported on October 15 and 16. He saw no aircraft associated with the noise. Three days later, seven people waiting at the Knoxville Airport "saw an object traveling to the southwest at a great rate of speed. [name censored], who has considerable flying experience, was extremely excited and stated that this object was not an aircraft. He described it as a circular object, leaving a trail of smoke."

There were two reported sightings on November 5. At 9:29 A.M. an object was detected on radar traveling over the restricted area at a speed of eighty mph. A fighter aircraft attempted an intercept, and then trailed the object for twenty miles. The pilot reported no visual contact. Two- and-a-half hours later, at 11:55 A.M., Don Patrick of the NEPA Division saw a very strangely shaped object travel by, apparently just above the mountain range. It seemed to change rapidly from a pear-shape to a bean-shape and other sausage-like shapes as it traveled. Although the shape changed, the overall size was about constant. It seemed translucent but had definite out-lined edges as seen against the sky and background clouds. There was no particular color, and there were no bright highlights. Patrick at first thought it was a balloon but then realized that the shape changes and rapid motions meant it was something else. He told the CIC investigator that "the core [dark triangular portion] remained constant and the apex of the core varied only a few degrees while the body of the object seemed to change shapes rapidly and would become elongated during a quick move-ment of the object." Project Blue Book files list this sighting as unidentified.

As part of the CIC agent's attempts to explain these sightings, he asked Mr. J. Holland, chief of the Weather Section of the AEC at Oak Ridge, to provide information on balloon launches at the times of the sightings. There was no correlation. The only sighting that could have been a balloon was the October 20 sighting, and even that was not correlated with the Weather Section data. With regard to the radar detections during the pre-vious month, Holland said radar can be reflected from patches of ionized air and, if a large quantity of radioactive material were released, it might provide sufficient ionization of the air. However, he didn't believe any such release had occurred. According the CIC agent's report, the Weather Sec-tion would carry out research to determine whether or not "radioactive energy ejections" could cause radar returns. There is no report on the results of the radar research.

Between 5:00 and 11:00 P.M. on November 29, radar targets returned to the Oak Ridge area. Fighters were scrambled. They saw nothing. However, at 7:00 P.M., during this period of radar sightings, graphic records of Geiger counter detections in the restricted area of Oak Ridge indicated an abnormal increase in alpha and gamma radiation that could not be attributed to a known source. Apparently this was "too much" for the officials in charge of Oak Ridge security. They held a two-day meeting to discuss the "operational difficulties" of the early warning radar of the Air Defense Command at Knoxville. AFI was asked to inves-tigate the situation and to set up a separate radar set for comparison.

The suggestion that some radar targets might be the result of ioniza-tion of the air by nuclear radiation must have been on the mind of Mr. Gray, SAC Knoxville, because on December 4 he called FBI headquarters and speculated that releases of radioactive material could have caused the anomalous radar targets observed. The next day Hoover sent an urgent teletype to SAC Knoxville: "Arrangements should be made to obtain all facts concerning possible radar jamming by ionization of particles in the atmosphere. Conduct appropriate investigation to determine whether incident occurring northeast of Oliver Springs, Tennessee, could have had any connection with alleged radar jamming." Unfortunately any information that might have been available on the "Oliver Springs" case has not been released. Nor is there any response to Hoover's teletype message.

On December 5 and 6, there was a discussion of the technical aspects of the radar sightings with ATIC and intelligence officials. They concluded that the targets were probably "radar angels," which are reflections of objects on the ground observed only because of a temperature inversion that bends the radar radiation downward. On the other hand, that did not mean that there were no flying saucers around. At about 12:50 P.M., December 5, the wife of one of the security officers saw an unusual object north of her position, flying apparently over the Post Office building in Oak Ridge. It appeared to be a couple of miles away, and 500 feet above the ground. It appeared to be made of highly polished aluminum or metal that reflected the sun. Its shape was round and flat, or disk-like. She saw the object for about a minute as it flew in a direct course eastward. Ten minutes later, another woman at a different location observed the same, or a similar, object heading westward. The OSI agent who investigated this case learned that there was an east wind at six mph and a clear sky. No balloons had been launched near that time. He also learned that there were two aircraft airborne at the time, but both were about fourteen miles south of the witnesses. ATIC subsequently claimed that the witnesses saw an aircraft.

Although ATIC would eventually claim that most of these events were mundane (radar anomalies, balloons, aircraft) and leave only two of the Oak Ridge sightings unidentified, the local military officials and scientists were not so certain of easy identifications. They planned to begin their own scientific investigation. Lt. Col. John Hood, the AMC Field Engineering Officer, outlined the plan in a December 5 memorandum titled "Technical Approaches to the Problems of UFOs." He proposed placing radiation counters over a wide area. After there had been sufficient anomalous object reports to establish a pattern, the data recorded by these counters would then be compared for time and location with the sightings "to see if any change in the background [radiation] occurs with the presence of sighted objects." He also proposed that portable counters be made available and taken to the area of a sighting. Along with the counters, he proposed that an aircraft with Geiger counters, and also a magnetometer, be made available. The magnetometer would indicate any fluctuations in the local magnetic field associated with sightings. He also proposed more accurate radars, capable of measuring height as well as range and azimuth. This plan was to begin operating near the end of December.

The next anomalous event in the Oak Ridge area was yet another appearance of radar targets that "blanketed the radar scopes in the area directly over the government Atomic energy Commission projects . . . these objects could not be identified from the radar image and a perfect fighter interception met with negative results."

The last Oak Ridge sighting of any consequence occurred at about 8:30 A.M. on December 18. Groups of people, in separate cars traveling to work, saw an unusual object fly over the Oak Ridge area. To the Air Force officers in one of the cars, it appeared as would a bright reflection from a very distant aircraft. It was southwest of them and they only saw it for a few seconds. At the same time, several other NEPA project employees were in another car at a different location. They saw this object for about thirty seconds before it was obscured by the nearby hills. They described it as a bright circular light with an intensity greater than that of the full moon. It was between fifteen and thirty degrees above the horizon as it moved in a northwesterly direction. They observed a strange effect on the circular light: it seemed to "darken, starting at approximately 7:00 to 9:00 o'clock along the perimeter and continuing to darken along the perimeter and inner area until the light was concentrated in approximately 1:00 to 3:00 o'clock position of a very small diameter, at which point it appeared somewhat similar to a large star."

About the time that Col. Hood's research plan was to be put into effect, the last two Oak Ridge sightings occurred. These were on December 20 and January 16. The December 20 case was another radar-only event (no visual contact), and the January 16 sighting involved sightings of stars. The Oak Ridge flap was over. There were no further sightings, until a single one in the late fall of 1951. By that time, the research project had effectively died. Thus, as happened with Project Twinkle in New Mexico, just as the local scientists and security agencies were about to carry out precise research that could prove the UFOs were real anomalous objects—they disappeared!

In retrospect, although it might be possible that some of the radar detections were weather anomalies, often called "radar angels," caused by temperature inversions in the atmosphere, the visual sightings cannot be so easily dismissed.

CHAPTER 17

Immediate High Alert: For Flying Saucers

One of the most important documents about secret activities of the Air Force in the early years was written in November 1950. It did not involve the FBI, but it is important because it provides further support for the idea that the government has been covering up conclusive evidence of an extraterrestrial reality.

It should be apparent from previous chapters that the Air Force appeared to take a two-faced or "split-personality" approach to the UFO problem. Sometimes an Air Force representative would tell the FBI or the general public that there was nothing to UFO sightings, and there was no research being conducted. At other times, an Air Force representative would tell the FBI, *but not the general public,* that investigations were ongoing because the sightings around "vital installations" and military bases were important enough to require continued attention.

During this period of time, roughly twenty percent of the sightings were unidentified according to Project Blue Book Special Report #14, written in 1953. (Of course the Air Force didn't tell anyone that fact.) There were only three classes of phenomena that could explain the unidentified sightings (natural phenomena having been ruled out):

extraterrestrial craft, man-made missiles (Soviet), or "mass hysteria." The staff at ATIC rejected the ET possibility in spite of any strong evidence they might have because they felt that "extraterrestrial" was not an acceptable explanation. The ATIC staff did not believe that Soviet missiles could be responsible for the unexplained sightings. The only remaining phenomenon was "mass hysteria" caused by the societal tensions of the time. This was the conclusion stated in the May 1950 ATIC document that responded to Capt. Rickenbacker's public statement (see chapter 14). On the other hand, the "mass hysteria" explanation was not particularly "tasteful" either because it implied that Air Force and commercial pilots were in a "hysterical" state whenever they reported unidentified flying objects. Rejection of the mass hysteria hypothesis threw the explanation back to the previous two, or to a fourth possibility, which was that the unexplained sightings could have been explained *if there had been more information.* Accepting this fourth possibility was equivalent to saying that even the twenty percent unidentified could be explained, *but without having to specify exactly how.*

The FBI heard this "non-explanation," as well as the "man-made missile" explanation for saucer sightings, from the lower brass (colonels and below) at the Pentagon. But at the Top Secret, Special Access level, the story was different.

Enter one Wilbert B. Smith, a scientist working for the Canadian Department of Transport. He had a Master's of Science in electrical engineering, and had set up a network of stations in Canada to measure changes in the ionosphere, which is important for long-range radio transmission. When he first heard of flying saucers, which were reported in Canada as well as the United States (and most other countries), he began to toy with the idea that these were craft that made use of the earth's magnetic field for propulsion. By the fall of 1950, he had concluded that the saucers were probably small extraterrestrial craft that came to Earth from a large "mothership" in orbit around the Earth at some great distance.

Smith did classified work for the Canadian Department of Transport, and had a Top Secret clearance. In September he attended an electronics conference in Washington, D.C., just after reading the books by Donald

Keyhoe and Frank Scully. During his visit to Washington, according to his own records, he made contact, through the Canadian Embassy, with an American missile control expert, Dr. Robert Sarbacher. Smith wanted to know what the United States was doing with respect to the flying saucer mystery. Dr. Sarbacher had done military research during the Second World War, but by 1950 he no longer worked for the government. However, as a "dollar-a-year-man" who still had his clearance for classified material, he was an unpaid consultant to researchers at Wright-Patterson Air Force Base. The WPAFB researchers told him about some of the developments in flying saucer research. In handwritten notes dated September 15, 1950, Smith recalled that Dr. Sarbacher told him: (a) flying saucers exist, and the facts regarding crashed saucers in Scully's book are substantially correct; (b) they did not originate from Earth; and (c) the subject of saucers is classified higher than the hydrogen bomb, which was the most highly classified publicly known research program at that time. Two months later, on November 21, Smith wrote a Top Secret memorandum for the Canadian Department of Transport in which he suggested doing research into the possibility of obtaining power from the Earth's magnetic field, and also suggested the possibility that "our work in geomagnetics might well be the linkage between our technology and the technology by which the saucers are designed and operated." Smith then summarized his conversation with Sarbacher as follows: (1) the matter is classified more highly than the H-bomb; (2) saucers exist; (3) their "modus operandi" is unknown, but a small group "headed by Dr. Vannevar Bush" is attempting to determine how they work; and (4) the matter of flying saucers is considered to be of great significance.

Considering that this information from Smith is found in a formerly Top Secret document released in the late 1970s by the Canadian government, it must be taken seriously. Several UFO investigators interviewed Dr. Sarbacher in the early 1980s before died. I was one of those investigators. He told me that, although he had never seen a saucer himself, he did know some engineers who worked at Wright-Patterson AFB in the late 1940s, and they told him there was *wreckage and bodies!* Furthermore he told me he had gained the impression from their descriptions that these creatures were lightweight and composed somewhat like

Dr. Vannevar Bush (left) and Dr. John von Neumann (right), who were involved in saucer research.

insects. He said he did not know why the subject was still secret in the 1980s. He also recalled that Dr. Vannevar Bush, Dr. John von Neumann, and Dr. Robert Oppenheimer were among the scientists working on the saucer problem. These men were, of course, top scientists of the day, with Bush being "the top of the top" as far as political connections were concerned, having organized virtually all of the U.S. military research carried out during the Second World War.

According to Smith and Sarbacher, at the Top Secret level, flying saucers were considered very important. The following teletype message found in the FBI file further indicates the level of importance that the intelligence community sometimes attached to saucer sightings. Recall that on December 5, Hoover sent a teletype message in which he asked SAC Knoxville to investigate "radar jamming" at Oak Ridge (see the previous chapter). Then, three days later, FBI headquarters received the following message from SAC Richmond, Virginia:

URGENT. DECEMBER 8. RE: FLYING SAUCERS.

This office very confidentially advised by Army Intelligence, Richmond, that they have been put on immediate high alert for any data whatsoever concerning flying saucers. CIC here states background of instructions not available from Air Force Intelligence, who are not aware of reason for alert locally, but any information whatsoever must be telephoned by them immediately to Air Force Intelligence. CIC advises data strictly confidential and should not be diseminated [sic].

How very strange for the Counter Intelligence Corps to be put on immediate high alert for any data regarding objects/phenomena/craft that ATIC claimed can all be explained, and are no threat to the security of the United States! Are we to presume the CIC has nothing better to do than to run around chasing "will o' the wisps" and similar ethereal things of *no consequence to national defense?* Of course not! This teletype message proves that Air Force Intelligence at the Pentagon, which requested the immediate high alert, considered the subject of flying saucers to be important—*very important*—contrary to the publicized ATIC opinion.

And well they might, because saucers and other unexplained phenomena had been reported numerous times near vital installations. This teletype also shows that AFI treated its interest in utmost confidence. The existence of an alert was strictly confidential and not for dissemination. One gets the impression that merely by telling the FBI of the alert, the local CIC agent was breaking security. Further evidence of the level of secrecy is the fact that AFI had not informed the CIC agent of the reason for the alert, and *even the local AFI agent, who told the CIC agent, didn't know the reason.* Apparently the reason for the alert was only known to the Top Brass who had a Top Secret/Special Access/Need-to-Know level of clearance for classified information.*

The existence of this teletype message raises at least two related questions: why an immediate high alert, and why on December 8? Neither of these questions can be definitely answered at the present time because the CIC and AFI records relating to this simply have not been found, even after a search of CIC records by the Army Security agency. However, I speculate that it was related to the possible crash of a flying saucer

---

* In order to do their jobs, the local agents, who also had Top Secret clearances, didn't need to know *why* AFI Headquarters wanted information; they only needed to know *that* AFI wanted information.

just south of the Texas-Mexico border on or about December 6, 1950, or that it might be related to a strange incident that almost led to a *declaration of national emergency on December 6!* The reason for the first conjecture is based on the testimony of a retired Air Force colonel who said that a flying saucer was detected by radar and then tracked as it flew over Texas, and then crashed just south of the Mexican border. Of course, there is nothing about this in the Project Blue Book file, just as there is nothing on the 1947 Roswell crash case in the Blue Book file. However, there were sightings on December 6 which are in the Blue Book file: one at Westover Air Force Base in Massachusetts, and one at Fort Myers, Florida. The latter case is listed as unidentified.

The story behind the odd incident that did cause the United States Defense Department to go into heightened state of alert during the morning of December 6 is not completely known but the available information is intriguing. While reading the following, keep in mind that the global political situation was much less settled than it is these days. Russia and China were becoming potent adversaries with the stated purpose of overthrowing the capitalist democracies. The war in Korea was viewed as the first real military contest between communism and capitalism, and it was not going well for the United States and South Korea. Ever since the beginning of the war, six months earlier, the U.S. government had been worried about the Chinese response to the United Nations attempts to preserve the independence of South Korea. These worries increased after Gen. MacArthur landed at Inchon in September, and succeeded in driving the North Korean army back across the 38th parallel (the agreed-upon northern boundary of South Korea). In October and November, U.N. troops pushed into North Korea under MacArthur's orders to destroy the North Korean army. Finally, on November 25, the Chinese counterattacked with about 200,000 men, a number which doubled over the next month. United Nations forces, numbered at about one half the Chinese force, were once again in danger of complete defeat. This was causing a near-panic situation in the States. President Truman was worried about the possibility that the war would widen, even bringing on World War III, which may have necessitated a nuclear response. The Joint Chiefs of Staff (the "top brass" of all the armed services) had sent a warning to U.S. forces commanders throughout the world of a heightened possibility for world war. It was during these parlous and frightening times that a large group of "unidentified aircraft" were detected approaching the United States from the north!

There are three published versions of what happened during the morning of December 6. The first version comes from the autobiography of Secretary of State Dean Acheson, *Present at the Creation.*† The second version, published in *The Wise Men* by Walter Isaacson and Evan Thomas, is based in an interview with Acheson.‡ It differs slightly from Acheson's own version. The third is in *Memoirs of Harry S. Truman: Years of Trial and Hope 1946–1952.*§ Looking first at Secretary Acheson's autobiography, we find that on the morning of December 6:

> ... soon after my arrival at the [State] Department, Deputy Secretary of Defense Lovett telephoned a report and an instruction from the President. Our early warning radar system in Canada had picked up formations of unidentified objects, presumably aircraft, headed southeast on a course that could bring them over Washington in two or three hours. All interception and defense forces were alerted. I was to inform but not advise the Prime Minister [Clement Atlee of Britain]. The Pentagon telephones would be closed for all but emergency defense purposes and he could not talk again. Before he hung up, I asked whether he believed that the objects that were picked up were Russian bombers. He said that he did not. Getting Oliver Franks on the telephone, I repeated the message. He asked whether the President had canceled the eleven-thirty meeting with Atlee, and was told that he had not. We agreed to meet there. Before ending the talk, he wondered about the purpose of my message. I suggested fair warning and an opportunity for prayer. As we finished, one of our senior officials burst into the room.

† W.W. Norton, NY; 1969; pages 479–480.
‡ Simon and Shuster, NY; 1986; pages 544–545.
§ Doubleday, NY; 1956; Vol. 2, page 405.

How he had picked up the rumor I do not know, perhaps from the Pentagon. He wanted to telephone his wife to get out of town, and to have important files moved to the basement. I refused to permit him to do either and gave him the choice of a word-of-honor commitment not to mention the matter to anyone or being put under security detention. He wisely cooled off and chose the former. When we reached the White House, Lovett told us that the unidentified objects had disappeared. His guess was that they had been geese.

There are several important points to keep in mind as you read the following versions of what happened. Acheson said that "early warning radar in Canada" had detected "formations" (plural) of "unidentified objects, presumably aircraft" which were headed "southeast" in a direction that could put them over Washington, D.C., in two to three hours. Using an estimated top speed of 300 mph for Soviet bombers, this would put them a mere 600 to 900 miles from Washington. Acheson ended his story by saying that, after he arrived at the White House, that is at about 11:30 A.M., Defense Undersecretary Lovett told him he thought that the objects had turned out to be geese.

The next version of the story, told in *The Wise Men,* is based on an interview with Acheson:

> For a moment on the morning of December 6, he thought his nightmare [of world war] had come true. At 10:30 A.M. Bob Lovett called him from the Pentagon and abruptly informed him in his laconic voice: "When I finish talking to you, you cannot reach me again. All incoming calls will be stopped. A national emergency is about to be proclaimed. We are informed that there is flying over Alaska at the present moment a formation of Russian planes heading southeast. The President wishes the British ambassador to be informed of this and be told that Attlee should take whatever measures are proper for Attlee's safety. I've now finished my message and I'm going to ring off." Acheson cut in, "Now wait a minute, Bob, do you believe this?" "No," Lovett replied, and

hung up. Acheson sat in his office and waited. The Air Force scrambled. A senior official burst in asking permission to telephone his wife to get out of town and wondering if he should begin moving files to the basement. Acheson tried to soothe him. A few minutes later Lovett calmly called back. The radar blips were not Soviet bombers after all. They were flocks of geese.

This version makes it seem that the alert period was very short, only a few minutes. However, by combining the information in this version about the beginning time, 10:30 A.M., with the information in Acheson's biography about the ending time (after Acheson arrived at the White House), about 11:30 A.M., we find that the alert lasted about an hour. This version is more specific as to where the objects were: they were detected over Alaska, which is over 3,000 miles from Washington, D. C. If that were true it would have taken much more than ten hours for the planes to arrive over Washington. President Truman wrote about the same episode:

> Shortly before we went into that morning meeting, Under Secretary Lovett called from the Pentagon, reporting that the radar screens of some air defense installations in the far north were reporting large formations of unidentified planes approaching. Fighter planes were sent up to reconnoiter and alerts were flashed to air centers in New England and beyond. But about an hour later—while I was meeting with [Clement] Attlee-Lovett notified me that the report had been in error. Some unusual disturbance in the Arctic atmosphere had thrown the radar off.

President Truman's version of the event suggests that the objects may have been detected north of the eastern United States rather than over Alaska. The fact that fighter aircraft were scrambled indicates that this alert was treated as a serious event by the Continental Air Command. Truman's explanation is somewhat different from Acheson's. Here we learn that the radar detections were caused by some sort of atmospheric disturbance.

President Harry S. Truman was informed about the "High Alert" situation in December 1950.

An unpublished version of this event is found in the official transcript of the meeting between Truman and Atlee, which is preserved at the Truman library:

> At this point [in the meeting] Mr. Connelly entered the room and handed the President a report from Deputy Secretary of Defense Lovett. Mr. Lovett was reporting that the "alert" that had reached the President an hour earlier when it was thought that a large number of unidentified airplanes were approaching the northeast coast of the United States, had now been due to erroneous interpretation of atmospheric conditions. The President informed the Prime Minister that the report of the planes was in error. The Prime Minister expressed relief and gratification.

This version, based on notes made at the time rather than upon memories years afterward, says the unidentified objects were approaching the northeast coast of the United States, clearly contradicting Acheson's assertion that they were detected over Alaska—unless, of course, there were *two* groups of objects. Furthermore, this version indicates Lovett was the source of the "atmospheric effects" explanation mentioned by President Truman. But Lovett was also the source of the "geese" explanation reported by Acheson. So, which explanation was right? Or was neither correct?

A report carried by the International News Service reported yet another explanation:

> Washington D.C., 6 December 1950 (INS): A warning of an impending air attack resulted in a false alarm in this capitol city today. No air raid alarms were sounded, but functionaries charged with the Civil Air Defense of Washington were alerted that an unidentified aircraft had been detected off the coast of the State of Maine at mid-day. Later, a spokesman for the Air Force stated that interceptor aircraft had been dispatched , and that the object in question had been identified shortly thereafter as a North American C-47 aircraft which was approaching the continent from Goose Bay, Labrador. The warning was said to have been useful in verifying the efficiency of the Washington Civil Defense System. Civil Defense officials declined to comment on the incident.

This report, supposedly based on an Air Force statement, says the radar target was from a single aircraft approaching from a location near Goose Bay, Labrador. It says nothing about Alaska.

It appears that this supposed attack did have repercussions in Alaska. The *New York Times* published a story with a December 7, Anchorage, Alaska, dateline reporting:

> All military personnel in Alaska were called on "alert" tonight, but Air Force officials said that the order was purely a "precautionary measure." Military police rounded up soldiers and theatres and radio stations made special announcements that troops were to return to their posts. Within a few hours there were no military personnel to be seen on Anchorage streets. Officials at Elmendorf Air Force Base said the alert had been in effect since the outbreak of the fighting

194 · Immediate High Alert: For Flying Saucers

in Korea. But they added that the air force had increased its vigilance here in recent days.

Further evidence of the official "jitters" is in the statement in the *Washington Post* on December 10 that "President Truman is 'seriously considering declaration of national emergency' which could lead to an 'immediate all-out mobilization.'"

Flocks of geese? Arctic atmospheric effects? A single C-47 aircraft? Or something else? Not until 1987 was further information on this event released by the Air Force, and sparse information at that. On December 6, Air Force Col. Charles Winkle, Assistant Executive in the Directorate for Plans, wrote a memorandum for Secretary of Defense George Marshall about the event. It confirms the alert:

SUBJECT: Air Alert - 1030 Hours,
6 December 1950

1. The ConAC [Continental Air Command] Air Defense Controller notified the Headquarters USAF Command Post that at 1030 hours a number of unidentified aircraft were approaching the northeast area of the United States and that there was no reason to believe the aircraft were friendly.

2. This information was further amplified at 1040 hours as follows. By radar contact it was determined that approximately 40 aircraft were in flight, at 32,000 feet, on a course of 200 degrees in the vicinity of Limestone, Maine.

3. The emergency alert procedure went into effect immediately.

4. The Office of the President was notified. Brigadier General Landry returned the call and stated that the President had been notified and that:

   a. All information in this matter was to be released by the Department of the Air Force.

   b. Office of the President would release no information.

   c. The substance of a and b above was to be passed to the Office of the Secretary of Defense.

5. At 1104 hours the ConAC Air Defense Controller state that the original track had faded out and it appeared that the flight as originally identified is a friendly flight.

6. ConAC took immediate action to dispatch interceptors on the initial contact.

The technical information in this document is sparse, but there are details that call into question all of the previous explanations. By combining the information from these various sources, I estimate that these objects were first detected in the direction of Goose Bay, Labrador (which is about 500 miles north-northeast of Limestone, Maine). Their distance when first detected might have been close to the 200-mile limit of the capability of the search radar in Maine. The radar operators then tracked these objects for ten minutes and determined that they were traveling south-southwestward (a course of 200 degrees). This course would take them over the eastern United States. They must have appeared, or "painted," as convincingly solid, moving targets on the radar screen. If they were detected 200 miles from Limestone and ten minutes later reached "the vicinity" of Limestone, the speed would have been nearly 1,200 mph; if detected at 100 miles, the speed would have been nearly 600 mph. Even this lower speed would be much too fast for the Soviet bombers of those days (with a top speed of about 300 mph).

The statement that there was "no reason to believe the aircraft were friendly" means that the Continental Air Command officials were not able to identify the aircraft from a known flight plan, nor were they able to communicate with the aircraft by radio. Ten minutes after the initial detection the radar operators had determined that there were forty objects at an altitude of about 32,000 feet. Evidently the radar images were so good that the operators were certain that these objects were unidentifiable yet solid targets, presumably aircraft, flying at a high altitude. This is decidedly different from what the operators would have concluded had the radar showed relatively slow-moving geese, or atmospheric effects, or a single C-47. Geese, C-47s, and atmospheric effects don't travel at 600 mph.

According to Winkle's document the radar track "faded out" at 11:04 A.M., or about twenty minutes after the objects were near Limestone. If the objects had continued on the 200-degree course at the same speed—for example at 600 mph—they would have been beyond the range of Limestone radar, which would explain the fading of the track.

The strangest statement in the document is: "it appears that the flight as originally identified is a friendly flight." What does that mean, "*it appears*"? Didn't they know for certain? Didn't they track the "friendly aircraft" until they were positive? Are we to believe that they scrambled aircraft and put the U.S. into a state of *immediate high alert,* and then weren't able to positively identify the aircraft?

One would expect if there had been upwards of forty friendly aircraft coming from the north toward the U.S. border, someone would have been aware of it. There would have been a flight plan. At the very least, these aircraft would have acknowledged the attempts to contact them by radio, attempts that must have been made numerous times, starting with the first detection by radar. Either the flight plan or the radio identification would have been passed to the local commanders of the Continental Air Command aircraft to prevent needless scrambling of aircraft.

If they were friendly aircraft, why did Undersecretary of Defense Robert Lovett tell Dean Acheson that flocks of geese flying over Alaska caused the radar targets? Why did Undersecretary Lovett tell the President that arctic atmospheric conditions caused the radar targets? Why did the Air Force tell the press that a single C-47 caused the entire high alert?

Presumably these were the explanations offered by the Top Brass after being told the details by the people who were directly involved with the radar detections and the scramble. Was the Top Brass embarrassed by the initial misidentification of a "friendly flight," and afraid to admit it? (I doubt that.) Or did Top Brass tell the President and the Undersecretary of Defense what these targets really were, but these gentlemen, for some reason, when writing about it years later, still could not reveal the exact nature of these objects to anyone else?

There must be other Air Force documents not yet released that clarify the December 6 situation. However, based on the information available in this document, combined with the fact that CIC was put on *immediate high alert for flying saucer information only two days later,* I can suggest another explanation. *The radar targets were flying saucers.*

One ominous implication of these events was that we, or the Soviets, might have failed to immediately identify groups of flying saucers and, thinking an attack was imminent, scramble atomic bomb-carrying aircraft, *thereby accidentally starting a war!* I suspect that this possibility was not overlooked by the highest government officials.

The failure of the Air Force to immediately identify unknown aircraft in other incidents was to play an important role in the involvement of the Central Intelligence Agency with saucer sightings a year and a half later.

CHAPTER 18
I've Been Lied To

The FBI's "X-File" has few entries for the year 1951, probably because this was a "down" year for UFO sightings. The Project Blue Book master list has 240 sightings in 1950, but only 171 in 1951.

In January 1951, the FBI added to its file a copy of a *Look* magazine article based on interviews with ATIC director, Col. Harold Watson. Recall that Col. Watson was the person who had virtually shut down Project Grudge in 1949. He did this in spite of orders from Gen. Cabell to carry out a good investigation. Perhaps he downplayed Project Grudge because it was poorly funded. Perhaps he just thought that saucer investigation was a waste of time. For whatever reason, during the interviews Col. Watson followed the "party line": all sightings were explainable, and saucer investigation was a waste of time.

The magazine article, "The Disgraceful Flying Saucer Hoax," by Robert Considine, didn't give UFO witnesses an even break. It characterized them as "true believers," "members of the lunatic fringe," "gagsters," and "screwballs," and claimed that the sighting reports were a result of "Cold War jitters," "mass hysteria," hallucinations," and "mirages." This was like a recycling of Shallett's article almost two years before.

The FBI memorandum that mentions this article indicates that it was filed "for information purposes." One can only imagine what the FBI officials thought about this article after what they had been through in the previous two years, with the frightening information from Col. Gasser, the sightings in New Mexico, and the sightings over Oak Ridge. To add to the confusion, during the month after Considine's article, *Time* magazine carried an article by Navy scientist Dr. Urner Liddel, in which he claimed that all credible sightings were Skyhook balloons. This was followed by several newspaper articles in which Dr. Anthony Mirarchi rebutted Liddel and said the saucers were Russian missiles (see chapter 15).

The only FBI teletype message about a sighting in 1951 was received at FBI headquarters on September 20. It discussed an important series of radar and pilot sightings at Fort Monmouth, New Jersey. These sightings, which occurred on September 10 and 11, involved radar detections of objects that could alternately hover or move at high speed. Not mentioned in the FBI teletype is the report of a pilot in a training aircraft who saw a UFO moving in the area at the same time. There is no evidence that the FBI responded in any way to these events. However, the Air Force certainly did respond, and in a big way. In fact, as a result of immediate top level interest, these sightings played an important role in the history of the Air Force UFO project.

You may recall that, about a year earlier, Maj. Gen. Cabell, the Director of Air Force Intelligence, had ordered a revitalization of Project Grudge. He delegated the responsibility for sighting analysis to Col. Harold Watson, a former test pilot, who was the director of Project Grudge. Cabell was serious about discovering the real nature of UFOs. He told Col. Watson and Watson's second-in-command, Col. Frank Dunn, that he, Cabell, was to be notified immediately when a major sighting occurred. Unfortunately Watson and the Grudge staff did not take this job seriously. When the report of sightings at Fort Monmouth arrived at Project Grudge, Watson did not even tell Gen. Cabell. Nevertheless, they assumed that the general would want an explanation so they tried to think of a good one. From the teletype messages they learned that the sightings had taken place at a radar school. They assumed the radar operators were unskilled and the pilot was inexperienced. Based on these assumptions, the Project Grudge staff concluded the sightings were errors caused by lack of experience. This satisfied Watson, so he planned to eventually give this answer to Cabell. Unfortunately for Col. Watson, the news media learned of the sightings, and on September 28 they were featured in the national press. This was how Cabell learned of the sightings. He was very angry that he had not been informed and he wanted an immediate briefing on the investigation. Of course, there had been no investigation, so Watson immediately dispatched two of the Grudge staff to Fort Monmouth. This was something they never did, but to pacify the general they tried to make it look as if they had planned an investigation all along ("Yes, General. Of course we were planning to go there, General.").

Two members of the ATIC staff immediately flew to Fort Monmouth. While there they learned that Gen. Cabell expected a briefing immediately after they completed the investigation. They interviewed the radar operators and the pilot and passenger in the aircraft. The evidence seemed strong that a real UFO was involved, rather than atmospheric effects or inexperience. Hence they were not pleased that the press had been allowed to interview a pilot and publish a story on the sightings because: (a) many people thought UFOs were from outer space and ATIC didn't want the fact of project interest in the sightings to cause any alarm, (b) Col. Watson wanted to keep a low profile in the hopes that if "you stuck your head deep enough into the sand" the problem would go away, and (c) Col. Watson had told the press that the project had been closed in the hope that the press would lose interest in the subject of UFOs. (Gen. Cabell knew Watson had told the press that the Project was closed, but Cabell assumed that Watson was lying in order to cover up the real investigative activity. It was all right with Cabell if Watson lied to the press, as long as he told the truth to Cabell. However, as a result of these sightings Cabell learned that Watson had been telling the truth to the press and lying to Cabell!)

The two ATIC officers flew to Washington and reported what they found to Gen. Cabell during a special meeting at the Pentagon. After hearing the Monmouth report, Gen. Cabell asked about Project Grudge itself, how well was it going? With Col. Watson absent (he had not been part of the investigating team, and had not flown from ATIC to attend the meeting), one of the ATIC officers felt it safe to "spill the beans." He told the general that Project Grudge was essentially dead. There was no real sighting analysis. Each sighting was explained in any way that seemed feasible and the explanation was sent on to Washington. The sighting files were scattered and many sighting reports had been boxed up and put away.

Gen. Cabell now realized what had happened. The lower brass had taken to heart the official Air Force "dogma" that flying saucers don't exist and saucer reports are mistakes or just plain garbage. They had stopped taking the project work seriously, even after he had ordered a revitalization in the summer of 1950. Even worse, to cover up their inactivity, they had lied to him during the previous months and years when they reported that Project Grudge was alive and well and analyzing sightings. Gen. Cabell was very angry. "I've been lied to," he said several times to his staff of colonels. He wanted the lying to stop and the project once again revitalized. "I want an answer to the saucers and I want a good answer." It was Gen. Cabell's feeling that as long as there was any question as to whether or not all sightings could be explained the Project should continue. Gen. Cabell criticized the December 1949 Project Grudge report saying it was the "most poorly written, inconclusive piece of unscientific tripe" he had ever read. (He did not say why he had kept his mouth shut about this feeling for over a year and a half.) In contrast to the official Grudge conclusion (everything is explainable), Gen. Cabell said, "Anyone can see that we do not have a satisfactory answer to the question." Gen. Cabell took the attitude that as long as there was the slightest question as to what was being seen, the project should continue. (Writing many years later in a personal memorandum which included much of the information related in the above paragraphs, Edward Ruppelt characterized Cabell as a "believer!" Cabell, in his autobiography, *A Man of Intelligence, Memoirs of War, Peace and the CIA*, has written that he "reminded our people that their jobs were to prove that the 'flying saucers' did exist because the alternative method, that something does not exist, approaches impossible."*

* Impavide Publications, Colorado Springs, CO, 1997.

Here was the man sitting at the top of Air Force Intelligence telling his "employees" that they had screwed up because they had taken the public Air Force statements to be the "gospel truth" and hadn't obeyed direct orders, which were to provide good analyses of sightings. When the general speaks, the colonels, etc., listen. Project Grudge was reorganized. The person brought in to carry out the reorganization was Capt. Edward Ruppelt.

Ruppelt took over Project Grudge in late September 1951. He immediately began planning for the future. He was the first director since the early Project Sign days to proceed in a straightforward scientific manner with a minimum of bias and prejudgment. On his staff, he wanted only those people who could approach the subject seriously, and with an open mind. Part of his reorganization plan was to have ATIC hire scientific consultants. This was approved, and ATIC hired the Battelle Memorial Institute in Columbus, Ohio, to analyze sightings using what were then advanced computer-based methods and to develop a standard sighting form. In early 1952, the reorganization was formalized as the project name was changed to the name which dominated the press reporting on saucer sightings for the next seventeen years, Project Blue Book. Moreover, plans were developed to get proof of saucer reality by obtaining photos of radarscope traces of UFOs, and photos of the UFOs themselves. This was a decided improvement in the approach to solving the saucer mystery.

However, if the Air Force had known what was going to happen six months later, it would have done more than change the project name and buy a few cameras.

It would have prepared for a *nationwide saucer "attack."*

CHAPTER 19

1952: The Year of the UFO

An entire book could be written about this one year, during which ATIC received *over a thousand sighting reports*. The title would be *1952*, and the subtitle, *The Year of the UFO*. What I present here will only scratch the surface of that amazing year.

During the latter half of 1951, there were important changes in the UFO project at ATIC, and also in Air Force Intelligence at the Pentagon. In November, Gen. John A. Samford replaced Gen. Cabell as Director of Intelligence (Cabell became the Director of the Joint Staff for the Joint Chiefs of Staff at the Pentagon and a year or so later retired from the Air Force and became an assistant director of the CIA). The new Air Force Intelligence Director soon learned that that the subject of UFOs received top-level attention. There was also a change at ATIC: Col. Frank Dunn replaced Col. Watson. Dunn asked Samford if the United States had a secret weapon that could explain the saucer sightings. Once again the answer was a firm "no."

On January 3, 1952, Brig. Gen. William M. Garland, Assistant for the Production of Intelligence, wrote a memorandum for Gen. Samford with the title "(SECRET) Contemplated Action to Determine the Nature and Origin of the Phenomena Connected with the Reports of Unusual Flying Objects." This memorandum begins as follows:

1. The continued reports of unusual flying objects requires positive action to determine the nature and origin of the phenomena. The action taken thus far has been designed to track down and evaluate reports from casual observers throughout the country. Thus far, this action has produced results of doubtful value and the inconsistencies inherent in the nature of the reports has given neither positive nor negative proof of the claims.

Here we find a general in Air Force intelligence admitting that there was no *negative proof* of the claims. Yet the Air Force had been saying publicly for several years that there was "negative proof"—that all sightings had been explained. Clearly the men "on the inside" were more honest with each other than with the American people about the fact they had not been able to prove flying saucers were only mistakes or figments of the imagination.

By this time it had become a standard procedure to appeal to the "Soviet Menace" in order to legitimize requests for action and the expenditure of funds. Gen. Garland, too, justified the added effort he would propose by referring to the potential Soviet threat:

2. It is logical to relate the reported sightings to the known development of aircraft, jet propulsion, rockets, and range extension capabilities in Germany and the U.S.S.R. In this connection, it is to be noted that certain developments by the Germans, particularly the Horton wing, jet propulsion, and refueling, combined with their extensive employment of V-1 and V-2 weapons during World War II, lend credence to the possibility that the flying objects may be of German and Russian origin. The developments mentioned above were contemplated and operational between 1941 and 1944 and subsequently fell into the hands of the Soviets at the end of the war. There is evidence that the Germans were working on

these projects as far back as 1931 to 1938. Therefore, it may be assumed that the Germans had at least a seven- to ten-year lead over the United States in the development of rockets, jet engines, and aircraft of the Horton-wing design. The Air Corps developed refueling experimentally as early as 1928, but did not develop operational capability until 1948.

Notice how "cleverly" the general has described the possible threat from Russian developments based on German war research and has concluded that the Russians *might* have a seven- to ten-year lead on the United States in producing advanced aircraft. Nowhere does he mention that the same argument had been rejected in previous years because *(a) the ATIC and AFI investigators in 1947 and again in 1948 could not accept the idea that the Soviets were that far ahead of us and (b) even if they were that far ahead, they would never fly their advanced aircraft over the United States (we wouldn't do the same over the Soviet Union).* Could it be that he didn't know about the previous rejection of the "Soviet hypothesis?" Could it be that he was not sufficiently intelligent to deduce for himself that the idea of the Soviets testing their advanced aircraft over the United States was ridiculous? Or could it be that he actually doubted the Soviet hypothesis but used it anyway to *justify spending money on saucer investigation?* (We will shortly see how this same ploy was used by a scientist to get money for a trip to Europe.)

Having established a "credible" threat, Gen. Garland continued:

3. In view of the above facts and the persistent reports of unusual flying objects over parts of the United States, particularly the east and west coast and in the vicinity of the atomic energy production and testing facilities, it is apparent that positive action must be taken to determine the nature of the objects and, if possible, their origin. Since it is a known fact that the Soviets did not detonate an atomic bomb prior to 1949, it is believed possible that the Soviets may have developed the German aircraft designs at an accelerated rate in order to have a suitable carrier for the delivery of weapons of mass destruction. In other words, the Soviets may have a

carrier without the weapons required while we have relatively superior weapons with relatively inferior carriers available. If the Soviets should get the carrier and the weapon, combined with adequate defensive aircraft, they might surpass us technologically for a sufficient period of time to permit them to execute a decisive air campaign against the United States and her allies. The basic philosophy of the Soviets has been to surpass the Western powers technologically and the Germans may have given them the opportunity.

In the preceding paragraph the general pressed two "hot buttons." One was the reference to sightings of UFOs/saucers over atomic installations (green fireballs, etc.). These installations were considered the keystone to our development of "defensive" atomic weapons ("weapons of mass destruction"). Although the Air Force publicly played down the importance of these sightings is clear that they had had an impact "at the top." The other hot button was the fact that the Soviets, now with a known nuclear capability, might have a delivery system superior to the bombers of the United States and her allies.

The general concluded:

4. In view of the facts outlined above it is considered mandatory that the Air Force take positive action *at once* to definitely determine the nature and, if possible, the origin of the reported unusual flying objects. The following action is now contemplated:

a) require ATIC to provide at least three teams to be matched up with an equal number of teams from ADC [Air Defense Command] for the purpose of taking *radar scope photographs* and *visual photographs* of the phenomena;

b) select sites for these teams based on concentrations of already reported sightings over the United States [these areas are, generally, the Seattle area, the Albuquerque area, and the New York-Philadelphia area] and,

c) take the initial steps in this project during early January 1952 [emphasis underlined in the original].

It is obvious that the general wanted action, ostensibly to protect the United States from the possible Soviet advancements in aeronautical research. However, information contained in a memorandum written by Capt. Ruppelt suggests that Garland may have had *an ulterior motive*. According to Ruppelt (from his personal papers), "Gen. Garland was my boss at ATIC from the Fall of 1952 until I left. He was a moderately confirmed believer. He had seen a UFO while he was stationed in Sacramento, California. He was Gen. Samford's assistant in the Pentagon before he came to ATIC . . ."

Since he had seen a UFO it is possible that he already knew it wasn't a Soviet device, and he was really using the Soviet ploy to justify an investigation of *interplanetary vehicles*. This possibility gains further support from what he did only a month or so after this document was written. He suggested the interplanetary hypothesis to writers of a *Life* magazine article, to be described later.

Ruppelt began the process of carrying out Garland's recommendations, but it was slow going. By the time things were starting to move in the late spring, Project Blue Book was swamped with sightings. The investigation teams proposed by the general were never formed but a plan for instrumentally recording sighting information was carried out. According to a Project Blue Book Staff Study (written in July), in June the ADC issued a requirement that radar scope cameras be available to radar operators. During the spring and summer of 1952, the Collection Division of ATIC developed a stereo camera with a diffraction grating for color analysis of photographed objects. ATIC ordered 100 of these special cameras, to be delivered in September. Blue Book planned to give these cameras to military and civilian control tower operators and to the Ground Observer Corps. Too bad these cameras arrived too late for the *big flap!*

As of March 1952, it had been more than three years since Col. Gasser had told the FBI that saucers were Soviet missiles, and more than two years the green fireballs had caused a minor panic among security agencies. It was over a year since the UFO scare at Oak Ridge and over a year since the public controversy sparked by the Considine article and the Liddel-Mirarchi debate. There had been scattered news stories about flying saucers during 1951, and there had been many sightings, but the FBI was not involved with any of them. If Hoover thought about saucers at all, he probably assumed they had all been explained by the Air Force, and that saucer sightings had simply faded away.

If that is what he believed, then he was in for a shock. The first inkling that something was still going on came on March 25 when FBI headquarters received a report from an artist living in Chicago. The local Chicago agent reported that an artist (his name is censored in the released document) contacted the FBI, and described the following sighting:

> . . . he saw a flying disc at 9:00 A.M. on March 6, 1952. Mr. [name censored] stated that he was looking out of a window at his home, which faces south, when he saw a flying disc at approximately 7,000 feet above Fullerton Avenue. The angle of elevation of the disc above the horizon was 45 degrees. The disc came out of a cloud in the east, stopped and hung motionless in mid air for a split second, then flew south at great speed. He described the disc as approximately six feet in diameter, circular, white in color with a bluish tinge. The disc, he said, appeared to have been constructed out of a metal similar to aluminum. He also stated that he saw no exhaust, lights, or heard no sound connected with its movements . . . He said it disappeared out of sight in approximately three seconds . . . He said it went so fast it appeared to flutter.

Special Agent in Charge Chicago reported that he sent a copy of the sighting report to AFOSI. However, this is another sighting that did not get into the Project Blue Book file.

On April 7, FBI headquarters received another report, this time from Nashville, Tennessee. A Navy serviceman (his name censored) reported to the FBI that on March 13, at 10:20 P.M.:

> . . . while standing in the backyard . . . and looking toward the moon, which was in the southwest section of the sky, he observed an object which was approximately 20 degrees above the horizon. ———— described this object as being circular in shape, approximately one-half the [angular] size of

the moon, deep bright blue in color, very vivid blue. He stated the object had a slight reddish fringe on the aft end. The object appeared to be moving from the northwest to the southeast. He stated that the object was not in his vision more than three seconds. It made no sound. —––––— stated that at the time he observed this there were no clouds in the sky, the stars were out, and the moon was full.

This is one more sighting that is not included in the Blue Book sighting collection.

Ten days after this sighting one of the assistant directors at FBI headquarters added to the file a copy of an article that appeared in the April 7 issue of *Life* magazine, an issue that would not soon be forgotten.

The *Life* cover was an irresistible combination of sultry sex and saucers. It showed a dreamy Marilyn Monroe, her eyes half closed and her luxuriously loose dress slid well down below her shoulders. The cover asserted she was "the talk of Hollywood." In the upper right corner of the cover there was a statement that must have come as a shock to readers: "There is a case for interplanetary saucers."

The case for interplanetary saucers was made by H. B. Darrach, Jr. and Robert Ginna, in their article "Have We Visitors from Space?" Next to the title was the attention-grabbing answer to this question: "The Air Force is now ready to concede that many saucer and fireball sightings still defy explanation; here *Life* offers some scientific evidence that there is a real case for interplanetary flying saucers." The article, based on a year-long investigation by Ginna, included information directly from the Air Force file. Ginna had visited ATIC on March 3 and, with the complete cooperation of Capt. Ruppelt and the Project Blue Book staff, he had reviewed sighting reports and analyses, some of which were declassified at his request. The authors also interviewed high-level Air Force officials at the Pentagon. They were told that the Air Force was carrying on a "constant intelligence investigation" and would attempt to get radar and photographic data, and that "attempts will be made to recover such unidentified objects." They were also told that the Air Force was, for the first time, since December 1949, inviting "all citizens to report their sightings to the nearest Air Force installation."

The authors discussed ten previously unpublished sightings (several of which have been presented) and concluded that Russian weapons, atmospheric phenomena, Skyhook balloons, secret weapons, hallucinations, and psychological aberrations could not explain these cases. According to the authors, "These disclosures, sharply amending past Air Force policy, climaxed a review by *Life* with Air Force officials of all facts known . . ." and "the Air Force is now ready to concede that many saucer and fireball sightings still defy explanation." Furthermore, they quoted Dr. Walther Reidel, a German rocket scientist, who, in his opinion, said these objects "have an out-of-this world basis." To top it off, the authors quoted an intelligence officer, "The higher you go in the Air Force, the more seriously they take the flying saucers." A reader of the article might well have gotten the idea that top Air Force officers were thinking "interplanetary." (This idea would be conveyed to the FBI *as fact* several months and *many hundreds of sightings later!*) The article ended with a series of questions, which pointed toward the interplanetary answer: "What power urges them at such terrible speeds through the sky? Who, or what, is aboard? Where do they come from? Why are they here? What are the intentions of the beings who control them? . . . Somewhere in the dark skies there may be those who know!" Although they did not so much as mention Maj. Donald Keyhoe and the startling conclusion he had published in *True* magazine two-and-a-half years before, you can bet that he was cheering for Darrach and Ginna!

The *Life* magazine statement that the Air Force was taking saucers seriously was diametrically opposed to many previous public statements but, of course, the Air Force had not stated that the saucers might actually be extraterrestrial vehicles. Even in private at ATIC, there was no endorsement of the interplanetary hypothesis. In a Secret monthly status report on the activities of Project Blue Book, dated April 30, 1952, Capt. Ruppelt wrote "It should be noted here that the conclusions reached by *Life* are not those of the Air Force. No proof exists that these objects are from outer space." Actually Ruppelt should have been more specific in saying that the ATIC/Project Blue Book staff did not endorse the *Life* conclusion because, as he admitted in *The Report on Unidentified Flying Objects,* other Air Force officials did endorse that conclusion. According to Ruppelt, some "high-ranking officers in the Pentagon—so high that their personal opinion was almost policy" did believe the saucers were extraterrestrial and expressed that opinion to Ginna. At least one of these high ranking officers was none other than Gen. Garland! Recall that Ruppelt, in his personal papers, noted that Garland had seen a UFO while he was stationed in Sacramento, California. Ruppelt also wrote the following: "[Garland] was the inspiration behind the *Life* article by Ginna. He gave Ginna his ideas and prompted *Life* to stick their necks out."

According to Project Blue Book records, the *Life* article was mentioned in more than 350 newspapers across the United States, and ATIC received 110 letters concerning the article. *Life* itself received more than 700 letters. The letters discussed old sightings and theories about sightings. Blue Book braced for an onslaught of new sightings that didn't come—*at least not right away.* On the day after the magazine hit the stands Blue Book received nine sightings, but then only a couple on the next day.

In the following days other publications disputed the *Life* article. The *New York Times* criticized Darrach and Ginna for being "uncritical." The *Times* author claimed that the Project Grudge report of two years proved that all sightings could be explained. Of course he did not know that Gen. Cabell had described the Grudge report as so much "tripe."

Ruppelt's claim that high-level officers actually believed saucers were interplanetary is confirmed in an indirect way in a memorandum written on April 29, 1952. This document was written to justify a trip to Europe by Dr. Stephen Possony and Lt. Col. Sterling, both members of a "special study group" that had been organized to study "advanced delivery systems," i.e., advanced aircraft. Possony, an Air Intelligence Specialist with high-level connections in the Pentagon, and Sterling, Chief of the Special Study Group, wanted a five-week trip to visit various military headquarters in Europe. They began their memorandum by stating that the Air Force can remain effective only by anticipating future developments of enemy weapon systems. However, they wrote, "there is no tenable and convincing estimate of future Russian delivery systems" and, furthermore, "current estimates do not reflect the possibility that the Russians may have overtaken the U.S. in advanced guided missile research and development." The memorandum then describes

Dr. Stephen Possony wrote that the Air Force could not "assume that flying saucers" are extraterrestrial.

the activities of the Special Study Group in this regard and includes a statement which shows that saucer sightings were definitely not ignored:

> The Special Study Group has undertaken a comprehensive study of Russian capabilities in the field of advanced delivery systems. This study is expected to determine the nature of such systems, their strategic implications and probable time tables as to development and operational availability. As an important side product, it is hoped that some much needed light can be shed on the vexing "flying saucer" problem.

Obviously this memorandum justifies the trip by appealing to the "Soviet Menace" in a manner similar to the previously discussed memorandum written by Gen. Garland about four months earlier. This memorandum is unique, however, because it contains an argument against the "ET hypothesis" in order to make the "Soviet hypothesis" seem reasonable. In essence it says that saucers could not originate from nearby planets, or be from far outer space because astronomers would see them coming. However, this document also points out the difficulty with the

Soviet hypothesis: "Nothing in this argument is designed to brush over the improbability that the Russians have such a considerable lead over the U.S. In order to fly saucers over the U.S., the Soviets would have to be at least twenty years ahead of us. They would have attained such superiority by keeping a large-scale development in complete isolation, even during the last war." In other words, the memorandum provides reasons to reject both hypotheses.

The following statement from the memorandum is the most interesting, since it reflects the thinking "at the top" of the Air Force:

> In connection with flying saucers the Group is attempting to develop a proper framework for fruitful analysis. The Air Force cannot assume that flying saucers are of non-terrestrial origin, and hence they could be Soviet.

Whoa there! Let's look at that last sentence again and rewrite it a bit: The [high-level] Air Force [officers] cannot [simply] assume that flying saucers are of non-terrestrial [i.e., of extraterrestrial] origin, and hence [ignore them because there still is a slight possibility that] they could be Soviet [aircraft]. The fact that Possony and Sterling included this statement in their memorandum means that the "impossible" may have been true. Top Air Force officers assumed that saucers were interplanetary and therefore disregarded the Soviet secret weapon hypothesis. (I suppose this could explain why the top Air Force officials seemed to treat the saucer sightings casually; they knew the saucers were extraterrestrial vehicles about which they could do nothing, so it was "best" to try to get the public to ignore them.)

In order to justify his trip to Europe for saucer investigations, Possony first argued against the ET hypothesis, and then he made it seem plausible that the Soviets had in some unimaginable way achieved a twenty-year lead on the U.S. in the development of "advanced delivery systems." This "reverse" argument worked. He got his trip, probably because the most important person he had to convince was none other than *Gen. Garland!* (Note: Ruppelt characterized Possony as a "believer" who had a direct "channel" to Gen. Samford, and who traveled around the United States and Europe studying advanced weapon systems and collecting UFO reports.)

By the end of the April, the sighting report rate on a daily basis had picked up and Ruppelt and the Blue Book staff attributed this to the *Life* article, and the resulting press interest. What Ruppelt didn't know was that the onslaught that would make this the year of the UFO was just beginning.

It is instructive to list the number of objects reported per month to see how this sighting flap developed.* According to the *Scientific Study of Unidentified Flying Objects*, which is the final report of the Air Force sponsored UFO study at the University of Colorado in 1967–1968, the monthly numbers starting with September 1951 and going through June 1952 are: Sept.(16), Oct. (24), Nov. (16), Dec. (12), Jan. (15), Feb. (17), Mar. (23), Apr. (82), May (79), Jun. (148).† The sudden upsurge in April, May, and June is obvious. What was happening? Were people going crazy? Did a magazine article and the associated publicity cause ordinary people to report any unfamiliar objects they might see in the sky? That's what ATIC and Capt. Ruppelt thought, or at least that's what they *said* they thought, but it was clearly not the whole story.

On May 12, the FBI got another jolt. Unidentified Flying Objects were seen at yet another "vital installation," the Savannah River atomic bomb fuel processing plant:

```
FBI, Savannah URGENT 7:58 P.M. 5-12-52
Savannah River Plant,
Atomic Energy Commission, Flying Disc.
```

At approximately 10:45 P.M., May 10, four employees of Dupont Co., employed on the Savannah River plant near Ellington, S.C., saw 4 disc shaped objects approaching the 400 area from the south, disappearing in a northerly direction. At approximately 11:05 P.M., above mentioned employees saw two similar objects approach from south and disappear in northerly direction. At approximately 11:10 P.M. one similar

---

* Note: This is the number of objects reported by witnesses. Some of these objects were subsequently identified, so they are not all UFOs.

† *Scientific Study of Unidentified Flying Objects,* Bantam Books, NY; January 1969; p. 514.

object approached from the northeast and disappeared in southwesterly direction. One more object sighted about 11:15 P.M. travelling from south to north. Employees described objects as being about 15 inches in diameter having yellow to gold color. All of these other objects were travelling at high rate of speed at high altitude without any noise. The ... object which approached the 400 area from the [northeast] was travelling at altitude so low it had to rise to pass over some tall tanks in 400 area. This object was also flying a high rate of speed and noiseless. Witnesses stated observed objects weaving from left to [right] but seemed to hold general course. Also stated due to speed and altitude they were only visible for few seconds. Savannah office is not actively conducting investigation in this matter and is furnishing this info to bureau for whatever action they deem advisable.

FBI headquarters immediately reported this to the head of the AFOSI. Project Blue Book lists this sighting as unidentified.

In early July, an article in *Look* magazine partially reversed its stance of a year and a half before. Recall that in the January 1951 issue, Robert Considine had trashed the subject, claiming that the Air Force had explained everything and that witnesses were essentially kooks and nuts, deluded, or publicity seekers. The author of the new *Look* article, J. Robert Moskin, took a more positive attitude. He visited Project Blue Book two weeks after the publication of the *Life* article. He received full cooperation from the Blue Book staff. He quoted Gen. Hoyt Vandenberg, the Chief of Staff of the Air Force, as saying that as long as there were any unexplained sightings the Air Force would continue to study the problem. Moskin went on to summarize the Project Blue Book plans to obtain better scientific data. He pointed out that many atomic installations had been "visited" by UFOs, but that there was no evidence that anyone, meaning the Russians, was spying on our country even though "this fear still lies deeply in some responsible minds." He also pointed out that the Air Force had given up trying to explain sightings as "Cold War jitters," societal tension, publicity about saucers, or mass hysteria. Instead, the Air Force was sure that the answer would be found as misinterpretations of conventional objects, optical phenomena, man-made objects, or *extraterrestrial objects*. Regardless of what the final answer might be, it was clear from Moskin's article that the Air Force was actively investigating, verifying the claim made in the *Life* article two months earlier.

Although Project Blue Book, after months of organizational work, was now prepared to handle the typical flow of sightings, it was "whelmed many times over" (i.e., *over*-overwhelmed) by what happened in July. During previous months the sightings had been coming in at a rate of one every two days or so. In the latter half of April, this increased to a rate of several per day and stayed that way until the latter half of June. Then the sighting rate increased to four per day, then five then ten, and during the latter half of July, it was running at more than twenty per day from all over the U.S. and some from foreign countries as well.

The locations of the sightings read like a geography lesson. Between early morning July 20, and midnight July 22, there were sightings in New Jersey (7), Colorado (2), Illinois (2), Michigan (2), Pennsylvania (1), Kentucky (1), California (3), Texas (5), North Carolina (1), Florida (2), Georgia (1), Missouri (1), Massachusetts (5), Maine (1), Indiana (1), New Mexico (1), Alabama (1), Oregon (1), New Hampshire (1), South Dakota (1), New York (1), Maryland (2), Virginia (1), and Washington, D.C. (3). There were also two reports from Germany and single reports from Mexico and Morocco. Fourteen of these fifty-one sightings were from military observers, six of whom were at Air Force bases. From Project Blue Book's point of view, the whole flying saucer mess was getting far out of hand.

As if this weren't bad enough the pot really began to boil over when flying saucers were reported over the nation's capitol. At least, that's the way it appeared to the experienced radar controllers at National Airport the night of Saturday, July 19, and again a week later. Several times, targets were detected by two independent radars, one at National and one at Andrews Air Force Base. These targets appeared as strong point returns rather than as diffuse, blobby images that characterize the effects of "anomalous propagations" or "radar angels." During the sightings, F-94 jets were scrambled from Newcastle Air Force Base in Delaware. Usually the scrambled aircraft did not see lights associated with the targets, but there were at least two visual confirmations. On the other hand, civilian aircraft flying in the area at the time reported several visual sightings of unusual moving lights, as did ground observers.

The events began at about 11:40 P.M. on Saturday, July 19, when the Washington Air Route Traffic Control Center (WARTCC) radar at National Airport detected targets moving toward Andrews AFB (AAFB). Then, at five minutes past midnight, a phone call was received at AAFB control tower advising that there was an orange lighted object to the south. A control tower operator, while talking to the person on the phone, looked south and saw the "orange ball of fire, trailing a tail . . . it was very bright and definite and unlike anything I had ever seen before. . . . It made a kind of circular movement . . . [then] took off at an unbelievable speed. It disappeared in a split second." The person on the phone saw the same thing. A few seconds later the tower operator "saw another one, same description. As the one before, it made an arc-like pattern and then disappeared." During the next twenty-five minutes, five AAFB personnel saw two more lights, reddish-orange in color, moving erratically on a generally southeastward track through the eastern sky. They were seen from five to thirty seconds on three occasions. At 1:20, and again at 1:25, fast moving lights with an orange hue and a tail were seen by AAFB tower personnel. At 2:35 WARTCC received a call from an airline pilot who said he had seen three objects near Herndon, Virginia, west of Washington, and reported that "they were like nothing he had ever seen."

A week later, on July 25 at 9:15 P.M., WARTCC again detected from four to eight anomalous targets "described by radar operators as 'good sharp targets.'" According to the AFOSI report, at 11:20 P.M., two F-94's were scrambled from Delaware, and one of the jets,

> . . . reportedly made visual contact with one of the objects, and at first appeared to be gaining on it, but the object and the F-94 were observed on the radar scope and appeared to be traveling at the same approximate speed. However, when it attempted to overtake the object, the object disappeared both from the pursuant aircraft and the radar scope. The pilot of the F-94 remarked of the "incredible speed of the object."

The next night was a repeat. At 8:15 P.M., July 26, the pilot and stewardess of a National Airlines plane flying at 1,700 feet and 200 mph saw a lighted object, which appeared similar to the glow of a lighted cigarette (dull red) which passed "directly over the airliner." They estimated the object speed to be 100 mph. At 8:54 P.M., AAFB radar began detecting ten to twelve unidentified radar targets in the Washington area. An hour and a half later, at 10:23, WARTCC detected four targets at various locations in the suburbs of Washington. According to a document not released until 1985, a Civil Aeronautics Administration official flying at an altitude of 2,200 feet at 10:46 P.M. saw "five objects giving off a light glow ranging from orange to white." The same document says, "Some commercial pilots reported visuals ranging from 'cigarette glow' [red yellow] to 'a light' [as recorded from their conversations with ARTC controllers]." At 10:38 P.M. the USAF Command Post was notified of unidentified targets and at 11:00 P.M. two F-94's were scrambled. The document says that "one pilot mentioned seeing four lights at one time and a second time as seeing a single light ahead but unable to close whereupon the light 'went out.'"

During the sightings on July 26, two members of the Project Blue Book staff, one of whom was a radar expert, were in the Washington area. They were notified quickly of the radar sightings and arrived at AAFB shortly after midnight. When they arrived they could see "seven good, solid targets." The radar expert checked with the airport radar and determined that there was a slight temperature inversion. The expert believed that the inversion was too weak to cause targets such as these, so a second intercept flight was requested. By the time it arrived the strong targets had departed. That ended the Washington, D.C., sightings, but the Air Force response was only just beginning.

As far as the general public was concerned, the first hint of something unusual happening came in an increase in local and national press reports of saucers. Then, on July 19, the national press reported the Air Force's admission that people were really seeing something unusual, that the numbers of reports had doubled over what had occurred years ago and that the Air Force couldn't track all the saucers. Some details of the Saturday and Sunday, July 19–20, sightings in Washington, D.C., were leaked to the press and were reported the following Tuesday. Capt. Ruppelt, who was in Dayton, Ohio, at the time, was not told about these sightings. When he arrived in Washington on routine business on Monday, July 21, he still did not know about them. He read about them in the Tuesday morning paper, and immediately began phoning people to find out what had happened because he was responsible for supplying the technical backup for whatever the Air Force would tell the press. Unfortunately he had no answers, only questions. His predicament was not helped when a general told him that *President Truman wanted to know what was going on.* Apparently, some of the radar targets had been *over the White House restricted area.* By late in the afternoon, Ruppelt had an "answer" for the press. The Air Force would have "no comment" on the sightings because investigation was ongoing. The next day the newspapers interpreted this as meaning that the Air Force "won't talk."

The press activity related to saucer sightings and Air Force investigations increased on a daily basis. Local papers throughout the country were loaded with the reports of local sightings. As just one example, the *Indianapolis News* carried the following front page headline on July 28, "Hundreds in state see 'flying saucers.'" The story reported that military personnel and police officers "kept a running check on saucers for more than four hours."

The reports of the Washington, D.C., sightings of July 25 and 26–27 only added to the furor. And then on July 28, newspapers across the nation carried a startling story, from the International News Service, which read:

> . . . jet pilots have been placed on 24-hour "alert" against "flying saucers" with orders to "shoot them down" if they refuse to land. It was learned that pilots have gone aloft on several occasions in an effort to shoot the mysterious objects to the ground but never came close enough to use their guns.

It was nearly a panic situation. What on earth—or *off the earth*—was causing all the sightings? The press and the public wanted answers—not soon, but *now!* The Air Force was about to give them some.

Several days earlier, on July 24, Lt. Col. W. K. Smith, in the Policy and Management Group of the Directorate of Intelligence, had written a memorandum summarizing the situation. This memorandum was written at the request of Maj. Gen. Samford and was sent to Gen. White, the Deputy Chief of Staff for Air Force Operations. According to the memorandum, there had been "between 1,000 and 1,050 [reports] since 1947," and the recent influx of reports was a result of the April *Life* magazine article and the subsequent press coverage. The memorandum stated that "there is no significance attached to the location of these sightings, other than that they are random in nature." According to Col. Smith's notes, used in preparation of the memorandum, there were 180 unexplained sightings, only fifty-three of which "came from what are considered reliable sources." In other words, the fraction of unexplained sightings was nearly twenty percent and the "hard core" unexplained was about five percent of the 1,000 reports.

At the bottom of the memorandum Gen. Samford had written a note to Gen. White, which said that a briefing by ATIC officers had been scheduled for July 29 "at such time as you may desire." As it turned out, Gen. Samford was "lucky" that he had prepared a briefing because he did give one on that date—but not to Gen. White!

During this time UFO reports were coming in like snow in a blizzard. On July 28, ATIC received about fifty reports, of which forty-three occurred on that day. The remainder were older reports that had been delayed for various reasons. Months later the Project Blue Book staff discovered that this day had the largest daily sighting rate ever recorded by the Air Force. During the following week the sighting rate dropped back to less than ten per day, which was still very large. However, on July 28, Capt. Ruppelt, the Project Blue Book staff, and AFI didn't know the sighting rate was about to decrease; they didn't know what to expect. It may well have seemed to them that an extraterrestrial craft landing or a shootdown would soon occur. What would happen after that? A real-life *War of the Worlds?*

July 29 began with more sightings, including one which provided further proof that radar could detect UFOs. A fighter-interceptor was flying on a routine training mission from Selfridge AFB in Michigan, when ground control asked the fighter to check on an object picked up by the ground radar. This object was moving southward over Saginaw, Michigan, at a speed of about 625 mph, which was within the capability of jet fighter. Was it simply an intruding Canadian military jet?

The pilot began a right turn and the copilot picked up a radar target at sixty degrees to the right. The plane kept turning until the target was straight ahead and the radar locked on to the object. The lock-on lasted for about thirty seconds as the plane flew at high speed toward the object. The copilot determined that the object was four miles ahead and, at the altitude of the plane, about 20,000 feet. The copilot later said he saw "the target . . . putting off what seemed like a changing light in definite sequences of white, red, and bluish-green. That is the only means of identification we had. From a bombardier, radar observer, navigator, I have never experienced any sighting like this before."

During this time, ground control announced that it had both the jet and the unidentified target on the radar screen. Then suddenly the object broke the airplane's radar lock. Before the jet could react, the object reversed its course. Ground radar, which had been tracking both the jet and the unidentified target, was startled to see the unidentified object make a 180-degree turn and head northward toward Canada. The F-94 gave chase but could not catch up as the unknown increased its speed in an erratic manner. The top speed of the unidentified was unknown because the radar only determined its location once during every ten-second sweep. However, typically it would travel about four miles during that time (four miles/ten seconds = 1,440 mph). This was about twice the top speed of the jet. The jet followed the object for about twenty minutes, but then radioed that it was running low on fuel and would have to break off the chase. The jet turned home, at which point the ground control saw that the speed of the unknown suddenly drop back to its original value. Months later, Project Blue Book would leave this as an unexplained case. Two of the other sightings on the morning of July 29 occurred near Roswell, New Mexico, and at Los Alamos. The Los Alamos sighting resulted in a scramble from Kirtland Air Force Base.

Meanwhile back in Washington, D.C., the press was in an uproar because of the July 28 announcement that the Air Force had directed pilots to shoot if necessary. Did the Air Force really mean it? Were things out of control? Had any saucer been shot down? What would the Air Force do if one *were* shot down? Everyone wanted answers, and Nathan Twining was about to provide some. Gen. Twining, the head of AMC in 1947, had left that post in January 1948 (Gen. Benjamin Chidlaw replaced him) and was now Chief of Staff of the Air Force, having replaced Gen. Vandenberg. Twining ordered Samford to hold a press conference to outline the official Air Force position regarding Unidentified Flying Objects. During the morning of July 29, Gen. Samford's press officer announced that a flying saucer conference would be held at the Pentagon late that afternoon. Gen. Samford was about to give to the assembled press part of the briefing that had been prepared for Gen. White. He was also about to accomplish in public what Vandenberg had accomplished in private four years earlier: Gen. Samford would put a major damper on interest in UFO sightings by telling the press that no reported saucer was an interplanetary vehicle. And, intentionally or not, Samford was about to lie.

At 4:00 P.M. the longest post-WWII press conference to that date began. It lasted eighty minutes. Gen. Samford brought with him several military experts in radar, Capt. Ruppelt, and a person who was mentioned in the first chapter, Maj. Gen. Roger Ramey. Gen. Ramey had been the head of the 8th Air Force when he invented and publicized the "weather balloon" explanation for the Roswell crash debris. Now he was in charge of Operations of the Air Defense Command.

Gen. Samford told the assembled press that because American secret weapons did not cause the sightings, the Air Force was obligated to investigate them. He further said:

> We have received and analyzed between 1,000 and 2,000 reports that have come to us from all kinds of sources. Of this great mass of reports we have been able adequately to explain the great bulk of them, explain them to our own satisfaction. However there have been a certain percentage of this volume of reports that have been made by credible observers of relatively incredible things. It is this group of observations that we are now attempting to resolve. We have, as of this date, come to only one firm conclusion with respect

to this remaining percentage, and that is that it does not contain any pattern of purpose or of consistency that we can relate to any conceivable threat to the United States.

Gen. Samford gave few explicit answers to the questions from the press. The discussion concentrated on the Washington sightings, even though the general and his "support team" did not have all the information needed to decide what caused them. Gen. Ramey provided some information about the jet scrambles, and Samford advanced the opinion, ostensibly based on the work of Air Force radar experts, that an atmospheric "inversion" had caused the radar targets. Various members of the press pushed hard to get a definite answer as opposed to an opinion, but he would not give a definite answer. He did say the Air Force was giving all reports "adequate but not frantic checks."

Gen. Samford rejected the extraterrestrial theory, implying that all the unexplained sightings were the results of natural phenomena. However, he could not be pinned down as to *which* natural phenomena because whenever he was asked questions about specific sightings, he would plead a lack of information. There were no witnesses at the conference, not even the Blue Book staff members who were in the control tower at AAFB during the July 26 and 27 sightings. (Those staff members had indicated that the radar targets were like strong aircraft returns, and not like diffuse "anomalous propagation" targets.) Because there were no witnesses at the conference, members of the press could not directly confront the general with witness testimony. Some of the reporters were aware of sightings by military personnel, and of sightings near the "vital installations." They asked the general about these, but he again pleaded a lack of information. The most they could do was get him to admit that about twenty percent of the sightings were unknown—an admission that, by itself, was quite startling.

The next day the national press, in front-page headlines, had distilled the whole conference down to the simple answer the Air Force wanted the public to believe about the Washington, D.C., sightings: summer heat had warmed the air above the Earth's surface and caused temperature inversions which, in turn, caused the unidentified radar targets, and that was it. Most members of the press, skeptical of saucer sightings and not radar experts, accepted this simple answer, albeit with reservations. A few news articles expressed a minority viewpoint that the Air Force was trying to debunk the whole phenomenon. Drew Pearson, a famous columnist, pointed out that the Air Force had now admitted for the first time that radar detections had occurred at the same time as visual observations. Pearson went so far as to suggest the objects might be from another planet. Other dissenting press organizations did not go that far, but did criticize the Air Force for boasting about scientific advances when it was clear the Air Force did not completely understand the saucer phenomenon.

During the following days and weeks, there were scientists and radar experts who publicly disputed the general's explanation of the Washington sightings. However, their arguments did not carry the weight of the pronouncements of Gen. Samford and his staff. No one outside the Air Force had all the information so his explanation could not be carefully examined for accuracy. When interviewed many years later, the air traffic controllers who were involved at the time still rejected the official explanation, saying that they were thoroughly familiar with the types of radar images that appear during periods of anomalous propagation, and the images seen that night emphatically were not anomalous propagation images.

Perhaps the Air Force felt that Gen. Samford's conference was not enough to dampen the saucer frenzy. Gen. Vandenberg was interviewed a day later and expressed his dismay at the continued "mass hysteria about flying saucers." Vandenberg told the press that the objects were not extraterrestrial craft nor secret weapons. He said that the Air Force had been investigating reports for several years and had found no convincing evidence. Then Gen. Ramey appeared on television. He repeated what Samford had said at the big press conference, and admitted the Air Force had been forced to come up with some quick answers to prevent a public panic.

To the outside world it may have seemed that the Air Force had everything under control. Not so, to the "inside" world. If the press had known what Gen. Samford's staff was telling other "insiders" *on the same day as the press conference,* the lid would have blown off the government's *UFO cover-up!*

CHAPTER 20
Ships from Another Planet

On **July 29**, 1952, several hours before Gen. Samford's press conference, Gilbert Levy, Chief of the Counter Intelligence Division of the Office of the Inspector General of the AFOSI, decided to contact AFI to find out how the press had learned so much about the Washington, D.C., sightings. He may have wondered if someone had broken security and leaked the information. He reported the result of his "investigation" to Gen. Carroll, the Director of AFOSI. His report is contained in the AFOSI section of the Project Blue Book file released in 1975:

1. In light of recent wide publicity concerning the [radar sightings at National Airport] I caused a check to be made for the purpose of determining the basis of recent releases to news media.

2. We were advised by the Current Intelligence Branch, Estimates Division, AFOIN, [i.e., Gen. Samford's office], which has staff responsibility with respect to these reports, that much of the publicity of the past few days is the result of a

radar sighting of unidentified aerial objects by the Civil Aeronautics Administration at National Airport at 2115 hours, 25 July 1952. These sightings continued from 2115 hours, 25 July until 0010 hours on 26 July, and were described by radar operators as "good sharp targets." They were observed in numbers from four to eight.

3. At 2320 hours, 25 July 1952, two (2) Air Force F-94's were dispatched from New Castle AFB, Delaware, for the purpose of intercepting objects which have been sighted by radar. One of the F-94's reportedly made visual contact with one of the objects and at first appeared to be gaining on it, but the object and the F-94 were observed on the radar scope and appeared to be traveling at the same approximate speed. However, when it attempted to overtake the object, the object disappeared both from the pursuant aircraft and the radar scope. The pilot of the F-94 remarked of [sic] the "incredible speed of the object."

4. The Director of Intelligence advises that no theory exists at the present time as to the origin of the objects and they are considered to be unexplained. Much of the publicity has been based on authorized news releases by the Air Force.

Oops! Now the cat is out of the bag. Reread paragraph four. The Director of Intelligence said that *no theory exists* to explain the sightings, which are *considered to be unexplained.* That's not what he told the press only a few hours later!

In the absence of any other information, one might assume that this is a mistake. Perhaps Levy misunderstood what he had been told. However, there is other information that is consistent with what Levy wrote. In fact, there is a lot more information that was withheld from the American people until it was released in the *FBI X-File!*

On the same day, and perhaps even at about the same time as Levy's contact with AFI, the FBI also asked AFI for information about the sightings. Mr. N. W. Philcox, the FBI liaison with the Air Force, arranged to be briefed through Gen. Samford's office by "Commander Randall Boyd of the Current Intelligence Branch, Estimates Division, Air Intelligence, regarding research into the numerous reports regarding flying saucers and flying discs." (This is exactly the same branch that provided the above information to Levy!) Philcox was told:

> Commander Boyd advised that Air Intelligence has set up at Wright-Patterson Air Force Base, Ohio, the Air Technical Intelligence Center which has been established for the purpose of coordinating, correlating and making research into all reports regarding flying saucers and flying discs. He advised that Air Force research has indicated that the sightings of flying saucers goes back several centuries and that the number of sightings reported varies with the amount of publicity. He advised that immediately if publicity appears in newspapers, the number of sightings reported increases considerably and that citizens immediately call in reporting sightings which occurred several months previously.

Comm. Boyd erred in his statement that ATIC was set up to investigate saucer sightings. ATIC was set up at Wright-Patterson Air Force Base with the mission to investigate all foreign aviation technology, particularly Soviet aircraft. Blue Book was a project involving some of the ATIC personnel. Comm. Boyd's claim that the number of sighting reports was correlated to press reporting on the subject was a statement of belief on the part of the Blue Book staff, but it had not been proven true. In fact, important evidence to the contrary would occur within days of this statement as the press kept up a barrage of sighting stories, while the sighting rate actually *dropped* precipitously.

Agent Philcox's report continues:

> Commander Boyd stated that these reported sightings of flying saucers are placed into three classifications by Air Intelligence:
>
> 1. Those sightings which are reported by citizens who claim that they have seen flying saucers from the ground. These sightings vary in description, color and speeds. Very little credence is given to these sightings inasmuch as in most

instances they are believed to be imaginative or some explainable object which actually crossed through the sky.

2. Sightings reported by commercial or military pilots. These sightings are considered more credible by the Air Force inasmuch as commercial or military pilots are experienced in the air and are not expected to see objects which are entirely imaginative. In each of these instances, the individual who reports the sighting is thoroughly interviewed by a representative of Air Intelligence so that a complete description of the object sighted can be obtained.

3. Those sightings which are reported by pilots and for which there is additional corroboration, such as recording by radar or sighting from the ground. Commander Boyd advised that this latter classification constitutes two or three percent of the total number of sightings, but that they were the most difficult to explain. Some of these sightings are originally reported from the ground, then are picked up by radar instruments. He stated that in these instances there is no doubt that these individuals reporting the sightings actually did see something in the sky. However, he explained that these objects could still be natural phenomena and still could be recorded on radar if there was some electrical disturbance in the sky.

Comm. Boyd's statement indicates that about three percent of sightings constitute the "hard core" of the phenomenon. This percentage agrees closely with the approximately five percent (fifty-three sightings out of about 1,000) that Col. W. Smith said on July 24 came from "reliable sources" (see previous chapter). Although not a large percentage, these were the sightings (a few of which have already been presented in this book), which absolutely could not be explained without resorting to such bizarre hypotheses such that several witnesses could all go insane or hallucinate the same vision, at the same time, perhaps even at the same time that instruments (e.g., radar, theodolite telescopes) malfunction, *and then immediately after the sighting the witnesses and instruments would be normal again!* Comm. Boyd did not tell the FBI that, at that time, the fraction of unexplained sightings was about twenty percent, which included the three percent "hard core" sightings. Presumably the other seventeen percent unexplained sightings had elements or features that would allow them to be *possibly* explained if enough reasonable assumptions about erroneous reporting were made. The "hard core" three percent, on the other hand, required unreasonable assumptions before any explanation could be offered.

Agent Philcox's report continued:

> He stated that the flying saucers are most frequently observed in areas where there is heavy air traffic, such as Washington, D.C., and New York City. He advised however, that some reports are received from other parts of the country covering the United States and that sightings have also recently been reported as far distant as Acapulco, Mexico; Korea, and French Morocco.

It is amusing to note Comm. Boyd's claim that saucers were most often seen in areas of high air traffic, which typically are areas of dense population, because one of the reasons offered against the reality of flying saucers was this: "If saucers are real, why are they only seen by the unsophisticated witnesses in the countryside, and not over cities?" The Battelle Memorial Institute study, which was going on even as Comm. Boyd spoke, discovered many months later that there was a degree of correlation between the number of sightings and *areas with military and civilian airports.* However, this does not mean that there were more misidentified aircraft reported as saucers in the vicinity of airports. Instead, the correlation may have resulted from a greater tendency of people living near airports to look upward and see the saucers.

Many years later I discovered that the Battelle sighting data also showed essentially no correlation between area population and the number of sightings in the same area. That is, an area with several hundred thousand people could have the same number of sightings over the years as an area with millions of people. That is not what would be expected if the skeptics were correct in saying that many sighting reports were "people-generated," that is, from psychopathological people who reported hallucinations or other mental aberrations. The number of reports such as these would be correlated with the population.

Continuing with Agent Philcox's report:

> He advised that the sightings in the last category [category 3 above] have never been satisfactorily explained. He pointed out, however, that it is still possible that these objects may be a natural phenomenon or some type of atmospheric disturbance. He advised that it is not entirely impossible that the objects sighted *may possibly be ships from another planet such as Mars.* [emphasis added] He advised that at the present time there is nothing to substantiate this theory but the possibility is not being overlooked. He stated that Air Intelligence is fairly certain that these objects are not ships or missiles from another nation in this world. Commander Boyd advised that intense research is being carried on presently by Air Intelligence, and at the present time when credible reporting of sightings are received , the Air Force is attempting in each instance to send up jet interceptor planes in order to obtain a better view of these objects. However, recent attempts in this regard have indicated that when the pilot in the jet approaches the object it invariably fades from view.

Oops, again! Another cat out of the bag? *Ships from another planet?* If the press had found out what Gen. Samford's staff had told the FBI, there would have been an explosion at the press conference!

In retrospect, it appears that the good general told the American people a lie when he rejected the interplanetary hypothesis and then offered his opinion that the Washington sightings could be explained as temperature inversions and implied that all sightings would be explained as natural phenomena. It was a lie because he didn't really believe they were all inversions and natural phenomena. *There is no theory to explain these,* Levy was told. Did the general lie simply to calm down the saucer hysteria? Or did he lie because the Top Brass didn't want the American public to know that *some Unidentified Flying Objects are identifiable—as extraterrestrial craft?*

Soon after Samford's press conference Stephen Possony, the top-level scientist and consultant mentioned before (who wrote in April 1952, that the Air Force could not assume that flying saucers were interplanetary; see the previous chapter) provided his opinion on the increase in sightings. Notice in what follows that he starts off by assuming saucers are natural phenomena, consistent with Samford's opinion stated at the press conference, but in contrast to his April memorandum in which he suggested that they could be Soviet devices. Notice, also, his direct refutation of Samford's claim that an "atmospheric inversion" could explain the Washington, D.C., sightings of July. Also, his reference to warming of the Northern Hemisphere of the earth is interesting, considering that this was written almost fifty years ago.

```
SECRET: 1 August 1952
MEMORANDUM FOR GENERAL SAMFORD
SUBJECT: USAF Interest in Flying Saucers.
```

At the risk of boring you with a tedious subject, I want to submit a few ideas which may be helpful in making a proper decision.

What are the Flying Saucers?

It is a well-established heuristic principle that the unknown must be made intelligible by referring to the known. If we ask the question: "What known phenomena bear the greatest similarity to saucers?" The answer seems to be that saucer behavior follows the pattern of electromagnetic phenomena. Assuming for the time being, that the saucers are a natural phenomenon of some electromagnetic kind, and accepting the fact that saucer phenomena have occurred at infrequent intervals throughout history, we should inquire as to the cause of the increased frequency of the occurrence. (The increase is about 4,000-fold from 19th-century reports, though elimination of current sightings would tend to reduce this figure). Since the increase in sightings started in 1946–47, it may be fruitful to tie the sightings to events preceding them and of which there were no counterparts at earlier periods. Prior to the upsurge in saucer sightings, the following new activities took place:

1. The carrying of radioactive particles into the upper atmosphere by means of atomic explosions and production;

2. The penetration of the upper atmosphere by guided missiles, new types of balloons, and perhaps aircraft;

3. The production of shock waves at higher altitude, due to the breaching of the sound barrier;

4. The increased output in radio and radar signals, including television;

5. The seeding of clouds for purposes of weather control;

6. The great increase in commercial and private flying.

Moreover, the present era is characterized by a general "warming up" of the climate in the northern hemisphere. Furthermore, the solar system may be passing through an area in the universe where there is a great deal of debris and where, therefore, an increase in the intensity of the meteoric bombardment may be expected.

It is probable that flying saucers are not caused by any single one of these factors, but by a convergence of causes. If the saucers are really electromagnetic phenomena, there is a possibility that they are connected primarily with atomic activities, and that they are caused by the encounter of radioactive particles and small meteors. In other words, they may be ionized air brought about by the entry of very small meteors into the atmosphere. During burn-up of the meteor metal, the natural degree of ionization may be increased greatly through available radioactive particles, with the possible result that after the destruction of the metallic core, there would be a gaseous rotating ion ball subject to movements in the atmosphere. This "interpretation" occurred to me after an illuminating discussion with General Maxwell, and I emphasize it merely to indicate what type of approach the Air Force should take in tackling the phenomena.

Incidentally, there was no temperature inversion in Washington for a long time, and therefore, the mirage theory does not explain the latest sightings.

What is the Air Force interest?

1. The Air Force continuously will be "on the carpet" as long as no satisfactory explanation can be given. Should the saucer activity increase, pressure by the press and even Congress will be quite considerable.

2. We cannot yet rule out entirely that saucers do represent a threat.

3. If there is any validity to the assumption that the saucers are partly the result of atomic activity, the phenomenon would tie in directly with long range detection and if solved, might lead to an increase in our intelligence capability . . . I suggest therefore, that before the ATIC program be undertaken, a very small panel of scientists be brought together and be briefed on the documentation which is in the files right now.

I presume that the "ATIC program" referred to here is the study carried out by the Battelle Memorial Institute.

By early August, the UFO flap was tapering off. The sighting rate generally exceeded ten per day from July 19 through August 3. After that it dropped to five to ten per day through the rest of August. By the end of September it was below five per day even though the publicity about the sightings continued at a high level. Months later, the Project Blue Book staff determined that the sighting rate had, in fact, peaked about the time of the order to shoot, and just before the press conference. *Could it be that the saucers reacted to the fact that jet aircraft were now pursuing them whenever possible?*

Although the sighting rate diminished, Air Force investigative activity continued at a high rate. At ATIC, there were eight full-time people working on the sightings, and the Battelle Memorial Institute had assigned two full-time employees. There was also a panel of experts to be called upon as needed. The FBI officially learned of the high level of activity on August 15, when the AFOSI told the FBI it would accept reports and transmit them to Wright-Patterson Air Force Base. A few days later, the AFOSI liaison at Bolling Air Force Base contacted FBI headquarters and requested that any information be telephoned to him immediately. According to a memorandum dated August 18, "the Air Force is greatly concerned about [flying saucers] and would appreciate the Bureau's cooperation in immediately advising of details received concerning such complaints." A few days after that, a review of communications from the field offices showed that the local FBI agents were not following the instructions issued in 1947 and 1949 to report sightings to the local AFOSI offices, so a new SAC letter, #83, was issued on August 29 to reiterate the instructions. The same letter pointed out the FBI should do no more than collect the basic sighting information to forward to the AFOSI because the investigation of such reports was the responsibility of the Air Force, not the FBI.

On August 26, the Air Force contacted the FBI with a rather strange request: *please analyze a hat that was burned by a flying saucer!*

The incident occurred after dark on August 19, in Florida. A scoutmaster, "Sonny" Desvergers, and three Boy Scouts were driving near West Palm Beach, when they saw a lighted object descend quickly into some woods across a field. Sonny felt that he had to stop in the event that it was a crashed airplane. Before he left the boys to walk into the woods, he told them if he didn't return in ten minutes they should walk to the nearest phone and alert the police. As Desvergers approached the edge of the woods, the boys could see the light from his flashlight. Then another light appeared and reddish ball of fire moved downward and seemed to knock Desvergers down. Then a reddish thing, like a disc, moved upward and disappeared. The boys panicked and ran to a farm, where the farmer phoned the police. The deputy sheriff and another officer arrived about half an hour later, in time to see Sonny stumbling out of the woods. He said he had been knocked unconscious by a flying saucer. The deputy sheriff said that Desvergers looked terrified. As they rode to the sheriff's office, Desvergers noted that his arms, face, and the cap on his head were all burned. It was this cap that showed up at the FBI testing laboratory.

The FBI found no residue on the cap and no way to explain the burning. They did not think it had been burned by a flame. The Boy Scouts testified that the cap seemed to be in perfect condition before the event. The Air Force (Capt. Ruppelt) investigated this case and sent soil samples to the Battelle Memorial Institute for analysis. It was found that the grass above water in this marshy area seemed healthy, but *the roots had been burned.*

Ruppelt and the Project Blue Book staff discovered that people who knew Desvergers did not trust him. Many people thought he had made up the sighting. The Air Force investigators decided that the Scouts probably had misidentified aircraft lights or something else and had not really seen a flying disc in the woods. Consequently they decided that the sighting was probably a hoax. However, they never did explain the burned cap and the burned grass roots!

The FBI did not want the public to know about its minimal involvement with the saucer phenomenon. Therefore, when an article appeared in the *New Yorker* magazine on September 6, stating that the FBI conducted certain inquiries for the Air Force, the FBI contacted several of the AFOSI offices and the office of Gen. Samford to find out who had leaked the information. No one knew where the reporter might have gotten the impression that the FBI investigated sightings. The FBI contacted ATIC. Capt. Ruppelt responded that ATIC did not in any way implicate the FBI, and he offered his opinion that the reporter had made it up. He also said that, so far as he knew, the FBI had never been called upon to furnish saucer information. (His incorrect belief that the FBI had never investigated was published in the book he wrote three years later.) Finally the FBI contacted the Air Force public affairs officer. He, too, denied giving the reporter any information about the FBI. The FBI never did learn where the reporter got his information, or whether Ruppelt was correct is assuming that the reporter had simply made it up.

While the FBI was trying to get its field agents straightened out on how to handle the saucer business and, at the same time, not reveal its minimal, but secret involvement, the sighting rate slowed but did not stop. To get an overview of what had happened, consider the number of sighted objects for every month from April through December of 1952: Apr. (82), May (79), Jun. (148), Jul. (536), Aug. (326), Sept. (124), Oct. (61), Nov. (50) and Dec. (42). Clearly something strange had happened, with the maximum strangeness occurring in July and August. The total of all sightings of 1952 together came to 1,501 objects sighted—*the year of the UFO!*

Needless to say, the Blue Book and Battelle analysts were kept busy. The time lag between a sighting and its analysis could be months. Such was the case with a very famous photographic sighting that occurred on July 2, 1952, a sighting which had a major impact on the insiders.

Navy Warrant Officer and Chief Photographer Delbert Newhouse, his wife, and family were driving through Utah on their way to California. They were about seven miles west of Tremonton, when Mrs. Newhouse saw strange-looking objects moving erratically through the sky. She pointed them out to her husband. After twenty-one years in the Navy and 2,000 hours as an aerial photographer, he knew what ordinary objects in the sky looked like, and these weren't ordinary. According to Newhouse, they were circular and looked like two pie pans, one inverted on top of the lower one. After pulling the car to the roadside, he hurried to get his movie camera out of the car's trunk. During this time, the objects were moving away from him and by the time he got the camera going they were quite far away. They made small images on the film, with no particular features. Newhouse immediately turned his film over to the Navy for evaluation. The Air Force photo lab at Wright-Patterson AFB also studied the film. After several weeks of work, they ruled out birds, balloons, and other aircraft. No one knew what they were. Word of this extraordinary evidence worked its way up through the ranks and finally showed up in the X-File. An FBI memorandum written on October 27 reads:

> Air Intelligence advised of another creditable and unexplainable sighting of flying saucers. Air Intelligence still feels flying saucers are optical illusions or other atmospheric phenomena but some military officials are seriously considering the possibility of interplanetary ships.

You will recall that Air Intelligence has previously kept the Bureau advised regarding developments pertaining to Air Intelligence research on the flying saucer problem. Air Intelligence has previously advised that all research pertaining to this problem is handled by the Air Technical Intelligence Center located at Wright-Patterson Air Force Base, Dayton, Ohio; that approximately 90 percent of the reported sightings of flying saucers can be discounted as products of the imagination and as explainable objects such as weather balloons, etc., but that a small percentage of extremely creditable sightings have been unexplainable.

Colonel C. M. Young, Executive Officer to Major General John A. Samford, Director of Intelligence, Air Force, advised on October 23, 1952, that another recent extremely creditable sighting had been reported to Air Intelligence. A Navy photographer, while traveling across the United States in his own car, saw a number of objects in the sky which appeared to be flying saucers. He took approximately thirty-five feet of motion picture film of these objects. He voluntarily submitted the film to Air Intelligence who had it studied by the Air Technical Intelligence Center. Experts at the Air Technical Intelligence Center have advised that, after careful study, there were as many as twelve to sixteen flying objects recorded on this film; that the possibility of weather balloons, clouds or other explainable objects has been completely ruled out; and that they are at a complete loss to explain this most recent creditable sighting. The Air Technical Intelligence Center experts pointed out that they could not be optical illusions inasmuch as optical illusions could not be recorded on film.

Colonel Young advised that Air Intelligence still feels that the so-called flying saucers are either optical illusions or atmospheric phenomena. He point out, however, that some military officials are seriously considering the possibility of interplanetary ships.

Oops, again! Military officials are seriously considering *interplanetary ships?* Had newspapers published this in 1952, the history of the UFO subject would be entirely different!

This FBI report clearly indicates the confusion within the middle ranks of the Air Force about what was really going on. Experts in film analysis had ruled out optical illusions or atmospheric phenomena as an explanation for Newhouse's film, *and subsequent analysis has proven that optical illusions and atmospheric phenomena could not have explained this sighting.* Nevertheless the Air Force was holding out the *hope*—that's the only way one can explain it, hope—that saucer sightings could be explained as optical illusions and atmospheric phenomena.

However at times it must have appeared there was little hope. Things looked bleak for the explainers. At a January 23, 1953 briefing for the Air Defense Command (ADC) on the status of UFO investigations, the Project Blue Book personnel admitted in private what they would never say publicly. Based on a statistical breakdown of about 1,000 sightings received through military channels in 1952, the Blue Book staff concluded that—get this—*only eleven percent of the reports could be positively identified.* These reports fell into the categories astronomical, balloons, aircraft, other, and hoaxes. Most of the remaining sightings were labeled *probably* identified (17%), *possibly* identified (29%) and *unknown* (20%). There was also a separate category for sightings that were indeterminate. That is, they couldn't make a definite decision whether or not these sightings were identifiable because of "insufficient information" (23%). Considering that a large proportion of these sightings had been generated by ADC personnel (pilots, air traffic controllers, etc.) on duty at the times of their sightings, the ADC officials, who were in charge of protecting the United States from a Soviet attack, must have been sorely dismayed to learn how many sightings were not immediately identifiable. It is to be noted, by the way, that the low percentage of positive identifications was not public knowledge. Whenever public statements were issued regarding the percentages of unknowns and knowns the *possible, probable and insufficient information* cases were all *added* to the positively identified cases, thereby creating a statistic which showed the *largest portion of sightings* (roughly 80%) *as (positively) identified.* Appealing to the "logic" of the situation (based on the assumption that there was no evidence to show saucers were real), the Air Force would then claim that the unknown sightings could have been explained, too, if there had been more information about them. In other words, they essentially reclassified the *unknowns* as *insufficient information* even though there was a separate category for those indeterminate cases and the unknowns could have been placed into that category initially, if the analysts had thought there was not enough information for a clear decision for, or against, identification.

After learning what happened in 1952, one wonders just how many times the saucers would have to beat the Air Force over the head before the military would admit they were real. Could it be that the people having delusions were not the witnesses, but the Air Force intelligence experts who so desperately wanted to *disbelieve* the information pouring in from all over the United States, the evidence that was right in front of their noses?

Or was this denial of evidence effectively orchestrated from above, from the top of the military and government command structure, in order to cover up something about flying saucers that certain government officials didn't want people to know? Another secret government agency decided it was time to find out just what was going on. Too bad this agency contacted the Air Force first, before doing its own independent investigation!

Enter the CIA.

CHAPTER 21

The X-File: CIA Version

The Central Intelligence Agency also had a file on the unexplained. A large portion of that file is even related to psychic phenomena, a subject for another book. What is of interest here is the file on Unidentified Flying Objects. Let's look into how that file happened to come about.

One very important effect of the 1952 UFO flap is not what happened in the press, but what happened behind closed doors. Recall that in July, ATIC received 536 reports. Apparently this tremendous flow of reports, and the sightings over Washington, were too much for the Director of Central Intelligence (DCI), Walter Bedell Smith. He decided that it was time to find out what was really going on out there.

The CIA had been monitoring the flying saucer sightings worldwide on a very casual basis since 1947. A memorandum written on March 15, 1949 indicates that at least one CIA employee was unimpressed by sightings he had studied. The memo suggests some of the usual explanations (meteorological balloons, meteors, psychological effects) and rules out the possibility that secret aircraft or guided missiles by either the United States or the Soviet Union could account for the sightings. Another

Walter Bedell Smith,
Director of Central
Intelligence.

memorandum, dated March 31, 1949, mentions the conclusion of Project Sign, that sightings can be categorized generally as explained (misidentifications of conventional aircraft, balloons, natural phenomena, or as hoaxes) and unexplained, and goes on to offer the following possibilities for the unexplained sightings:

a) Natural terrestrial phenomena:
   (1) Meteorological (ball lightning)
   (2) Some type of animal
   (3) Hallucinatory or psychological phenomena

b) Man-made terrestrial phenomena:
   (1) Advanced type of aircraft

c) Extra-terrestrial objects:
   (1) Meteors
   (2) Animals
   (3) Spaceships

The memorandum concludes by mentioning the scientists involved in the investigation and their conclusions regarding the unexplained cases:

Studies on the various possibilities have been made by Dr. Langmuir of GE [General Electric Corporation], Dr. Valley of the MIT [Massachusetts Institute of Technology], Dr. Lipp of Project Rand, Dr. Hynek of Ohio State and [by the] Aero Medical Laboratory.

That the objects are from outer space or are an advanced aircraft of a foreign power is a possibility, but the above group have concluded that it is highly improbable.

Following the date of this memorandum, the CIA maintained a continuous review of sighting data. Evidently there was nothing found of interest to the CIA because there are no further entries in the CIA file until 1952. The 1952 concentration was, however, just too much to ignore.

On July 29, the same day as Gen. Samford's press conference, Acting Assistant Director for Scientific Intelligence of the CIA, Ralph Clark, wrote a memorandum for the Deputy Director of Intelligence stating that the CIA had been "maintaining a continuing review of such reported sightings for the last three years," and that a special group had been formed to study the situation. Three days later, a member of the study group, Edward Tauss, Chief of the Weapons and Equipment Division of the Office of Scientific Intelligence, responded to Clark's request "for an overall evaluation" of the saucer situation. He said most of the large number of (nearly 1,500) reports received by AMC/ATIC had been explained, but about 100 credible sightings had not been explained. He pointed out that there was no discernible pattern to the unexplained reports and offered his opinion: ". . . it is probable that if complete information were available for presently 'unexplainable" reports, they, too, could be [explained]." If his opinion were correct, there would be no need for CIA involvement. However, he added a cautionary note, which formed the basis for continued CIA involvement:

> Notwithstanding the foregoing tentative facts, so long as a series of reports remains "unexplainable" (interplanetary aspects and alien origin not being thoroughly excluded from consideration), caution requires that intelligence continue coverage of the subject.

He recommended continued "CIA surveillance of subject matter" in coordination with AMC/ATIC, and said that he had arranged for a briefing by ATIC personnel on August 8. He recommended that "no indication of CIA interest or concern reach the press or public, in view of their probable alarmist tendencies to accept such interest as 'confirmatory' of the soundness of 'unpublished facts' in the hands of the U.S. Government."

CIA memoranda written by several study group members dated August 14, 15, and 19 provide details on what the CIA learned from ATIC and from the CIA's own study of sightings. According to the August 14 memorandum, the CIA made its own check on the "U.S. secret project" explanation. The Chairman of the Research and Development Board denied, at the Top Secret level, that any U.S. development could account for saucer sightings. Not satisfied with this top-level denial, the author of the memorandum pointed out "two factors which tend to confirm the denials—first, the official action of alerting all Air Force commands to intercept, and second, the unbelievable risk of such flights in established airlanes."

On August 20, the Director of Central Intelligence (DCI), Walter Bedell Smith, was briefed on the flying saucer situation. He directed his staff to prepare a memorandum for the National Security Council that would state the need for an investigation, and direct various agencies to cooperate in the investigation.

A document titled "The Air Force Stand on 'Flying Saucers,' as stated by the CIA in a briefing on 22 August 1952," contains the following information based on the CIA visit to ATIC:

I. The Air Force has primary responsibility for investigating the "flying saucers." The unit concerned with these investigations is a part of the Air Technical Intelligence Center at Dayton, Ohio, and consists of three officers (a Captain in charge) and two civilians. They receive reports of sightings, analyze and attempt to explain them. A standard reporting form has been prepared which is used on a world-wide basis. The Air Force Office of Special Investigations checks into each sighting attempting to determine its authenticity and the reliability of the observer.

II. (A) The Air Force officially denies that "flying saucers" are:

    (1) U.S. secret weapons

    (2) Soviet secret weapons

    (3) Extra-terrestrial visitors

II. (B) It is believed that all sightings of "flying saucers" are:

    (1) Well-known objects such as balloons, aircraft, meteors, clouds, etc., not recognized by the observer

    (2) Phenomena of the atmosphere which are at present poorly understood, e.g., refractions and reflections caused by temperature inversion, ionization phenomena, ball lightning, etc.

III. Not a shred of evidence exists to substantiate the belief that "flying saucers" are material objects not falling into category II B(1), above.

IV. A study of "flying saucer" sightings on a geographical basis showed them to be more frequent in the vicinity of atomic energy installations (which is explained by the greater security consciousness of persons in those areas). That by-products of atomic fission may in some way act catalytically to produce "flying saucers" has not been disproved. The greatest number of sightings has been made at or near Dayton, Ohio, where the investigations are going on.

V. Of the thousands of "flying saucers" sighted of which there are records, the Air Force says that 78% have been explained by either II B(1) or II B(2) above, 2% have been exposed as hoaxes and the remaining 20% have not been explained, primarily because of the vague descriptions given by observers.

VI. The Air Force is mostly interested in the "saucer" problem because of its psychological warfare implications. In reviewing publications designed for Soviet consumption, there has not been a single reference to "flying saucers." On the other hand, several "saucer" societies in the United States have been investigated. Key members of some of these societies which have been instrumental in keeping the "flying saucer" craze before the public have been exposed as being of doubtful loyalty. Furthermore the societies , in some cases, are financed by an unknown source. The Air Force realizes that a public made jumpy by the "flying saucer" scare would be a serious liability in the event of air attacks by an enemy. Air defense could not operate effectively if the Air Force were constantly called upon to intercept mirages which persons had mistaken for enemy aircraft.

Evidently the opinion of the "saucer craze" as expressed by the Project Blue Book staff to the CIA study group was considerably different from the opinion expressed by AFI personnel in the Pentagon to the AFOSI and to the FBI (see the previous chapter). The AFI personnel admitted that there was a "hard core" amounting to about three percent of the sightings, such as many reported by commercial and Air Force pilots, which could not be explained and this led some top-level officials to believe that saucers could be interplanetary vehicles. Because the Project Blue Book personnel were very skeptical, even cynical, about UFO sightings, they did not tell the CIA study group about the "hard core." Instead the CIA representatives were told that "20% have not been explained, primarily because of the vague descriptions." This was misinformation provided (perhaps intentionally) to the CIA by the Blue Book personnel. The fact is that the hardcore three percent of the total number of sightings (fifteen percent of the unexplained sightings) had well-reported, explicitly described details which *prevented* identification as known phenomena.

Instead of being told that saucers were most often reported in the vicinity of airports, as Comm. Boyd had correctly told the FBI, the CIA was told, incorrectly, that saucers were most frequently seen near Dayton, Ohio. The Blue Book personnel did not tell the CIA representative that whenever a pursuing jet tried to get close to a saucer, it invariably would fade from view, nor did they tell the CIA that the extraterrestrial hypothesis was not being overlooked. Instead, as the CIA perceived it, the Air Force had officially taken a rigid stand against the extraterrestrial hypothesis: anything *but* ET.

Why would the Blue Book personnel do such a thing? We know from the FBI documents that the Top Brass at the Pentagon did *not* flatly deny that flying saucers could be ET visitors. We also know that there was a considerable amount of highly credible testimonial evidence available to the ATIC personnel to show that saucers could not be explained as II (B) above. We also know that the hardcore unexplained cases did not have "vague descriptions" that prevented identification. In fact, the Battelle Memorial Institute study was finding the opposite: the unexplained cases had lots of details that prevented identification as mundane objects. Furthermore, Battelle discovered that, on a statistical basis, the better sighting, with more details and more credible observers, the more difficult it was to explain. (A year or so later the Battelle study would discover that nearly thirty-three percent of the best sightings by military witnesses were not explainable!) Several examples of such cases have been presented in previous chapters. So the question is, why did Project Blue Book misinform the CIA? Was it because the Blue Book staff really believed there was no ET evidence at all, or was to it to prevent the CIA from looking more deeply into the saucer problem and perhaps *discovering something the Air Force wanted to keep secret?*

Although the document contains some incorrect information, it also provides some information not found elsewhere. It states a geographical study that showed saucer sightings occurred more often at nuclear installations. This contradicts Gen. Samford's statement to the press that there seemed to be no threatening pattern to saucer sightings.

The comment about the "publications designed for Soviet consumption" (the Soviet press) not having any saucer reports, while the U.S. press was full of them, was intended to indicate a disparity that could work to the advantage of the Soviets if there were an attack. The importance of this disparity is clarified in the last sentence which indicates that public reporting of saucers during an attack on the United States could be a "serious liability," whereas the Soviets would have no such liability. In fact, in the future months this would develop into three fundamental worries of the CIA: (1) a large flux of saucer sightings, whether saucers were "real" or not, during a time of national emergency could have a negative psychological impact on the American people, (2) saucer reports could act as "decoy unknowns," diverting the limited number of defensive aircraft from protecting against attacking aircraft, which would initially also appear on radar sensors as "unknowns," and (3) a large flux of saucer reports could clog defense communications channels.

One more thing to note in the CIA document is the statement that individuals and groups that promoted saucer studies had been investigated to check on the possibility of subversive activity. The reference to groups being funded by an unknown source indicates that the CIA suspected that some saucer groups might actually be funded by the Soviets. Evidently the CIA did not know that the FBI had already looked for subversion and hadn't found any in 1947. However, in the 1950s both the CIA and the FBI did keep track of some saucer enthusiasts and groups. (Yes, Big Brother *was* watching!)

By early September the CIA staff had collected enough information to make an informal report to the DCI. Dr. H. Marshall Chadwell, the Assistant Director for Scientific Intelligence, reported that the study had been undertaken to determine "whether or not adequate study and research is currently being directed to this problem in its relation to national security implications," and what further work should be carried out. He reported that the only work on the problem was that being done by the Air Technical Intelligence Center under the authority of the Air Force Directorate of Intelligence. Chadwell wrote:

> OSI [Office of Scientific Intelligence within the CIA] entered into its inquiry fully aware that it was coming into a field already charged with partisanship, one in which objectivity had been overridden by numerous sensational writers, and one in which there are pressures for extravagant explanation as well as for oversimplification. The OSI Team consulted with a representative of the Air Force Special Studies Group; discussed the problem with those in charge of the Air Force Project at Wright Field; reviewed a considerable volume of intelligence reports; checked the Soviet press and broadcast indices; and conferred with three OSI consultant, all leaders in their scientific fields, who were chosen because of their broad knowledge of the technical areas concerned.

OSI found that the ATIC study is probably valid if the purpose is limited to a case-by-case explanation. However, the study makes no attempt to solve the more fundamental aspect of the problem, which is to determine definitely the nature of the various phenomena which are causing these sightings, or to discover means by which these causes and their visual or electronic effects may be immediately identified. Our consultant panel stated that these solutions would probably be found on the margins or just beyond the frontiers of our present knowledge in the fields of atmospheric, ionospheric, and extraterrestrial phenomena, with the added possibility that our present dispersal of nuclear waste products might also be a factor.

The consultant panel recommended the formation of a study group to analyze the fundamental sighting information, determine what fundamental sciences would be involved and make recommendations for further study.

Dr. Chadwell then got to the heart of the problem from the national security point of view. First there was the psychological aspect. The CIA could find no mention of saucers in the Soviet media, so the Russians were not being "conditioned" to believe in saucers by the Russian press, which was saying nothing about saucers. In the U.S., on the other hand, the recent continual press interest and "pressure of inquiry on the Air Force" indicated that a fair proportion of the population had been "mentally conditioned to the acceptance of the incredible. In this fact lies the potential for touching-off of mass hysteria and panic." In other words, if a nefarious group of individuals bent on destroying the United States were to start publicizing UFO reports, U.S. citizens might panic.

The second national security aspect was air vulnerability. There was the possibility that a flux of saucer sightings at a time of air attack could cause the Air Force to divert precious hardware (jet fighters) to check out spurious unidentified saucers, when they should be flying toward the unidentified aircraft. Dr. Chadwell suggested immediate steps should be taken to improve the methods of quickly identifying unknown objects or phenomena. He also suggested that U.S. intelligence agencies should determine the level of Soviet knowledge about the phenomenon so we could defend ourselves against attempts by the Soviets to use their knowledge to our detriment, while at the same time using our knowledge of saucers to our advantage. By this he meant using saucer sightings as part of psychological warfare against the Soviets. Finally, he recommended the National Security Council direct the CIA to begin a study along the lines he outlined.

Dr. Chadwell's memorandum to the Director apparently met with some favor, because in early October he wrote another memorandum in which he concluded that "flying saucers pose two elements of danger which have national security implications. The first involves mass psychological considerations and the second concerns the vulnerability of the United States to air attack." Chadwell then made the following recommendations:

(a) That the Director of Central Intelligence advise the National Security Council of the implications of the "flying saucer" problem and request that research be initiated.

(b) That the DCI discuss this subject with the Psychological Strategy Board, [and]

(c) That [the] CIA, with the cooperation of the Psychological Strategy Board and other interested departments and agencies, develop and recommend for adoption by the NSC a policy of public information which will minimize concern and possible panic resulting from the numerous sightings of unidentified objects.

A draft proposal was written for presentation to the Intelligence Advisory Committee (IAC) and Secretary of Defense, Robert Lovett. (Recall that he had been an Undersecretary of Defense at the time of the December 6, 1950, alert.) On December 2, Dr. Chadwell summarized the situation regarding the NSC directive, and included in his memorandum to the DCI the following statement, which indicates a level of concern that goes beyond what the Air Force had conveyed to the CIA months earlier:

Recent reports reaching the CIA indicated that further action was desirable and another briefing by the cognizant A-2 [air intelligence] and ATIC personnel was held on 25 November. At this time, the reports of incidents convince us that there is something going on that must have immediate attention. The details of some of these incidents have been discussed by AD/SI [Associate Director of the Scientific Intelligence Division] with DDCI [Deputy Director of the CIA]. Sightings of unexplained objects at great altitudes and travelling at high speeds in the vicinity of major U.S. defense installations are of such nature that they are not attributable to natural phenomena or known types of aerial vehicles.

Note that the meeting on November 25 was about a month after the FBI was told of the "extremely credible and unexplainable" sighting by Navy photographer Delbert Newhouse in Tremonton, Utah (see previous chapter). Note also that Dr. Chadwell did *not* say sightings *are* or *might be* attributable to natural or man-made phenomena; he said they *are not* attributable to natural or man-made phenomena. Could it be that he was convinced?

He went on to say that OSI was about to establish a "consulting group of sufficient competence and stature to review this matter and convince the responsible authorities in the community that immediate research and development on this subject must be undertaken." Notice that he expected the "consulting group" would be able to *convince* the "responsible authorities" to immediately undertake research on "this subject." This statement gives the impression that Chadwell was quite certain the consulting group would conclude, as he apparently had, that saucers were real objects flying around U. S. defense installations and other locations.

Chadwell's proposal was accepted, and on December 4, the IAC was briefed on the problem. Present at the meeting were representatives of the Air Force, the Army, the Navy, the Department of State, and six representatives from the CIA, including Dr. Chadwell. Gen. Samford represented AFI. Also present was Mr. Meffert Kuhrtz, acting for the Assistant to the Director, FBI.

The CIA version of the minutes of the IAC meeting shows only that the IAC approved having the CIA set up a review of the available evidence and scientific theories. Gen. Samford offered the AFI cooperation. Any further work would depend upon the result of the scientific study. Kuhrtz' report to the FBI, written December 5, provides a bit more information. It says that Dr. Chadwell talked about a theory of saucers that had been suggested by a German atomic scientist (his name was censored from the released document). He also said that a "recent" saucer sighting in Africa "presents some evidence that the 'saucers' are not a meteorological phenomena, which theory has been held to date by the Air Force." Kuhrtz said details of the African report were not given but that he would try to get the details from the Air Force. According to Khurtz's report, the IAC approved the idea of having a group of scientists study the sightings and try to identify the saucers. This would be carried out under CIA direction. The IAC would not get involved unless the scientists determined that the saucers were devices "under control of our enemy." (Presumably, then, if extraterrestrials controlled the saucers and if they were not our enemy, then the IAC would not become involved.) On December 23, Kuhrtz reported the CIA had information about an explosion in Africa that had been picked up on seismographs. There were reports "of unknown reliability" that associated the explosion with a flying saucer.

During December, Dr. Chadwell wrote several memoranda that show that he was impressed by the Tremonton, Utah, (Newhouse) film, and by the Florida scoutmaster ("Sonny" Desvergers) landing case (both discussed in the previous chapter). He also met with several scientists to brief them and get their opinions. Most of them agreed that the subject should be studied, but Chadwell's memoranda do not indicate they were enthusiastic about studying saucer sightings. Also during December and January, the CIA and ATIC (under Capt. Ruppelt) prepared for the big meeting that would decide the fate of the CIA study of UFOs. The CIA asked Dr. H. P. Robertson, a distinguished scientist, formerly of Princeton and the California Institute of Technology, and a consultant to the CIA, to establish a panel of "top scientists and engineers in the fields of astrophysics, nuclear energy, electronics, etc., to review this situation." AFI and ATIC offered full support, and Capt. Ruppelt and the Project

Dr. H. P. Robertson headed the CIA's Robertson panel, which studied saucer sightings.

Blue Book staff prepared a briefing for the scientists. Unfortunately the Battelle study was nowhere near completion (it wouldn't be finished for about a year), so the complete statistical analyses were not available.

The meeting convened on Wednesday, January 14. Attending were Dr. Robertson, Dr. Samuel Goudsmit (co-discoverer of electron spin), Dr. Luiz Alvarez (professor of physics; Nobel prize winner many years later), and Dr. Thornton Page (professor of astronomy). Two days later Dr. Lloyd Berkner (physicist; radar engineer) arrived in time for the closing sessions. The ATIC representatives had spent weeks preparing for this meeting, but because of time limitations were only able to present in detail about two dozen of the sightings they considered their best evidence. Two of these were the Newhouse film and the Washington, D.C., sightings discussed before. The panel of scientists, after a few hours of study, concluded that "reasonable explanations could be suggested for most sightings and 'by deduction and scientific method it could be induced (given additional data) that other cases might be explained in similar manner.'" One particularly egregious example of their explanations was that "birds" explained Delbert Newhouse's film, which the ATIC had said couldn't be explained. The claim by the photographic analysts that the images were too bright to be reflections from birds was discounted. And Newhouse's visual sighting of pie-pan-like objects before he started filming was not even mentioned!

Obviously these expert scientists did not get the full picture in their several day review of a five-year phenomenon that had generated thousands of reports. Hence their conclusions were based on a lack of information and a lack of understanding combined with a natural bias against anything unusual that wouldn't fit their scientific "worldview." Another example of a faulty conclusion based on insufficient information was that of Dr. Thornton Page. He argued that saucers couldn't be extraterrestrial craft because such craft wouldn't appear in only one country. Of course he was correct; they would show up all over the world. What he didn't know, and apparently no one told him, was that saucers *had* been seen all over the world.

The panel concluded that, even though they were not "real," the saucers were a danger for the reasons already cited above. An enemy could use an existing saucer flap or create one with balloons or some other devices in order to swamp the communications channels with sighting reports while using the objects as decoys for the actual attacking aircraft. To reduce the danger, the panel recommended stripping the saucers of their special status and starting a program of education and "debunking," or explaining, so the general public would be better able to identify normal aerial objects and phenomena. Once the subject had been sufficiently debunked, the general public would believe that all the sightings had been explained and so there would be less interest in reporting.

Although the debunking recommendation of the panel was not widely disseminated, it did have an effect. Over the next twelve months, after Ruppelt left the project (and retired), Project Blue Book went from being an active analytical organization to mere shadow of its former self, with investigations carried out by another organization (the 4602 Air Intelligence Service Squadron). The activities of the Project Blue Book were centered on categorizing sightings into two classes, those which they could explain and those which they could not explain, and then filing these sightings away, with no further study of the unexplained sightings. The other major Blue Book activity was handling the publicity surrounding UFO sightings. Whenever the press asked the Air Force about sightings, Blue Book provided an answer.

During the following year, the Air Force issued two new regulations that virtually guaranteed secrecy about saucer sightings by military people. These documents restricted information released to those sightings which had been explained, and threatened a fine and prison term for military people who intentionally released UFO information without proper authorization.

In the months and years following the Robertson panel, the number of sighted objects fluctuated from roughly 500 to roughly 1,000 per year. Project Blue Book claimed that all but about three percent could be explained and, without supporting evidence, claimed that even those could have been explained if more information had been available. Not only was there no supporting evidence for this claim, the Battelle scientists, many months *after* the Robertson panel, discovered evidence to contradict it. They discovered that the highest quality sightings with the *most* information were the *least* likely to be explainable. The most obvious example of well-reported sightings came from on-duty military witnesses between 1947 and 1952: *about thirty-three percent of these sightings were unexplained!*

And what happened to the CIA? Insofar as could be determined from the released documents, the agency essentially ignored the saucer phenomenon from then on. They collected some sightings from around the world and occasionally reviewed the situation, but never again did the agency officially take the same interest that was shown in the summer of 1952, before ATIC "pulled the wool over their eyes."*

---

*Note: Some employees of the CIA did become interested in saucer sightings in August 1955, but not because they thought saucers might be extraterrestrial craft or some unusual phenomenon. According to CIA historian Gerald Haines, writing in the journal *Studies in Intelligence* (Spring, 1997), they became interested because they believed that *their project was generating saucer sightings!* Their project was the U-2 high altitude spy plane. This airplane was designed to fly at 60,000–70,000 feet, where it would be essentially invisible to ground-level observers during the daytime. Nevertheless, these project employees believed that observers did see these aircraft in the early morning before sunrise and in the evening after sunset when direct illumination by the sun would cause bright reflections, perhaps reddish in color because of atmospheric reddening of the sunlight. The employees assumed that an observer, seeing the glint of sunlight and believing nothing could fly that high, would report a sighting of a flying saucer. Therefore these employees believed that there was an increase in reports when the U-2 started flying. Furthermore, according to Dr. Haines, the employees believed that U-2 flights in the late 1950s and into the 1960s caused as much as fifty percent of the UFO sightings.

However, a study of the statistical sighting data of Project Blue Book and civilian organizations, and especially a study of the sightings that occurred near sunrise and near sunset, shows no effect of the U-2 sightings when they began in August 1955. The statistical data provide no support for the claim that a large fraction of UFO reports were caused by U-2 flights.

CHAPTER 22

Government Witnesses

Over the next few years, the FBI received one or two reports per year (while the Air Force was still receiving hundreds per year). Two of these reports are worthy of mention.

Richard Russell saw two flying saucers while he was riding on a train. Now, by itself this wouldn't seem very important. There have been other reports by people on trains. However, those other people were not in charge of the Senate Armed Services Committee, but Richard Russell was. And those other people were not travelling through the Soviet Union when they had their sightings—*Senator Russell was.* And when those other people told their stories, few people paid any attention. But when Sen. Russell told his story, *the FBI and the CIA sat right up and listened closely.* According to the records of the Air Force, CIA, and FBI, this is what happened.

On October 4, 1955, at dusk, while Sen. Russell, Col. E. U. Hathaway, a U.S. Army Staff officer assigned to the Senate Armed Services Committee, Reuben Efron, a committee consultant who was keeping records and acting as interpreter, and another business man (possibly a covert CIA agent) were riding on a train through the Baku area of the Soviet

Union near the Caspian Sea. Sen. Russell, who was not feeling well at the time, was alone in one compartment with the lights off while the others were in the next compartment talking with the lights on. Sen. Russell happened to look outside when he saw a yellow-green light rise vertically upward from a location some distance south of the train. It moved upward at a moderate speed from some initial altitude to a higher altitude and then accelerated and traveled northward, passing directly over the moving train. He ran into the next compartment and yelled "Did you see that out there? I just saw a flying saucer." The three men in the compartment had not been looking outside. They turned out the lights and all four looked out the window. "I saw it coming up from over there. Here it is, coming up again." Suddenly a second one repeated the performance. After the second one had disappeared over the train, Sen. Russell said "We saw a flying saucer . . . I wanted you boys to see it so I would have witnesses." The verbal descriptions and the illustration presented by Col. Hathaway and Mr. Efron to the Air Attaché at the Embassy in Prague ten days later indicate that they saw a rotating, circular craft with two stationary lights. The Air Attaché wrote a report on what he was told and sent it to the Air Force. His report begins with the following statement by Col. Hathaway:

> I doubt if you're going to believe this but we all saw it. Senator Russell was the first to see this flying saucer and he called us to the window and we both [Hathaway and Efron] saw the second one. We've been told for years that there isn't such a thing but all of us saw it. There were two lights towards the inside of the disc which remained stationary as the outer surface went around. The lights sat near the top of the disc. The aircraft was circular [and] resembled a flying saucer. [It was] revolving clockwise or to the right. There was no noticeable color. The disc rose in the same position as it was in when it sped away. Some sparking or flame came out of the bottom as the craft rose.

The report contains an illustration showing an object that was flat on the bottom with a raised portion or dome on the top. The witnesses saw no protrusions or anything like wings. The Air Attaché's report also included conventional intelligence information on Soviet aircraft, radar installations, and railroads that had been observed by Sen. Russell's party during their trip. The report was classified Top Secret until 1959, when it was downgraded to Secret. It was not released until 1985.

Shortly after Sen. Russell returned to the United States, the CIA got into the act. Over the next month or so the CIA agents interviewed the witnesses and Herbert Scoville, Assistant Director for Scientific Intelligence, tried to make some sense out of the four somewhat divergent descriptions of what happened. One gets the impression that even before he interviewed all the witnesses, Dr. Scoville had more or less concluded they had not seen a "flying saucer." He suggested they had seen helicopters or jets taking off. He even mentioned the remote possibility they had seen a Soviet version of something like the Air Force's circular aircraft referred to as "Project Y," which at that time was being researched by the AVRO company in Canada under a USAF contract. The Chief of the CIA's Applied Science section pointed out that if the Soviets had, in fact, flown a circular "Y-type" craft, then they had jumped far ahead of our own work. However, he doubted that possibility since there had been no other reports to indicate such progress by the Soviets.*

The FBI first learned of this sighting during the IAC meeting of October 18. At that meeting the CIA Director, Allen Dulles, reported the very basic details of Sen. Russell's sighting, and the others. FBI Liaison Khurtz wrote that the IAC members thought it could have been a helicopter or something else, but that more information was necessary. Several weeks later, on November 8, an FBI agent summarized the information received from the CIA, which had by now interviewed all the witnesses. The CIA had concluded that the only testimony which "would support the existence of flying saucer or radically unconventional aircraft is that of Colonel Hathaway." The CIA claimed that:

> All other observations can probably be explained as [a] steep-climbing aircraft or missile or [the] exhaust of [a] normal jet aircraft in a dive, followed by a sharp pull-up in such

---

* Note the similarity here between the 1948–1949 time period when the Air Force considered the possibility that the green fireballs and saucers might be Soviet developments of atomic-powered aircraft and then rejected this possibility because the Air Force did not believe the Soviets had gotten that far ahead.

a way [that] nothing could be seen until [the] exhaust [became] visible to observers on [the] train, but [it is] possible [the] aircraft was indeed of the short or almost vertical take-off variety.

The implication was, of course, that if the other descriptions could be explained away, then probably Col. Hathaway's could be too, in spite of the fact that he was probably the most qualified of the observers.

A comparison of the November 1955 assessment with the initial interview a month earlier shows how much the information had been "watered down," with various important elements of the description being rejected one after another as necessary to arrive at an explanation. Perhaps the most surprising part of the description was the rotation of the outer surface, while the two lights, like "eyes," stayed constant. Obviously any man-made craft with wing lights or whatever that went into rotation would cause the lights to also rotate. Of course this portion of the description was ignored.

There probably was no likelihood that Dr. Scoville would have arrived at any conclusion other than "identified" considering what he had written in a memorandum to the DCI on this sighting *before* he had interviewed all the witnesses:

> Two years ago Dr. Robertson headed a group which investigated U.S. sightings of flying saucers. This group was able to explain almost all the sightings and reached the conclusion that these phenomena represented no threat to the security of the U.S. Even if the present sightings by Russell are confirmed, it should not be inferred that these unconventional aircraft have actually been flying around the U.S. and were the source of U.S. speculation.

Such was the stature of the Robertson panel that Dr. Scoville willingly believed that the panel had explained "almost all sightings," which, of course, it had not done. Furthermore, Dr. Scoville was willing to believe that even if by some chance Sen. Russell's sighting turned out to be a real flying saucer, that would not mean that saucers had actually been seen over the United States. Fortunately civilization persists even in the face of "logic" like this.

The next sighting of interest to the FBI was made about a year later *by an FBI employee* (Scully and Mulder, are you paying attention?):

> [Name censored] on 4/9/56 reported the following rather unusual occurrence which is in the "flying saucer" category. On 4/5/46 ——— left Washington by car with her fiancé —— ———(employee of the National Security Agency), to go to Morven, North Carolina to meet the ——— family. Around 5 A.M. on 4/6/56 as dawn was breaking and while driving on Route 1 north of Henderson, North Carolina, the pair was startled by what appeared to be a round low-flying object coming directly toward the car. The object appeared to pass over the car and [they] turned to see it appear to speed up and then veer off out of sight. She and ——— both felt they had seen something unusual which was difficult to explain and certainly did not appear to be an optical illusion. ——— stated that the object as she saw it appeared round, was spinning and was bright as though containing a series of lights in a zig-zag pattern. The object appeared to be flying very low as it came toward them, moving at a great speed and gave off no particular sound. The object, to the best of her belief, was at least as wide as the highway and appeared no more than two to four feet in thickness. ———, who is one of our best employees, stated heretofore she has placed little credence in "flying saucer" stories and felt that had she and her boyfriend not seen the same object she would be inclined to think she had imagined something. She appreciates that what they saw may have been some kind of optical illusion; however, at the time, the object appeared very real to them.

The FBI decided that she should be interviewed again before passing the information on to the Air Force. On April 12, she reviewed the information from the April 9 interview, and then added the following information:

She advised she had seen the object for only a few seconds, that it was still dark when she observed it, although it was near daylight on April 6, 1956. She stated when daylight came, she observed the sky to be cloudy and it started raining approximately 30 minutes after she had observed the object. She recalled the object had approached their car on the driver's side from straight ahead at a height which she thought to be less than 25 feet. She was unable to estimate the speed of the object. She described it as being oval shaped, being very bright and having a light blue color. It made no sound that she could hear. She advised her fiancé would be able to state exactly where they had observed the object in North Carolina, inasmuch as he was familiar with that area. She was unable to recall any additional pertinent information.

On August 16, the FBI wrote a letter based on the above information to Air Force intelligence. However, this appears to be yet another credible sighting that fell through the cracks. It does not appear in the Project Blue Book sighting file.

During the late 1950s and 1960s, the FBI typically received between zero and two "complaints" a year while, as pointed out before, Project Blue Book received hundreds of sightings, except in 1957, 1965, 1966, and 1967, when the totals were even greater (around 1,000 each of those years). Although the FBI was not very active in collecting sighting reports, it did receive and respond to letters from the general public, it did investigate a few cases, and it did keep track of some of the prominent UFO groups and personalities.

The last case investigated by an FBI agent is worthy of mention because it became one of the most important sightings in the history of the UFO phenomenon. This case was the "last straw" for Dr. J. Allen Hynek, who was the astronomy consultant to Projects Sign and Blue Book from 1948 through 1969. Until this case, he had remained very skeptical of the idea that flying saucers and UFOs were evidence of extraterrestrial visitations. This case shook his confidence. Although he still doubted that saucers were craft from other planets, he was now certain that the UFO problem deserved a better investigation than the Air Force was giving it. One effect of this case was that after Project Blue Book closed in 1969, Dr. Hynek decided to start a research group of his own, the Center for UFO Studies, which he founded in 1973. It exists today as the J. Allen Hynek Center for UFO Studies.

Hynek was not the only person who was intrigued by this sighting. Maj. Hector Quintanilla, Jr., the Director of Project Blue Book at the time, was so impressed that he wrote about it in a 1967 issue of the classified version of the CIA journal mentioned at the end of the previous chapter, *Studies in Intelligence.* The fact that an FBI agent was almost immediately on the scene and conducted an in-depth interview, even though in an "unofficial" capacity, was an important factor in establishing the credibility of the case.

CHAPTER 23

The Police Officer's Sighting

It had been several years since the
FBI received a sighting of any importance, when suddenly on April 25,
1964, the teletype machine at the Washington headquarters began to
chatter out an urgent message:

```
5:37 PM MOUNTAIN STANDARD TIME 4-25-64
URGENT
TO: DIRECTOR, FBI
FROM SAC, ALBUQUERQUE 62 - NEW MEXICO
UNIDENTIFIED FLYING OBJECT. SOCORRO, N.M.
APR TWENTY FOUR, NINETEEN SIXTY FOUR
INFORMATION CONCERNING
```

Information received APR twenty four and twenty five, from
[police officer] Lonnie Zamora, considered sober, depend-
able, mature, not of fantasy . . . that at about five fifty P.M.
MST, while in south area of Socorro noted flame in sky to

southwest, which he decided to check out in belief dynamite shack in area had blown up.

While traveling in isolated area approximately one mile south area of Socorro, noted in depression about eight hundred feet away whitish object which, upon glancing at same, appeared to be overturned automobile. Two persons in apparent white coveralls were adjacent to object.

Then traveled over rough road to spot about one hundred three feet from object and about twenty to twenty five feet higher. No persons visible. Heard two or three loud thumps, less than a second apart, then with a roar and bluish and orange flames, object slowly vertically rose to about car height, then noise and flame stopped and object took off at high speed in straight line and almost horizontally to disappear over distant mountain.

Zamora greatly frightened, radioed his observations and Officer Chavez and FBI Agent Byrnes quickly on scene, noted four small irregularly shaped smoldering areas and four regular depressed areas approximately sixteen by six inches in rectangular pattern averaging about twelve feet apart.

Zamora states object was oval shaped, similar to football, possibly twenty feet long, and had a red insignia about thirty inches high and two feet wide, centered on object. No other witnesses known to noise, flame or object.

The teletype message also reported that Agent Byrnes had immediately notified Army Capt. Richard Holder, Commander of the Stallion Range Center, at White Sands Missile Range tracking station south of Socorro. Byrnes also mentioned that by the time of the teletype message, the press was already showing considerable interest. Byrnes concluded by pointing out that the FBI was "conducting no investigation," but that he would advise headquarters of pertinent developments.

It may be that the FBI agent was conducting no official investigation, but it is clear from the record that he was a key factor in it. Within half an hour after Officer Zamora radioed a message to police headquarters for help, Agent Byrnes was on the scene.

Socorro, New Mexico, police officers Sam Chavez (left) and Lonnie Zamora (right) at time of the April 24, 1964 sighting.

On May 8 he wrote a summary of his activities related to the sighting:

> Special Agent D. Arthur Byrnes, Federal Bureau of Investigations, stationed at Albuquerque, New Mexico, was at Socorro, New Mexico, and at the State Police Office there on business late afternoon of April 24, 1964.
>
> At approximately 5:45 to 5:50 P.M. Nep Lopez, radio operator in the Socorro County Sheriff's office, located about thirty feet down the hall from the State Police Office, came into the State Police Office.
>
> Mr. Lopez advised Sargeant Sam Chavez, New Mexico State Police, that he had just received a radio call from Officer Lonnie Zamora to come to an area about one mile southwest of Socorro. The call was in relation to some unknown object which had "landed and has taken off." Agent Byrnes finished his work in the State Police Office at Socorro at approximately 6:00 P.M., April 24, 1964, and thereafter proceeded to the site where Officer Zamora, Socorro County Undersheriff Jim Luckie, Sargeant Chavez and Officer Ted Jordan, New Mexico State Police, were assembled.

It may be noted that it has been the observation of Agent Byrnes that Officer Zamora, known intimately for approximately five years, is well regarded as a sober, industrious and conscientious officer and not given to fantasy.

Officer Zamora was noted to be perfectly sober and somewhat agitated over his experience.

Special Agent Byrnes noted four indentations in the rough ground at the "site" of the object described by Officer Zamora. These depressions appeared regular in shape, approximately sixteen by six inches rectangular. Each depression seemed to have been made by an object going into the earth at an angle from a center line. Each depression was approximately two inches deep and pushed some earth to the far side.

Inside the four depressions were three burned patches of clumps of grass. Other clumps of grass in the same area appeared not to be disturbed. One burned area was outside the four depressions.

There were three circular marks in the earth which were smooth, approximately four inches in diameter and penetrated in the sandy earth approximately one-eighth of an inch as if a jar lid had gently been pushed into the sand.

No other person was noted in the area the night of April 24, 1964. No other objects were noted in the area possibly connected with the incident related by Officer Zamora.

So far as could be noted, there were no houses or inhabited dwellings in the area or in sight of the area.

In a message dated April 30, Agent Byrnes wrote that Officer Zamora was "a well regarded and capable officer who was noted to be perfectly sober and thoroughly frightened." Agent Byrnes said that he visited the site and saw the indentations and immediately contacted Capt. Holder. When Capt. Holder arrived later that evening, he and Agent Byrnes made measurements of the burned areas. They then interviewed Officer Zamora *at length* and learned that the sighting had begun when Officer Zamora was chasing a speeding motorist in Socorro. He happened to see a bright flash and hear a noise that made him think a dynamite shack on the other side of a hill had blown up. He broke off chasing the speeder, and turned onto a dirt road toward the shack. He got a first glimpse of the object as he came up the hill. It appeared to be an overturned car with two children next to it. He lost sight of it for a few seconds as he continued driving over the rough land. At the same time he radioed that he was going to check on an overturned car.

When he got to the top of the hill, he could see it again below him in a depression (arroyo). It was oval shaped and seemed to have two legs, and a red design or insignia on the side. As he was getting out of the car to call to the two "children," who were no longer visible, he dropped the microphone and turned to pick it up. At that moment he heard a "roaring noise" from the object, a noise that started at a low pitch and then increased in frequency. He turned and saw what appeared to be a bluish and orange flame beneath it. Thinking it was going to explode, he dashed around the car, losing his glasses as he ran, in order to put the car and the hill between himself and the object. As he ran, he turned his head to watch. After several seconds the oval-shaped object rose straight up. He ran for about fifty feet and dropped onto the ground, covering his eyes. He then realized the noise had stopped. He looked back in time to see the object moving away from him. He quickly got up and ran back to the car, picking up his glasses as he ran, to call Nep Lopez. He asked Lopez to look out the window but didn't think, in the heat of the moment, to tell Lopez to look out a west window. (The window in Lopez' office faced north.) Officer Zamora asked Lopez to send Sgt. Chavez immediately. The other officers who arrived at the scene shortly after (Luckie, Jordan) heard the radio message and also went there. When Chavez arrived a few minutes later, he found a pale and sweating Zamora, as well as slightly smoldering grass and brush where the object had been.

By 1:00 A.M. the next morning, Agent Byrnes and Capt. Holder had typed up the interview. In the following days, the Army and Air Force checked every known project in the area and could not find an explanation. Project Blue Book was contacted quickly and Dr. Hynek traveled to Socorro for his first visit five days later. He interviewed all the people involved and was not able to arrive at a conclusion. About five months later he visited again. Still no answers. Some people believed that Officer

Zamora had seen a top-secret military vehicle, or perhaps the NASA moon lander that was being discussed in the press at the time. A very few people thought it was a hoax, perhaps to draw tourists to Socorro. However, no evidence of a hoax ever turned up and Officer Zamora's credibility remained high.

Maj. Hector Quintanilla, Jr., Project Blue Book Director, took a special interest in the case. He was convinced that Zamora had told the truth about what he had seen, and that it was not a hoax. Writing in *Studies in Intelligence,* in 1967, Quintanilla summarized the sighting:

> Diagnosis: *Unsolved*
> There is no doubt that Lonnie Zamora saw an object which left quite an impression on him. There is also no question about Zamora's reliability. He is a serious police officer, a pillar of his church, and a man well versed in recognizing airborne vehicles in his area. He is puzzled by what he saw, and frankly, so are we. This is the best documented case on record, and still we have been unable, in spite of thorough investigation, to find the vehicle or other stimulus that scared Zamora to the point of panic.
>
> During the course of the investigation and immediately thereafter, everything that was humanly possible to verify was checked. Radiation in the landing area was checked with Geiger Counters from Kirtland AFB. The Holloman AFB Balloon Control Center was checked for balloon activity. All local stations and Air Force bases were checked for release of weather balloons. Helicopter activity was checked throughout the state of New Mexico. Government and private aircraft were checked. The reconnaissance division in the Pentagon was checked. The White House Command Post was checked. The Commander at Holloman AFB was interviewed at length about special activities from his base. Down range controllers at the White Sands Missile Range were interviewed. Letters were written to industrial companies engaged in lunar vehicle research activity. The companies were extremely cooperative,

Maj. Hector Quintanilla, Jr., director of Project Blue Book.

but to no avail. The Air Force Materials Laboratory analyzed soil samples from the landing area.

The findings were altogether negative. No other witnesses could be located. There were no unidentified helicopters or aircraft in the area. Radar installations at Holloman AFB and at Albuquerque observed no unusual blips; but the down-range Holloman MTI radar, closest to Socorro, had been closed down for the day at 1600 hours [4:00 P.M.]. There was no unusual meteorological activity, no thunderstorms; the weather was windy but clear. There were no markings of any sort in the area except the shallow "tracks" Chavez and Zamora found. The soil analysis disclosed no foreign material. Radiation was normal for the "tracks" and surrounding area. Laboratory analysis of the burned brush showed no chemicals that could have been propellant residue.

The object was traveling at approximately 120 miles per hour when it disappeared over the mountain, according to Zamora's best guess of the time it took. Not an interplanetary speed, at any rate; and the findings are also negative for any indication that the Socorro UFO was of extraterrestrial origin or that it presented a threat to the security of the United States.

Here is an example of a well-reported, well-researched sighting with more than sufficient information for identification, yet identification was impossible. Even Maj. Quintanilla admitted defeat: there was no explanation for Officer Zamora's sighting. Yet, according to Quintanilla, it was not evidence of an extraterrestrial device and it was not a threat to the United States. One can certainly ask how he arrived at that conclusion, considering the lack of identification? Apparently the speed, "not interplanetary," was evidence that the object was not interplanetary.

Maj. Quintanilla, being consistent with the official Air Force position on Unidentified Flying Objects, was skeptical of the extraterrestrial hypothesis, and his skepticism kept him from admitting that Zamora *might actually have seen an extraterrestrial craft.* There have been numerous civilian investigations of this case since Quintanilla's article. A couple of people have proposed that Quintanilla saw a new type (at that time) of hot air balloon with the flame from the heater causing the noise and the burned plants on the ground. To accept this explanation would require rejecting major portions of Zamora's testimony and certainly raise lots of questions such as why didn't Zamora recognize a large balloon? This shows how desperate some people are to avoid admitting there are unexplained objects/craft flying around. The investigations since Quintanilla's article have ruled out *every other man-made or natural phenomenon!* What remains?

There were physical effects caused by this object, burned grass, and depressions in the ground. One odd aspect of the physical evidence was the nature of the burned material. Chavez found it cold to the touch only minutes after the event. Therefore the burns were not made by an ordinary rocket-type blast of fire, which would have consumed whatever it contacted and would have started hot fires in nearby brush. Perhaps it was more like flash burning from an intense radiation source or extremely hot air (or a plasma?) that doesn't last long enough to heat the internal part of an object, but only long enough to "fry" the outer surface.

Another odd effect, not mentioned in the official reports, was noted by Officer Ted Jordan. He had a camera with him and took 35mm pictures of the site within half an hour of the event. The next day, one of the Air Force investigators asked him for the film with the promise to provide Jordan with duplicate copies of the pictures. Many weeks later Jordan asked about his film and was told that his film didn't turn out; *it had been ruined by radiation.* Sgt. Chavez took Polaroid pictures the next day which came out all right. Also, a Geiger counter was brought to the site almost forty-eight hours later. It registered no excessive radiation. Could it be that some intense form of radiation, that could affect film in a camera, was present at the site for a short time afterward, but then had decayed away by the next day?

It certainly appeared to Zamora that he saw a real, solid, structured, manufactured device, a large oval-shaped flying craft that made no noise as it traveled after the initial "take off." It did not look like any man-made flying craft (or balloon). But if it *we* didn't make it, then *who did?* And what was it doing near Socorro on that fateful day?

CHAPTER 24

The "X-Files" Today

During the late 1940s and 1950s, as we have seen, the FBI interviewed some witnesses and collected a lot of information supplied by the Air Force. The FBI also followed the activities of several prominent UFO "contactees" of the 1950s and 1960s. These were people who claimed to have had direct contact with generally benevolent outer space creatures. The FBI collected information about them because several of these contactees claimed that outer-space alien societies tended to be communistic and, of course, promotion of communism and communist subversion was always one of the prime concerns of the FBI. However, no contactee was ever arrested for subversive activities.

After the Zamora case in 1964, the FBI received only a few sighting reports from citizens over the next thirty years. These were immediately passed on to the Air Force, except for one discussed below. The FBI did receive letters asking for information, to which the FBI often replied that the investigation of UFO/saucer sightings is "not a matter within the investigative jurisdiction of the FBI" or that the investigation "is not and *never has been a matter* within the investigative jurisdiction of the FBI [emphasis added]."

During the 1970s farmers and ranchers in various Midwest and far western states discovered, in their fields, thousands of their cattle (and a few other types of livestock) had been mutilated and killed. In most cases it appeared to the ranchers and to investigators that predation by hunting animals and scavengers could not explain the nature of the mutilations. In many cases, there were reports of odd, lighted objects or "flying saucers" that were seen during the nights before mutilated cattle were discovered. Eventually some state politicians convinced the FBI to carry out an investigation. Although by the late 1970s there were thousands of mutilations on record, the retired FBI agent who carried out the investigation studied only a few mutilations, and decided that they were, after all, caused by predator animals. This man's final report did not satisfy the ranchers, who knew that normal predation could not explain such things as sharp, surgical cuts, or evidence that a dead animal had been dropped from some height to the location where it was found, but it did end the FBI involvement in this mystery.

During the 1976 presidential campaign, then-Governor Jimmy Carter reported that he had seen a UFO in Georgia in 1973. Aware of the continuing arguments over the subject, he promised to release all the government files if he were elected. (Apparently he did not realize that the Project Blue Book file had already been released in 1975.) In June 1977, Jody Powell, of President Carter's staff, initiated a search within the Executive Branch to find out if there were any group coordinating the flow of information on the UFO subject. As result of Mr. Powell's request, Stanley Schneider of the Office of Science and Technology of the White House contacted the FBI. The FBI told him:

> . . . as far as the FBI is concerned there appears to be no conceivable jurisdiction for us to conduct any inquiries upon receipt of information relating to a UFO sighting and, in the absence of some investigative jurisdiction based upon the information furnished, that information would be referred to the Department of the Air Force without any action being taken by the Bureau.

That is the present policy. Hence, if you contact the FBI to report a sighting, the local agent may accept your report and then he will turn it over to the Air Force. He may also send a copy to headquarters where it will join the *real X-Files.*

During the latter half of the 1980s, some UFO researchers investigated documents that appeared to be official descriptions of early attempts to retrieve and study crashed flying saucers (the "MJ-12" documents, referring to the Roswell crash discussed previously, and to a special committee of twelve people, assembled to study the evidence and to formulate a government policy for withholding the evidence). These documents had security markings on them. The FBI began an investigation of these documents, but the investigation was ended quickly when the Air Force told the FBI that the documents were fakes. No one has as yet, more than fifteen years after these documents were first obtained by researchers, determined their exact source.

Before closing the file on the UFO-FBI connection, one more sighting report is worthy of mention because it provides an answer to a question raised in recent years: considering that abduction of a human being is a federal offense, what would the FBI do if a person reported being abducted *by aliens?*

JANUARY 18, 1967
UNIDENTIFIED FLYING OBJECT
ALLEGEDLY [sic] SIGHTING, JANUARY 17, 1967

At 4:10 A.M., January 18, 1967, Mr. [name and address censored] advised that he desired to report that he had observed a large oblong-shaped object which alighted in the street in front of him when he was on his way home from his television repair shop, the [name censored], Chesapeake, Virginia. He believes that he was taken into this craft which he recalls as being made of a glass-like substance and being transparent. It was manned by several individuals who appeared to be undersized creatures similar to members of the human race, probably not more than 4 feet tall. They were allegedly wearing regular trouser pants and T-shirts. Mr. ——— believes that he was transported by this craft for an undetermined distance and returned to his point of take-off approximately one hour later.

Mr. ——— spoke in a coherent manner although he appeared to be under certain emotional strain. He claimed he had not been drinking any intoxicants but he was unable to account for the time between 8:00 P.M. and 4:00 A.M. He stated he was telephoning from his workshop but had no recollection of being elsewhere between 8:00 P.M. and 4:00 A.M.

The above is being furnished for your information.

Below the above message is a slightly "ominous" addition:

NOTE: Mr. ——— furnished information to night supervisor Special Agent [name censored], Special Investigative Division. A check of Bureau indices did not disclose any information which could be identified with Mr. ———.

So, if you contact the FBI to report being abducted, they may check their files to see if you have a record, but don't expect them to investigate.

Clearly the witness took this event seriously. He didn't wait until daytime to make his report. Instead, he called the FBI shortly after his "return" at 4:10 in the morning. The FBI, however, did not take this report seriously, as there is no indication that it was sent to the Air Force, although numerous other sighting reports do contain appended statements that say the reports were sent on to the Air Force.

CHAPTER 25

None Dare Call It Conspiracy

The UFO-FBI connection and the "X-Files" of Air Force intelligence show that as far back as fifty years ago some Air Force personnel knew that UFOs are real; i.e., that "flying saucers" were tangible objects with capabilities far exceeding our own aircraft. Not only that, but, as early as 1948, Project Sign personnel had concluded that the saucers had an interplanetary origin. In 1952, Dr. Stephen Possony indicated in a travel request memorandum that the Air Force "assumed" saucers were interplanetary (see chapter 20) and Capt. Ruppelt indicated in his personal memoranda that some top officials accepted the interplanetary explanation. This was confirmed in August and October 1952, when Air Force intelligence told the FBI that top officials were seriously considering the interplanetary explanation (see chapter 21). However, in public the Air Force presented a "unified front," consistently claiming that all saucer sightings could be explained as misidentified natural phenomena or man-made objects, with some being hoaxes or delusions. The Air Force consistently denied any evidence of a threat from, or extraterrestrial origin of, the saucers. This raises a major question. Why did the Air Force publicly deny what at least some top officials knew to be true? Was it because there was no universally accepted absolute proof; i.e., no hard evidence? Was it because the very top generals really were not convinced, and so they set forth a policy of denying the evidence? Or did they know the saucers were real and orchestrated a cover-up—a conspiracy to withhold the evidence—because they believed the information too dangerous to be released?

These questions cannot be answered directly. There are no documents as yet available that indicate the specific reasons why the Air Force consistently denied the evidence. All that can be demonstrated is that the Air Force *did* withhold the evidence by classifying the sightings and the internal discussions about the sightings and, through public statements, by giving the American people the impression that a good investigation was ongoing, but that nothing new had been discovered.

It is very likely that the failure of the Air Force to "come clean" or "level" with the American people can be traced to Gen. Vandenberg's rejection of the Estimate in late September or early October 1948. This rejection had a lasting impact by forcing the intelligence analysts to classify each unexplainable sighting as either an unknown (to them) domestic project, a foreign (Soviet) advanced aircraft, a misidentification of natural or man-made phenomena, a hoax, or a delusion. We know that the analysts rejected the first explanation because no one, not even the top military and government officials, was aware of any domestic aircraft project with the capabilities attributed to the flying saucers (and none has been discovered as a result of recent investigations into the status of formerly secret aeronautical research in the late 1940s and 1950s).

We now know that for several years the analysts clung to the foreign aircraft explanation, using it to justify the expenditure of funds for further research. However, this explanation was not really believed even as early as 1948, and it was not used after the big flap of 1952. The inadmissibility of the extraterrestrial explanation combined with the extreme unlikelihood of the domestic and foreign project explanations, resulted in a "logical default": logical analysis pointed toward real objects with highly advanced capabilities, but the only allowed explanations were misidentification, hoax, and delusion. In other words, the objects couldn't be "real." One might say that Vandenberg's rejection was the triumph of policy, or politics, over logic. Within half a year of Vandenberg's rejection, the ATIC personnel who had worked on Sign and the Estimate had been transferred to other projects. The remaining low-level personnel and the "new hires" who joined the project in later years realized that there was no "glory" and no promotion for those who went against the official policy, so the Grudge investigators simply treated the sightings as trivial wastes of time, to be studied only because of orders from above. The final Project Grudge report was a travesty of science, proposing unlikely or impossible explanations for sightings just so they could claim to have explained each sighting.

Yet in spite of the Air Force public attitude that saucer sightings signified nothing, by the early 1950s, as we now know, some top officials admitted to leaning toward, if not fully accepting, the interplanetary, or extraterrestrial, hypothesis. However, this was kept from the American public. Instead, the "Vandenberg Policy" carried the day when, at the peak of sighting fervor in 1952, with flying saucers seeming to be very real and appearing everywhere, Gen. Samford publicly stated that all unexplained sightings were natural phenomena. He said this even though privately his intelligence office told the AFOSI that there was no "theory" for the unexplained sightings, and told the FBI that the interplanetary explanation was under serious consideration. It would appear that the real intent of the Air Force generals who made public statements in July and August 1952 (Samford, Vandenberg, and Ramey) was *not* to provide the public with some real information about flying saucers, but rather to damp down the public near-hysteria over the sightings. To do this all they had to do was appeal to the previous public Air Force statements that all sightings could be explained, and those which weren't explained probably could have been if there had been more information (an outright lie, as we now know).

In 1953, the CIA proposed a defense-based reason to deny saucer reality. If people thought saucers were real, they might report more of them, and the reports could clog communication channels, especially if the Soviet sympathizers in the United States were to generate spurious saucer reports at the time of an attack. Furthermore, spurious saucer reports could cause dispatched jet fighters to be diverted from attacking the real Soviet aircraft. However, these reasons no longer applied in the 1960s (and afterward), so one might think that the Air Force could have admitted to saucer reality at least by the time of the Colorado University study in 1967–1968. But, no. This study, even though leaving about a third of its cases unexplained, claimed that there was nothing threatening or new about saucer reports which, according to project director Dr. Edward Condon, were made by "poor observers."

So the question arises, did the top Air Force officials orchestrate an effort to withhold information and downplay (debunk) saucer sightings? And, if so, was it because the Air Force officials didn't want egg on their faces for suggesting something that seemed ridiculous (extraterrestrial visitation)? Or was there another reason?

Consider again the early history of Air Force involvement. Within a couple of weeks after the first publicized sightings, and only a couple of days after the Roswell Army Air Base reported finding a crashed flying saucer, the Air Force (Gen. Schulgen) asked the FBI for help. It is at this point that the history of the Air Force involvement could be interpreted in either of two ways. The first way, "Interpretation A," is based on the available documents from the Blue Book file, from the FBI, CIA, State Department, Army, etc. These documents do not say there was "hard evidence" (in fact, some of them at the Secret level of classification, and one at the Top Secret level, indicate that there was no hard evidence). Therefore Interpretation A is based on the assumption that the Air Force never got hard evidence; i.e., the Roswell debris was *not* from an extraterrestrial vehicle, and there was no saucer crash in December 1950 (see chapter 17), or at any other time.

"Interpretation B" of the Air Force UFO history is based on the assumption, as yet not documented in an indisputable way, that the Roswell object was, in fact, an alien craft, probably with bodies. This latter interpretation is based upon the wealth of witness testimony collected over the last fifteen years by a number of researchers, and upon testimony such as that of Dr. Sarbacher and Wilbert Smith. Let us first consider Interpretation A.

Interpretation A:
The Air Force Had No Hard Evidence

If there never was hard evidence, then the policy to withhold information might be interpreted as follows: the Air Force investigators and the Top Brass, being truly as puzzled as everyone else, were trying honestly to find the explanation, and never were able to because the sighting data were never good enough. There was no conspiracy to withhold the "ultimate secret" of saucer reality because the sightings were unimportant and no one was sure the objects were real. Nevertheless, the Air Force withheld information to minimize public interest in the subject.

A more realistic interpretation of the Air Force policy is based on the idea that the Top Brass knew there was convincing evidence, it was just not "hard." The idea that the Top Brass knew of convincing evidence is based, in part, upon the 1952 FBI "X-File" documents that say the interplanetary explanation was given serious consideration, upon the April 1952 memorandum by Dr. Stephen Possony, wherein he indicated that some top Air Force generals *assumed* saucers were interplanetary, and upon the private notes of Capt. Edward Ruppelt. One may speculate that the top Air Force officials were afraid of the consequences of publicly admitting saucer reality because they would, at the same time, have to admit that the Air Force and the government didn't know what was going on, and couldn't do anything about the saucers. Therefore they covered up their belief in UFO reality and directed the lower-ranking officers to make it appear as if there were no convincing evidence. (Vandenberg accomplished this by rejecting the interplanetary, or extraterrestrial, hypothesis in 1948.) If this were the case, then there was a plan for "withholding of evidence" which required the acquiescence of the AFI personnel and those at ATIC where the sighting information was stored. This could be called a conspiracy to convince the American people, and the world, that there was nothing to flying saucer sightings.

Interpretation B:
From the Start, the Air Force Had Hard Evidence

This one is a "no-brainer," a slam dunk. If Roswell (or any other crash report, such as the one I suggested may have occurred in December 1950, when the Counter Intelligence Corps was put on immediate high alert) is true, if an alien craft *did* crash and the material and perhaps bodies *were* retrieved by the Army Air Forces, then we have collusion on a grand scale to prevent the American public from knowing the truth.

But, some might say, the open record as presently available shows that there was no hard evidence because no "evidence of the hard evidence" ever showed up in Air Force documents. In fact, in Secret level classified documents the Air Force repeatedly denied having hard evidence. However, recall the conversation that Wilbert Smith had with Dr. Sarbacher (see chapter 17). Smith's Top Secret memorandum about that conversation said that flying saucers are real. Dr. Sarbacher told me directly that he had been told of debris and alien bodies (composed somewhat like insects) at Wright-Patterson AFB. This testimony indicates that at the Top Secret/Special Access level, people were saying things they didn't say at the Secret level of classification.

Just because a Secret level document says something doesn't mean it's true! Subject matter, material, information, whatever you want to call it, which is very highly classified is not mentioned, and sometimes cannot even be alluded to in documents of lower classification. Statements can be made at the Secret level that tend to draw the reader away from the Top Secret truth. Hence Gen. Twining could put into a Secret level letter to Gen. Schulgen a statement that there is no hard evidence. Then at another time by directly communicating through Top Secret channels with Schulgen he could have told Schulgen that there *was* hard evidence, but it should never be mentioned in correspondence at the Secret level or discussed with people who did not have "special access" to the information. Why wouldn't it be mentioned at the Secret level? Because many more people had Secret clearances than Top Secret, and the more people who know, the better the chance that the information would leak out. Furthermore, people working at the Secret level, and even most of the people working at the Top Secret level, had no "need-to-know" that there was hard evidence. They could do their jobs perfectly well in response to a direct order without being told why the order was given.

In the realm of further speculation, assume that the Top Brass knew that saucers were real because of the hard evidence. They would not know just from the debris (and bodies) what saucers were doing, or where they were doing it. To find out this information they could order the lower brass to create an information collection and analysis project. A simple collection project would not be good enough, however, because there would be a lot of "noise,"—that is, false sightings. These false sightings would obscure the "signal," namely the *true* saucer sightings, and only the true sightings could provide information about what the extraterrestrials were doing. Therefore the project would also have to analyze sightings to weed out the signal from the noise. It wouldn't be necessary for the analysis project to do any more than separate the signal from the noise. However, if it went beyond that and tried to determine the nature of the signal, there could be a problem for the Top Brass. In fact, the worst thing would be for the sighting analysis project to actually discover the true nature of the signal. Then the "cat would be out of the bag," and the cover-up would be difficult to maintain. Hence if the sighting analysis succeeded in identifying the signal as extraterrestrial craft, then that analysis would have to be rejected for lack of convincing proof, *no matter how good the sighting information might appear to be.*

Something like this is what happened when Gen. Vandenberg rejected the Estimate of the Situation (see chapter 5) for lack of proof. The question we cannot answer based on the available documentation is: did he reject it to prevent the analysis project from finding out the truth, and thereby jeopardizing the top level cover-up, did he reject it even though he knew there was convincing sighting evidence but he didn't want the Air Force to face political consequences of admission (like, "What are you doing about these saucers, sir?"), or did he reject it because he simply was not convinced by the available evidence?

These questions cannot yet be answered. However, the important thing to understand is that, although the publicly known history of the "Air Force-UFO connection" does not prove there was a crashed extraterrestrial saucer and an orchestrated effort to withhold that information, the publicly known history is not necessarily incompatible with that possibility. That is, the history of Air Force activities as found in the available documents could appear just as it does even if an alien spacecraft crashed at Roswell, if all information related to Roswell were kept out of normal Secret and Top Secret intelligence information channels, and, of course, if no one leaked the information or provided hard evidence that would positively confirm the event.

But enough of speculation about crashed saucers. The fundamental questions of overriding importance are these: do the FBI and the Air Force files contain evidence that proves that flying saucers or UFOs are real, and that top Air Force officials knew it, but withheld that information from the public?

My answer is . . . *yes!* (Agent Scully would be probably surprised, whereas no doubt Agent Mulder would completely agree.)

As for myself, if sometime in the future a government or military official admits that there really was a crashed flying saucer near Roswell, or that there were alien bodies stored in "Hanger 18" at Wright-Patterson Air Force Base in Dayton, Ohio, or that there really was an alien flying disc tested at Area 51 north of Las Vegas in Nevada—*I won't be a bit surprised!*

Appendix 1: Acronyms Used

ADC:	Air Defense Command
AFCRL:	Air Force Cambridge Research Laboratory
AFI, AFOIN:	Air Force Intelligence
AFOSI:	Air Force Office of Special Investigations
AFSAB:	Air Force Science Advisory Board
AFSWP:	Armed Forces Special Weapons Project
AMC:	Air Materiel Command
ARTC:	Air Route Traffic Control
ATIC:	Air Technical Intelligence Center
CIA:	Central Intelligence Agency
CIC:	(Army) Counter Intelligence Corps
CONAC:	Continental Air Command
CUFOS:	Center for UFO Studies
EEI:	Essential Elements of Information
FBI:	Federal Bureau of Investigation
FOIPA:	Freedom of Information and Privacy Act
GRD:	Geophysics Research Division
IAC:	Intelligence Advisory Committee

JIC: Joint Intelligence Committee
NEPA: Nuclear Energy for the Propulsion of Aircraft
NSC: National Security Council
ONI: Office of Naval Intelligence
ONR: Office of Naval Research
OSI: see AFOSI

Appendix 2: Documents

The quotations presented in the text are from a number of sources including books and documents. The FBI's UFO documents consist of about 1,600 pages of material stored at FBI headquarters, starting in 1947. They can be obtained through an FOIPA request to the FBI or, more quickly, by direct transfer over the World Wide Web at http://foia.fbi.gov/ufo.htm. Some of the FBI documents may be found in the book *Clear Intent* (see following list of sources). The following documents are just a few examples of the information discussed in this book.

The CIA's own history of involvement with UFO investigation can be found on the Web at www.cia.gov/csi/index.htm. Click on "Online Publications" and then "Semiannual Edition #1, 1997," and finally on "A Die-Hard Issue" by Gerald K. Haines. The most extensive government UFO Website is that provided by the U.S. Navy at www.history.navy.mil/faqs/faq29-1.htm. This includes links to other sites, including the National Security Agency, the Department of Defense, as well as the FBI and CIA. Also referenced therein is Record Group 341 at the National Archives, College Park, Maryland, which contains most of the records of the Air Force Office of Intelligence (AFOIN, called simply AFI in this book), and Record Group 341.15, the files of Project Blue Book. Many government documents can also be found at the "Black Vault" Website at www.blackvault.com.

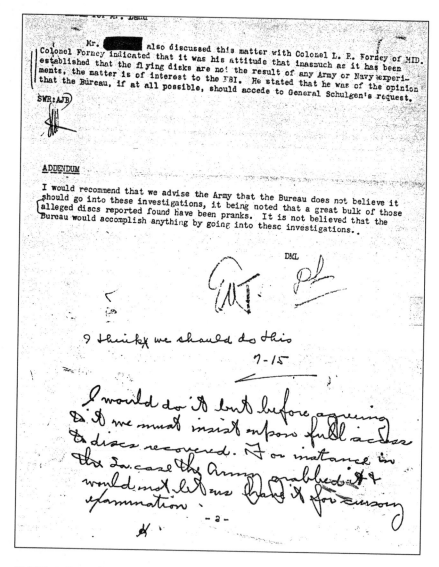

Exhibit A. Hoover's response (handwriting at bottom) to D. M. Ladd's recommendation (see chapter 1): "I would do it but before agreeing to it we must insist upon full access to discs recovered. For instance in the La. case the Army grabbed it & would not let us have it for cursory examination."

Office Memorandum • UNITED STATES GOVERNMENT

TO : MR. A. H. BELMONT

DATE: October 27, 1952

FROM : V. P. KEAY

SUBJECT: FLYING SAUCERS

SYNOPSIS:

Air Intelligence advised of another creditable and unexplainable sighting of flying saucers. Air Intelligence still feels flying saucers are optical illusions or atmospherical phenomena but some Military officials are seriously considering the possibility of interplanetary ships.

BACKGROUND:

You will recall that Air Intelligence has previously kept the Bureau advised regarding developments pertaining to Air Intelligence research on the flying saucer problem. Air Intelligence has previously advised that all research pertaining to this problem is handled by the Air Technical Intelligence Center located at Wright-Patterson Air Force Base, Dayton, Ohio; that approximately 90 per cent of the reported sightings of flying saucers can be discounted as products of the imagination and as explainable object such as weather balloons, etc., but that a small percentage of extremely creditable sightings have been unexplainable.

DETAILS:

Colonel C.M. Young Executive Officer to Major General John A. Samford, Director of Intelligence, Air Force, advised on October 23, 1952, that another recent extremely creditable sighting had been reported to Air Intelligence. A Navy photographer, while traveling across the United States in his own car, saw a number of objects in the sky which appeared to be flying saucers. He took approximately thirty-five feet of motion-picture film of these objects. He voluntarily submitted the film to Air Intelligence who had it studied by the Air Technical Intelligence Center. Experts at the Air Technical Intelligence Center have advised that, after careful study, there were as many as twelve to sixteen flying objects recorded on this film; that the possibility of weather balloons, clouds or other explainable objects has been completely ruled out; and that they are at a complete loss to explain this most recent creditable sighting. The Air Technical Intelligence Center experts pointed out that they could not be optical illusions inasmuch as optical illusions could not be recorded on film.

NWP/sjb

21 OCT 30 1952

Exhibit B. Air Intelligence report of October 27, 1952 and reaction to the Delbert Newhouse film of UFOs over Tremonton, Utah (see chapter 20). First page of two.

```
Memo to Mr. A. H. Belmont          RE:  FLYING SAUCERS
from V. P. Keay

                          YOUNG
          Colonel ████ advised that Air Intelligence still feels
that the so-called flying saucers are either optical illusions or
atmospherical phenomena.  He pointed out, however, that some
Military officials are seriously considering the possibility of
interplanetary ships.

ACTION:  ─

          None.  This is for your information.
```

Exhibit B (continued). Air Intelligence report of the Delbert Newhouse film. Note conclusion: ". . . some Miltary officials are seriously considering the possibility of interplanetary ships."

·*Office Memorandum* · UNITED STATES GOVERNMENT

TO : MR. A. H. BELMONT

FROM : V. P. KEAY

DATE: July 29, 1952

SUBJECT: FLYING SAUCERS —

PURPOSE:

To advise at the present time the Air Force has failed to arrive at any satisfactory conclusion in its research regarding numerous reports of flying saucers and flying discs sighted throughout the United States.

DETAILS: Mr. N.W. Pilcox ▓▓▓▓▓ the Bureau's Air Force Liaison Representative, made arrangements through the office of Major General John A. Samford, Director of Air Intelligence, U.S. Air Force, to receive a briefing from Commander ▓▓▓▓▓ of the Current Intelligence Branch, Estimates Division, Air Intelligence, regarding the present status of Air Intelligence research into the numerous reports regarding flying saucers and flying discs.

Commander Boyd ▓▓ advised that Air Intelligence has set up at Wright Patterson Air Force Base, Ohio, the Air Technical Intelligence Center which has been established for the purpose of coordinating, correlating and making research into all reports regarding flying saucers and flying discs. He advised that Air Force research has indicated that the sightings of flying saucers goes back several centuries and that the number of sightings reported varies with the amount of publicity. He advised that immediately if publicity appears in newspapers, the number of sightings reported increases considerably and that citizens immediately call in reporting sightings which occurred several months previously. Commander ▓▓▓ stated that these reported sightings of flying saucers are placed into three classifications by Air Intelligence:

(1) Those sightings which are reported by citizens who claim they have seen flying saucers from the ground. These sightings vary in description, color and speeds. Very little credence is given to these sightings inasmuch as in most instances they are believed to be imaginative or some explainable object which actually crossed through the sky.

(2) Sightings reported by commercial or military pilots. These sightings are considered more credible

RECORDED-136

NWP:hke

66 AUG 8 1952

Exhibit C. Air Force Intelligence memorandum of July 29, 1952, of interview with Commander Randall Boyd. First page of three.

by the Air Force inasmuch as commercial or military
pilots are experienced in the air and are not
expected to see objects which are entirely imaginative.
In each of these instances, the individual who reports
the sighting is thoroughly interviewed by a representative
of Air Intelligence so that a complete description of
the object sighted can be obtained.

(3) Those sightings which are reported by pilots and
for which there is additional corroboration, such as
recording by radar or sighting from the ground.
Commander ███████ advised that this latter classification
constitutes two or three per cent of the total number
of sightings, but that they are the most credible
reports received and are difficult to explain. Some
of these sightings are originally reported from the
ground, then are observed by pilots in the air and then
are picked up by radar instruments. He stated that in
these instances there is no doubt that these individuals
reporting the sightings actually did see something in
the sky. However, he explained that these objects could
still be natural phenomena and still could be recorded
on radar if there was some electrical disturbance in the
sky.

He stated that the flying saucers are most frequently
observed in areas where there is heavy air traffic, such as
Washington, D.C., and New York City. He advised, however, that
some reports are received from other parts of the country
covering the entire United States and that sightings have also
recently been reported as far distant as Acapulco, Mexico;
Korea and French Morocco. He advised that the sightings
reported in the last classification have never been satisfactorily
explained. He pointed out, however, that it is still possible
that these objects may be a natural phenomenon or some type
of atmospherical disturbance. He advised that it is not
entirely impossible that the objects sighted may possibly be
ships from another planet such as Mars. He advised that at
the present time there is nothing to substantiate this theory
but the possibility is not being overlooked. He stated that
Air Intelligence is fairly certain that these objects are not
ships or missiles from another nation in this world. Commander
███████ advised that intense research is being carried on presently
by Air Intelligence, and at the present time when credible
reportings of sightings are received, the Air Force is attempting
in each instance to send up jet interceptor planes in order to

- 2 -

Exhibit C (continued). Boyd interview page two. Note middle of third paragraph:
"[Boyd] advised that it is not entirely impossible that the objects sighted may possibly be
ships from another planet such as Mars . . . intense research is being carried on . . ."

obtain a better view of these objects. However, recent attempts in this regard have indicated that when the pilot in the jet approaches the object it invariably fades from view.

RECOMMENDATION:

None. The foregoing is for your information.

Exhibit C. Final page of Boyd interview.

Sources

The quotations presented in the text are from a number of sources including books and documents. The FBI's UFO documents consist of about 1,600 pages of material stored at FBI headquarters starting in 1947. They can be obtained through an FOIPA request to the FBI or, more quickly by direct transfer over the World Wide Web at www.fbi.gov. "Click" on Freedom of Information an Privacy Act. Then select Unusual Phenomena, and finally on Unidentified Flying Objects. Some of the FBI documents may be found in the book *Clear Intent* (see following list of sources).

The CIA documents are available directly from the CIA via the web at www.cia.gov, then "click" on Freedom of Information Act and then "Popular Document Collection" and finally on UFOs. A history of CIA involvement is presented in the Spring, 1997, issue of *Studies in Intelligence,* available from the CIA or at the CIA Website: www.odci.gov/csi. Click on "Studies in Intelligence," then on "On Line Publications," the "Semiannual Edition #1, 1997," and finally on "A Die Hard Issue."

The National Security Agency (NSA) has made available many documents at www.nsa.gov.

The Fund for UFO Research sells a CD with all the available NSA and FBI documents (Box 277, Mt. Rainier, MD 20712, or order at the Website, www.FUFOR.org) for $15.00.

The documents of the Army Counter Intelligence Corps are available from the United States Army Intelligence and Security Command, Freedom of Information and Privacy Act Office, Fort George Meade, MD 20755-5995.

The files of Project Blue Book and the Air Force Office of Special Investigations were transferred to microfilm (with names crossed off) in the early 1970s. They are available for reading at the National Archives, or can be purchased from the Archives. Numerous other documents declassified within the last fifteen years are also at the National Archives in Adelphi, Maryland.

Books that have been sources of information are:

Berlitz, Charles and William Moore. *The Roswell Incident.* Grosset and Dunlap, New York, NY. 1980.

Condon, Edward (Project Director). *Scientific Study of Unidentified Flying Objects.* Bantam Books, New York, NY. 1969.

Fawcett, Larry and Barry Greenwood. *Clear Intent.* Prentice Hall, New York, NY. 1984.

Friedman, Stanton and Donald Berliner. *Crash at Corona.* Paragon House, New York, NY. 1992.

Friedman, Stanton. *TOP SECRET/MAJIC.* Marlowe and Company, New York, NY. 1996.

Goode, Timothy. *Above Top Secret.* Sidgewick and Jackson, London. 1987.

Hynek, J. Allen. *The UFO Experience.* Henry Regnery, Chicago. 1973.

Jacobs, David. *The UFO Controversy in America.* Indiana University Press, Bloomington, IN. 1975.

Randle, Kevin and Donald Schmidt. *The Truth about the Crash at Roswell.* Avon Books, New York, NY. 1994.

Ruppelt, Edward. *The Report on Unidentified Flying Objects.* Doubleday, New York, NY. 1956; Ace Books paperback, 1956.

Index

☾ REACH FOR THE MOON

Llewellyn publishes hundreds of books on your favorite subjects! To get these exciting books, including the ones on the following pages, check your local bookstore or order them directly from Llewellyn.

ORDER BY PHONE
- Call toll-free within the U.S. and Canada, 1-800-THE MOON
- In Minnesota, call (651) 291-1970
- We accept VISA, MasterCard, and American Express

ORDER BY MAIL
- Send the full price of your order (MN residents add 7% sales tax) in U.S. funds, plus postage & handling to:

    Llewellyn Worldwide
    P.O. Box 64383, Dept. K493-6
    St. Paul, MN 55164–0383, U.S.A.

POSTAGE & HANDLING
(For the U.S., Canada, and Mexico)
- $4.00 for orders $15.00 and under
- $5.00 for orders over $15.00
- No charge for orders over $100.00

We ship UPS in the continental United States. We ship standard mail to P.O. boxes. Orders shipped to Alaska, Hawaii, The Virgin Islands, and Puerto Rico are sent first-class mail. Orders shipped to Canada and Mexico are sent surface mail.

International orders: Airmail—add freight equal to price of each book to the total price of order, plus $5.00 for each non-book item (audio tapes, etc.).

Surface mail—Add $1.00 per item.

Allow 2 weeks for delivery on all orders.
Postage and handling rates subject to change.

DISCOUNTS
We offer a 20% discount to group leaders or agents. You must order a minimum of 5 copies of the same book to get our special quantity price.

FREE CATALOG
Get a free copy of our color catalog, *New Worlds of Mind and Spirit.* Subscribe for just $10.00 in the United States and Canada ($30.00 overseas, airmail). Many bookstores carry *New Worlds*— ask for it!

Visit our website at www.llewellyn.com for more information.

Night Siege
The Hudson Valley UFO Sightings

Dr. J. Allen Hynek,
Philip J. Imbrogno, & Bob Pratt

In 1983, just a few miles north of New York City, hundreds of suburban-
ites were startled to see something hovering in the sky. They described it
as a series of flashing lights that formed a "V," as big as a football field,
moving slowly and silently.

It has been seen many times since then, yet the media has remained
silent about it, as has the military, the FAA, and the nation's scientists.
Now, in *Night Siege,* expert UFO investigators reveal the amazing evidence that cannot be denied and the more than 7,000 sightings that cannot be dismissed.

A classic in the field, *Night Siege* has been called one of the best
researched and factual UFO books to date. This second edition is revised
and expanded with sightings up to 1995.

1-56718-362-X, 288 pp., 5³⁄₁₆ x 8, 8 pp. b & w photo insert $9.95

UFOs Over Topanga Canyon

Preston Dennett

The rural Californian community of Topanga Canyon is home to 8,000 close-knit residents, the Topanga State Park—and an unusual amount of strange activity going on in the sky.

Like Hudson Valley, N.Y., and Gulf Breeze, Fla., Topanga Canyon is considered a UFO hotspot, with sightings that began more than fifty years ago and continue to this day. Here is the first book to present the activity in the witnesses' own words.

Read new cases of unexplained lights, metallic ships, beams of light, face-to-face alien encounters, UFO healings, strange animal sightings, animal mutilations, and evidence of a government cover-up. There are even six cases involving missing time abductions, and a possible onboard UFO experience.

1-56718-221-6, 312 pp., 5¾₆ x 8, illus.   **$12.95**

Contact of the 5th Kind

The silent invasion has begun—
What the government has covered up

Philip J. Imbrogno &
Marianne Horrigan

George and Maria have a daughter who is almost two years old. One day she brought out her doll and asked her mom to open its head. Maria asked her where she had seen something like that and she told her mom, "They do it to daddy at night."

How would the people of this country react if they knew that their government allowed an alien intelligence to abduct them and experiment on them in exchange for technological advances?

Contact of the Fifth Kind is a new approach to UFO research that is filled with hundreds of documented alien contact and abduction cases. Philip J. Imbrogno is one of the few researchers who actually goes out into the field to personally investigate the evidence. And the evidence, in some cases, is so overwhelming that even the most skeptical of readers will not be able to deny that there is an intelligence currently interacting with certain people on this planet.

1-56718-361-1, 256 pp., 5³⁄₁₆ x 8   **$9.95**

To order call 1-800-THE MOON
Prices subject to change without notice.

Out of Time and Place
Amazing Accounts that Challenge Our View of Human History

Complied and edited by Terry O'Neill from the files of FATE magazine

I held my hand out of the wagon window and caught four fat, brown little toads ... I had heard of fish and frogs falling from the clouds, but I had never heard of a fall of toads ...

— "Does It Rain Toads?"

Explore fascinating mysteries of history, archaeology, and the paranormal with this collection of amazing reports published only in the pages of FATE magazine. The writers of these fascinating articles follow the footsteps of Indiana Jones, seeking the lost and trying to solve the mysteries of the oddly found. Thirty original articles from the best of FATE over the past 40 years feature tales of lost cities, strange falls from the sky, extraordinary creatures, and misplaced artifacts that call into question our entire view of human history.

Despite studies by historians and scientists from many fields, these events and objects from out of time and place remain unexplained. Readers can't resist being enthralled by these mysteries and by the efforts to solve them.

1-56718-261-5, 272 pp., 5³⁄₁₆ x 8 $9.95

Strange But True

From the files of FATE magazine

Corrine Kenner &
Craig Miller

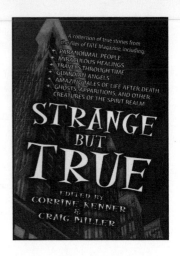

Have you had a mystical experience? You're not alone. For almost 50 years, FATE readers have been reporting their encounters with the strange and unknown. In this collection, you'll meet loved ones who return from beyond the grave . . . mysterious voices warning of danger . . . guardian angels . . . and miraculous healings by benevolent forces. Every report is a first-hand account, complete with full details and vivid descriptions:

- *"Suddenly, a vision appeared at the foot of my bed. It was a young woman, wearing a sad expression on her strangely familiar face . . ."*

- *"Running across the clearing from one thickly wooded area to the other was a thin, hunched creature, covered with light gray hair . . ."*

Whether you're a true believer or a die-hard skeptic, you'll find *Strange But True* a book you can't put down.

1-56718-298-4, 256 pp., 5³⁄₁₆ x 8   **$9.95**

To order call 1-800-THE MOON
Prices subject to change without notice.